INTERMEDIATE
INFORMATION
TECHNOLOGY

MOLLY WISCHHUSEN
ANDREW SCALES

Heinemann Educational Publishers
a division of Reed Educational and Professional Publishing Ltd
Halley Court, Jordan Hill, Oxford OX2 8EJ

OXFORD FLORENCE PRAGUE MADRID
ATHENS MELBOURNE AUCKLAND KUALA LUMPUR
SINGAPORE TOKYO IBADAN NAIROBI
KAMPALA JOHANNESBURG GABORONE PORTSMOUTH NH
CHICAGO MEXICO CITY SAO PAULO

First Published 1996

99 98 97
10 9 8 7 6 5 4 3 2 1

A catalogue record for this book is available from the British Library
on request

ISBN 0 435 45258 4

Designed by Roger Denning and typeset by TechType, Abingdon
Printed in Great Britain by Bath Press Ltd, Bath

Contents

Acknowledgements

Many people have helped and advised in the production of this book, all of whom are greatly appreciated. Special thanks must go to all my colleagues for being so long suffering in listening to my progress or lack of progress (!), especially Barbara Wilson, whom I can *blame/thank* for suggesting me as a possible author to Heinemann, Bob Crooks for his invaluable advice, Jenny Johnson and Camilla Moore for proof reading and constructive criticism, and Margaret Berriman and Jan Nikolic for their amazing patience and encouragement to 'keep bashing on'.

Above all my greatest appreciation goes to my fabulous family, to my granddaughter Hannah, whose occasional 'assistance' only delayed me slightly, to my children Mairion, Alun and Jackie, who have encouraged me not only in words, but also in practical help to give me time to write, and most of all to my husband Peter, who not only gave his support, encouragement, advice and practical help which have never wavered, but in addition even drew some of the flow diagrams!

Molly Wischhusen

I would like to express my gratitude to Margaret Berriman for giving me the opportunity, and for her invaluable advice and suggestions. I am also indebted to Jan Nikolic for her patience and tact, and for the high quality of her editing.

It is with particular pleasure that I thank my mother and father, Geoff and Betty Scales, for their encouragement in this and in all other things. Finally, I should like to thank my lovely wife, Anongluk, for her endless enthusiasm and confidence in me.

Andrew Scales M.A. (Lond)
University of British Columbia

The authors and publishers are grateful to the following for permission to reproduce photographs and other material:

Alton Towers
Bite Communications
British Telecommunications
The Daily Telegraph
IBM

The Image Bank
Steve Jackson
Pictor International
Science Photo Library

Introduction

Welcome to a GNVQ Intermediate programme of study, which is equivalent to approximately 4 to 5 GCSEs at Grade C or above. This book has been written to help you achieve your Intermediate GNVQ in Information Technology, a course directed towards acquiring and improving skills related to the business and computing world. If you are prepared to work hard and are really interested in IT, you will find the course an excellent introduction to a subject which is becoming more and more central to every type of business. It may be a stepping stone to higher level courses, or it may set you on the path for a career in one of many industries.

To be successful you must complete *at least* the four mandatory units, two of the optional units and the three core skills units.

The mandatory units are:

1 Introduction to Information Technology
2 Using Information Technology
3 Organisations and Information Technology
4 Communications and Information Technology

The optional units are:

5 Introduction to Software Development
6 Technical Support
7 Using Software Packages to Satisfy User Requirements through Teamwork
8 Presenting Information Using Application Software Packages

The core skills are:

1 Communication
2 Information Technology
3 Application of Number

There are also additional units and personal skills available, and if you do achieve more than two option units and/or any of the additional units or personal skills, these will be indicated on the final diploma.

What is meant by a unit?

A unit is similar to a subject or a topic, and each unit consists of **elements.**

Each element consists of a number of **performance criteria.**

Performance criteria span a **range** of activities.

All of these together make up the unit specifications, for which you have to provide evidence in order to be accredited with the unit.

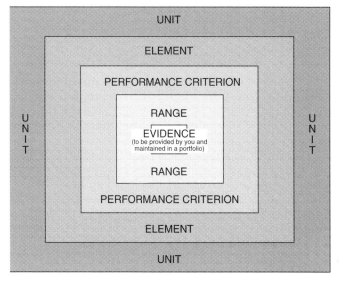

In the main, the core skills will be integrated with the mandatory or optional units.

What do you have to do to succeed?

You have to provide **evidence** to prove that you have covered and understand all the performance criteria in the units. The evidence will be filed and indexed in a portfolio. The evidence you must produce is varied, and examples may include:

■ assignments
■ questionnaires completed after watching a video
■ records of observations made by your tutors.

The assignments will often be in the form of a report, but don't panic. There are all kinds of reports, such as:

■ a printout from a database or spreadsheet
■ a leaflet/news-sheet designed using a word processor or desk-top publishing package
■ a slide show using a presentation package
■ a printout of a fax sent from a PC and the actual fax received
■ a diagram or chart produced using a drawing package.

Assignments allow you to generate the **evidence** which is saved in your **portfolio.**

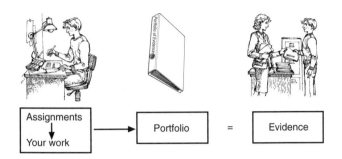

In addition to the assignments, which are internally assessed by your tutors, there will be external tests for the four mandatory units, which take the form of multiple choice questions. The pass mark is 70%, and although this is high, you do have three opportunities to pass the tests during the year. If at the end of the year you have successfully completed a mandatory unit *except* for the test, you have another chance to pass the test the following September.

Grading

You can achieve a grade of Merit or Distinction for the whole diploma (not each individual unit), provided that *at least one third* of the evidence in the portfolio meets the criteria for that grade.

Currently the themes that are assessed for grading are:

■ Planning
■ Information seeking and handling
■ Evaluation
■ Quality of outcomes

Please do *read* the Student Guide very carefully. It explains:

■ how this book has been designed to help you
■ how you can collect evidence for your portfolio
■ how you can achieve a Merit or Distinction grade
■ what is meant by the core skills and personal skills.

Your tutor will give you any other details you need, such as:

■ the name of your awarding body, which will be either BTEC (Business Technology Education Council), City & Guilds, or RSA (Royal Society of Arts)
■ which optional units you may study
■ how your evidence should be recorded and stored.

You will very probably find all this information overwhelming and confusing at first, but remember you don't have to do everything at once, and your tutors will be guiding you through the units and towards the completion of the portfolio. At the beginning, concentrate on those areas you *do* understand, and in particular make sure you work through any assignments which have been set for you. Gradually, you will find that you understand more and more about how the GNVQ programme works, until eventually everything fits into place!

We do hope you will enjoy your GNVQ programme, and that you will find this book helpful and interesting. We wish you every success in your studies.

Molly Wischhusen
Andrew Scales

May 1996

Student Guide

The layout of this book

The four main sections of this book correspond to the four mandatory units of Intermediate Information Technology. The chapters within each section correspond to the elements of each unit.

Each chapter is organised as follows:

- **The main text** gives information on all the topics which you need to understand, and which form the basis for questions in the unit tests. You will notice sub-headings which correspond closely to the performance criteria and range statements in the unit specification.
- **Activities** are provided to help your understanding, and they may produce evidence for your portfolio.
- **Did you know?** sections contain interesting snippets of information relevant to the topic being discussed, but which are not required for the tests.
- **Evidence Assignments** are case studies and other suitable activities which will give you the opportunity to collect the evidence necessary for the element.
- **Revision Tests** at the end of each element provide revision questions for the section. Try to answer the questions without looking at the main text, and then check your answers afterwards. This will help you identify any areas you do not understand, so that you can seek guidance from your tutor before the end-of-unit test.

If you work through each chapter, completing the activities and the Evidence Assignments, you should have enough evidence to prove that you have successfully completed each element.

Collecting evidence

The most important opportunities for collecting evidence are the Evidence Assignments. As this is an IT course, clearly almost all your evidence will be produced on the computer and will consist of various types of printouts, such as:

- a word processed report
- a spreadsheet printout showing data

- a spreadsheet printout showing formulae (this is very important, as your tutor cannot tell whether you just worked out the answers on the calculator and entered them into the spreadsheet, unless you print the formulae)
- a database report – form design, printout of records, printout of searches
- a graphics printout – a news-sheet, leaflet, diagram etc.

Quite often it is necessary to produce printouts at certain stages to show the development of an assignment. For example, you might be asked to create a *template,* which is a master document, rather like a blank form. In this case you would need a copy of the *blank template,* and then further copies of *completed examples.* It is very easy to spoil an excellent piece of work if you have not read each part of the assignment carefully. Most of us are impatient when we are reading instructions, but try to avoid the temptation to read only the first sentence, then think you know what is going to follow. Sometimes you will be right, but often you will miss something significant.

When you first read the assignments, highlight important points. For example, the Evidence Assignment for Element 4.1 includes this statement:

By **saving** and **printing** these two *uncompleted* fact sheets, and then returning to them for Element 4.3, you will provide evidence for IT Core 2.2 – editing information.

Once you become involved in producing your fact sheets for the assignment, it is very easy to forget this instruction, and lose the opportunity to provide the evidence for IT core skills, and yet it is quite simple to achieve.

Once you have finished the assignment, read it through again checking the tasks against the work you have produced. This is vitally important and should ensure that you do not hand in uncompleted work.

Grading

In order to pass the Intermediate GNVQ, you must provide evidence for all the performance criteria in each element. In addition, as mentioned in the introduction, there are four grading themes which give you the opportunity to achieve a Merit or

Distinction. The more you can prove you are capable of working independently, the more likely it is that you will achieve a Merit or a Distinction grade. We will examine the four themes below.

Planning

It is important *to draw up a plan* of action on your own before you start the assignment. The plan should clearly show:

- the *tasks* you need to carry out
- the *order* in which you need to undertake them
- the *dates* by which you aim to complete them (the final date should be 2 to 3 days *before* the deadline for the assignment, to allow for any unexpected problems or delays)
- if it is a group activity, your *personal* contribution to the plan.

You then need to *monitor* the plan regularly to show:

- whether you planned adequately
- whether you completed each task by the planned date
- if not, the reason why – network problems, disk corrupted, delay in receiving information requested from a company, tasks more difficult than anticipated or took longer than expected, illness, etc.

You should be completely honest when you are monitoring the plan, and if you can indicate how you overcame a problem this might help you achieve a Distinction. For example, the problem may have involved underestimating how long the task would take. If you overcame this and still achieved the deadline by going to the IT workshop in your own time, say so.

Information seeking and information handling

Firstly you must *identify* the information required for the task. Then, it is important to indicate the sources of your information. These might include:

- class notes
- text books/journals/newspaper articles – state exactly the source and the author
- videos – again, name the video
- research – which could be talking to people, especially if they use computers at work, conducting a survey, visiting an exhibition or a museum.

You should then indicate which sources were most relevant and why. For example, many IT text books will cover topics included in this book, but this book is likely to be more relevant because it is written specifically for your programme of study. You might, however, find further detail on a particular topic from other books or sources, which enable you to show initiative and to include additional detail.

Evaluation

After completing an assignment, you should look at the work and evaluate how successful the assignment has been compared to your original plan. Think about the following:

- Did you gather enough information/evidence?
- Do you feel satisfied with the report and its presentation?
- Could you have achieved the assignment in a better way – e.g. used more images, or made a presentation instead of producing a written report?
- What particular improvements in presentation are possible? For example, a long paragraph of text could have been listed in bullet points, as in this section.

Your tutor may provide suitable forms for you to use for these three themes, or alternatively you can simply write out your work by hand or word process it. Whatever method you use, it is essential that you do not ignore the grading themes.

Quality of outcomes

This theme will be judged through the actual assignments marked by your tutor. He or she will consider your work and decide:

- how well you have understood and explained the topic
- whether the work is well presented
- whether all the required aspects of the assignment have been covered.

You will not achieve a Distinction if you include only the minimum information required, e.g. if you state: 'There are four network topologies in common use as follows', and then add diagrams of the various layouts. The diagrams may be excellent for indicating all the network components, but unless you have explained what is meant by topology and the advantages and disadvantages of the four types, you may achieve only a pass, not even a Merit. Indeed, you may find the assignment returned for further work.

The portfolio

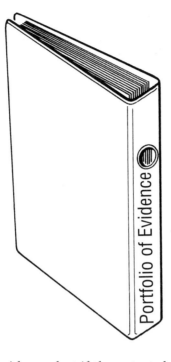

This is the file in which you store all *completed* assignments and activities, and it is essential that it is kept quite separate from your everyday file, where you keep notes and any current work. Apart from the unit test results, this is the only evidence you have to show that you have completed the programme. Portfolios should be well organised, clearly referenced, neatly filed, and contain the work the index says they contain. On opening such a file, the external verifier will naturally be impressed. A disorganised, messy portfolio may well contain all the necessary evidence, but if the external verifier cannot find it, he or she cannot confirm that the evidence actually exists.

Each piece of work in the portfolio must have a portfolio reference on the front. You might use a system such as Ass. 1.1, Ass. 2.1, etc. for the actual Evidence Assignments, and Q1, Q2 etc. for any questionnaires you have answered, possibly whilst watching a video. Your tutor will guide you on this, but whatever referencing system you use, you will need an index to the portfolio which may look something like this:

You will notice that in the example below the student has clearly planned very well, been less consistent on information seeking and handling, omitted to do the evaluation and achieved Merit for quality.

It is advisable to use file dividers to create sections for each of the units and also for the core skills, to show any evidence which is specific to them. File the work in the appropriate section, in the order in which it appears in the index.

Core skills and personal skills

As part of your GNVQ programme, you will study three compulsory core skills – Communication, Application of Number and Information Technology. Core skills are assessed at three levels – 1, 2 and 3. To gain a GNVQ Foundation programme you must pass Level 1 core skills, for Intermediate you must pass Level 2 core skills, and for Advanced you must pass Level 3. Core skills are assessed within the *vocational context,* which simply means that the work you produce for the core skills should be related to the subject you are studying, in this case Information Technology, and also to the world of work. Therefore, a report explaining the advantages of using IT in a particular organisation would be relevant, whereas an essay on autumn would not.

Core skills are very important for your future working life. Communication includes talking to people as well as writing documents (letters, memos and reports); Application of Number at the very least will help you calculate and check your bank statement; and Information Technology has so overtaken our lives that being able to use a computer and appreciate its benefits is almost essential in work today.

You won't have to write a poem, or a computer program, or use Pythagoras's theorem, but you will need to prove you are competent in the three skills, which means you should be able to perform them

Portfolio reference	Details of relevant unit	Indication of grading		Date
Ass 4.1	Unit 4.1 PCs 1-3 Comm: 2.2 PCs 1-5 　　　2.3 PCs 1-3, 2.4, PCs 1-4 IT: 2.1 PCs 1-4, 　　2.2 PCs 2 and 5, 2.3, PCs 1-5	Planning　　　M ☐　D ☑ Inf. S & H:　M ☑　D ☐ Evaluation:　M ☐　D ☐ Quality:　　　M ☑　D ☐		10/1/9-

easily, unaided and with confidence. You will find that many of the Evidence Assignments for your mandatory units will relate to a particular element of the core skills, but do remember that *one single piece of evidence is not likely to cover all the range.*

For Intermediate Information Technology, the three core skills must be achieved at Level 2. However, as this is an IT course, you have every opportunity to achieve the core skills for IT at Level 3 (equivalent to Advanced), and this book gives guidance on the additional requirements. These subjects are covered in the final section of the book, and tracking sheets are included to show you exactly which Evidence Assignments provide opportunities to achieve the particular performance criteria in the core skills.

Most of these opportunities to acquire evidence for the core skills will occur naturally through the assignments, but additional assignments have been provided where necessary. However, don't assume that when you complete an assignment you will *automatically* achieve the core skills indicated on the tracking sheets. You must *check* your work to ensure that you have also included suitable evidence for the core. For example, if you do not bother to use the spell checker and you submit work full of errors, you cannot achieve Communication Element 2.2 PC 3 – Follow appropriate standard conventions, including spelling.

For IT core skills, it is a good idea to create a log sheet like the one on page 186 to record any difficulties or problems that arise as you work through the course. This will help you fulfil the requirements for IT core Element 2.4 PC 4, for example.

Personal skills

These relate to your ability to take responsibility for yourself, your learning and self-improvement, and your skills in working with others as part of a team, making a valid and worthwhile contribution to the team effort.

Your tutor will monitor your progress in these areas during tutorials, and will discuss with you your strengths and weaknesses. Your ability to prepare and monitor action plans, revising them as necessary while ensuring that you keep to deadlines, will provide useful evidence of the personal skills.

It is possible that you will also be assessed on your ability to solve problems. In practice this means resolving difficulties which arise, and finding alternative methods when the original plan does not work.

In GNVQ programmes you are expected to take a great deal of responsibility for yourself. You will need to:

- manage your own assignments
- decide which tasks to complete and when
- keep track of your work – most students have some work returned indicating certain aspects not yet achieved, so *don't file it under the bed* and forget all about it!
- record completed work in the portfolio index
- store work neatly in the file
- revise knowledge for the unit tests – but your work in producing the assignments will help this process.

GNVQ programmes are challenging and the requirements may *sound* formidable at this stage. But they do not all have to be done at once, and if you follow the advice you will succeed. You will finish the course with a portfolio of which you can be justly proud. If you wish, you can then progress to an Advanced programme, and possibly continue to higher education at university, or if you prefer you can seek employment. You will have acquired very marketable skills that will always be useful in the world of work.

Element 1.1

Examine industrial and commercial information technology systems

To examine commercial and industrial information systems we are going to look at the hardware, software, staff and accommodation which together make information technology (IT) operations possible. We will begin by exploring examples of everyday commercial and industrial systems. We will then analyse their main benefits and limitations. To finish, we will consider their most important features.

After studying this chapter you should be able to:

1 describe the *benefits* and *limitations* of *commercial systems*
2 describe the *benefits* and *limitations* of *industrial systems*
3 explain the *features* of a selected *commercial system*
4 explain the *features* of a selected *industrial system*.

Information technology is the processor of modern society. Although we are usually unaware of its presence, commercial and industrial IT surrounds our everyday lives. We use its systems without thinking, often without even knowing they're out there, constantly working away for us.

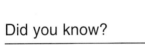

Did you know?

IT systems store and manipulate all kinds of data, from our bank accounts and medical records to secret police files. They control assembly robots in car factories and exploration robots on the seabed. They make it possible for communications systems to connect our phone calls by microwave or by satellite. They tell us what's on the television tonight and will video our favourite programmes when we're not at home.

All information systems are classified into two basic types – commercial and industrial. Commercial systems are used by businesses to help sell their goods or services profitably. For example, travel agents like Thomas Cook use them to check whether there are any free rooms in that Florida hotel where you hope to stay next summer.

Industrial information technology systems are used by factories to help them manufacture, produce or commercialise goods. For example, manufacturers from Ferrari to Ford use them to make their cars go faster by simulating wind resistance with computer-aided design (CAD) programs.

Figure 1.1 Automotive engineers working with computer-aided design programs

Commercial systems

Commercial IT systems are used to make bookings, transfer funds, provide point of sales information, control stock, process orders and process payrolls. Airlines, holiday or hotel booking systems, shops and mail-order companies are all typical commercial system users.

Booking systems

To *book* means to register or record something. In a booking system, the book is a list of all available places whether for college courses, Caribbean cruises, boxing matches or anything else. The system works by registering each place as no longer available once it has been booked.

For example, when you go to some cinemas, you can choose your seats from a diagram showing all the rows and seat numbers. The box-office clerk crosses off your choice which shows those seats are booked and no longer available. Although this is the basis of all booking systems, at modern multiscreen, multiperformance cinemas or at other big events, a lot more information needs to be registered.

Wembley Stadium holds nearly 100,000 people. Each time there is a major event such as a football match or pop concert, the Wembley booking system has to register each place as it is booked, making sure there are no double-bookings. It also has to record details such names and addresses, process the payments, print and send out the tickets.

Did you know?

For events such as a cup final or a Michael Jackson concert, tickets can be sold out in 24 hours. To handle that number of bookings, a team works around the clock on the same system. Each can see instantly on screen the availability of seats at a particular price, and they can book the seats knowing that they cannot be double-booked.

Activity

Write down the name of at least five local organisations that use booking systems. Discuss these with your tutor and the rest of the class when you finish.

Electronic funds transfer

Once a ticket or place has been booked, it has to be paid for. Your practice with estimates in the Application of Number unit will tell you that 100,000 tickets at an average of £22.50 is a great deal of cash to handle. Cheques would be easier but they still need handling and cause a lot of extra work if they bounce. The simplest and safest payments are in paperless money – electronic funds transfer.

Banks and credit-card companies like Visa and Access use a system that lets you pay for tickets by authorising the transfer of money from your account to the company's account. The same systems also allow you to withdraw money from ATMs (automatic teller machines) around the world. Unfortunately, you can only take out as much as you have put in.

Electronic fund transfer systems can move funds from one bank to another, in the same town or across the world in the space of a few seconds. You can put your money into your local branch, go to a town or city on the other side of the world and, using a charge card such as Visa, take it out again in the local currency.

Did you know?

At the end of the day, when the bank closes, they do not just leave your money lying around in a safe. Banks wire the money around the world, using it to buy and sell foreign currencies, make a profit and get the money back to your account before they open again in the morning.

Activity

Some people think that we will soon stop using coins and banknotes altogether and just use electronic funds transfer systems. What do you think the advantages of eliminating cash would be? And the disadvantages? Make two lists then discuss your ideas with your tutor and class.

Electronic point of sales systems

The *point of sale* is the place where a sale takes place. It could be in an agency or shop, or over the telephone to a software retailer like Windowline or PC World. When an agent makes a sale, it is not safe to accept credit or cheque cards without being sure they are legitimate, used by the actual owners and that there are sufficient funds to cover the price – especially over the telephone.

Electronic point of sales systems check credit or debit card details as you pay. The salesperson dials up the credit agency, entering card details and the amount of the sale. The credit agency's system compares that information with its database then approves or rejects the payment application.

Did you know?

In Canada and the USA, point of sales systems are usually attached to cash registers in the same way as printers are attached to computers. When you go to pay, the cashier swipes your card then hands you a box that looks like a fat calculator on a flex. You key in your personal identity number (PIN), verify the total, select the account you want debited and wait for approval. These systems will probably become common in Europe in the next few years.

Stock control

When you visit an electronics showroom you often see only one of each telephone, fax machine, PC, printer or other piece of hardware. That is because they are all demonstration models. The ones that you buy are kept safe, clean and unscratched in their boxes in the store or stockroom.

If a shop runs out of a particular model, the customer may well go somewhere else, in which case the first shop loses the business. No one likes to lose business so making sure there are enough items in stock is essential. On the other hand, too many of one item such as a TV takes up space that might be needed for other types of goods. This means that shops need to keep the right balance of stock – neither too few nor too many of an item at one time.

Keeping a check on stock by hand means counting up how many of each item are sold each week, and reordering when more are needed. In an electronics store checking stock by hand would be hard enough.

Imagine what it would be like in a supermarket! Fortunately, the bar-code readers that price goods at the checkout can also instantly calculate the stock level held by the shop, and reorder automatically when stock reaches the minimum level.

Order processing

Most people buy computer hardware and software over the telephone because it's cheaper than buying from shops. One of the main reasons for this is that shops have to pay rent for high street or shopping centre sites. Businesses that sell over the phone take advantage of order processing systems that allow them to operate out of town, and often in different parts of the country at the same time.

For example, a telesales person in Birmingham takes orders, credit-card details, address for delivery, and so on, over the phone, and enters these details in a computer. Credit-card details are automatically sent to Southampton to be checked for credit limits and whether the card has been stolen. The order details are sent down the line to the warehouse, which may be in Leicester. The computer in Leicester prints out all the necessary documents, such as labels, packing orders for the warehouse staff, and delivery instructions. The delivery service picks up the order and takes it to the customer in central London.

Payroll processing

When you get a job, whether it is full time, part time, temporary or permanent, the organisation you work for will put you on their payroll. A payroll is a record of the wages or salaries paid by the company to each and every employee. When you receive your wages you get a pay-slip that details your current payroll information. This includes:

■ your name
■ your payroll or works number
■ your gross pay and how it is made up (normal hours, overtime, etc.)
■ deductions (tax, National Insurance, pension contributions, etc.)
■ your net pay (what is left after the deductions)
■ your gross pay to date (so far this year)
■ deductions to date
■ your net pay to date.

The accounts department will make these calculations and write or print out the pay-slips. In a small company with just a few employees such as Microsoft was in 1978, when only 15 people worked

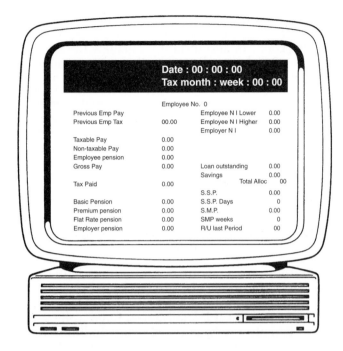

| | | Date : 00 : 00 : 00 | |
| | | Tax month : week : 00 : 00 | |

		Employee No. 0		
Previous Emp Pay		Employee N I Lower	0.00	
Previous Emp Tax	00.00	Employee N I Higher	0.00	
		Employer N I	0.00	
Taxable Pay	0.00			
Non-taxable Pay	0.00			
Employee pension	0.00			
Gross Pay	0.00	Loan outstanding	0.00	
		Savings	0.00	
		Total Alloc		00
Tax Paid	0.00			
		S.S.P.	0.00	
Basic Pension	0.00	S.S.P. Days	0	
Premium pension	0.00	S.M.P.	0.00	
Flat Rate pension	0.00	SMP weeks	0	
Employer pension	0.00	R/U last Period	00	

Figure 1.2 A payroll package on screen

there, this could be done by hand. It would be tedious and repetitive and the wages clerk would have to check carefully that all calculations were accurate – people do not like mistakes in their wages.

By 1992, Microsoft was employing over 10,000 people. A payroll clerk working by hand would have gone mad. Fortunately, payroll processing packages that make all the calculations, without making any mistakes, were introduced with some of the earliest software.

A small business that uses its payroll package once a month will choose a simple, straightforward system. That way the owner can remember how to use it. Larger organisations use integrated packages that link different systems together – for example, payroll software with stock control and accounting software.

Activity

Using computer magazines, local software retailers or other sources, find out the names of three payroll processing packages. When you have this information, discuss it with your tutor and compare it with the rest of your class to find out which packages seem to be the most popular.

Industrial systems

Industrial IT systems are used for design, process production control and robotics. Examples include domestic systems such as washing machines and central-heating systems; public systems such as traffic lights, car-speeding camera systems and photographic processing facilities; and manufacturing systems such as those used to produce electronic circuit boards, bottles, cars and plastic pipes.

Design

One of the best-known types of industrial system is *computer-aided design/computer-aided manufacture (CAD/CAM)*. In these systems, computers are used in the design and manufacture of products ranging from kitchen sinks to suspension bridges. The following is an outline of the way they might work to produce a mountain bike:

1 Design – at this stage, technical drawing and computer graphics are combined to produce a model of the bike.
2 The bike model is changed, redesigned and tested on video display screens until it has the best mix of features. This includes simplicity of production and manufacture, and cost considerations.
3 Shared databases are then used to integrate the bike's CAD information with CAM processes.

The CAM engineers also use *computer modelling* to obtain the best manufacturing procedures for the factory. For example, if the brakes and the gears are

made of the same materials and require some of the same machine tools, these might be manufactured first. The factory would then change production over to frames and welding, then to spraying and finishing. This process continues to testing and handling the finished product.

Activity

Follow the same procedure you used to find out the most popular payroll processing package earlier, but this time for two CAD packages.

Process production control

Process production control is a system of manufacture that uses machines to do the jobs that humans used to perform. As well as simple, routine tasks such as spot-welding in a car factory or taking photographs of speeding motorists, they are capable of controlling complicated sequences of operations without the need for people. For example, operators used to connect all telephone calls. Now, automatic telephone switching equipment selects the route and connects our calls.

Figure 1.3 Switchboard operators used to have to connect calls by hand

Robotics

Robotics is the science of making robots. Robots are basically IT systems that operate hardware. They are mostly used in industry (and scientific research) for boring, repetitive tasks. The advantages of using robot systems are that they can perform set routines faster, more cheaply and more accurately than humans.

Did you know?

One of the first robots was an experimental model called Shakey. It was capable of arranging blocks into stacks by using a TV camera as a visual sensor, then processing this information in a small computer. Robots can also operate in places or under conditions that are dangerous for people. These could be in outer space, at the bottom of the sea or on a factory floor (such as a nuclear processing plant).

Modern computers use a small microprocessor that can use the data they receive from sensors in the surrounding environment. With this information robots can then change what they do according to the information they receive.

Although robotics is still mainly an industrial area, robots are being increasingly commercialised. For example, all modern car factories use robots for many assembly tasks. Androids, robots in human form like Robocop and other Schwarzenegger characters, may only become possible in the future. Present-day information systems find it extremely difficult just to make a robot 'walk'.

Did you know?

People who study the sea – oceanographers – often use submarines for deep-sea exploration. One of the most famous is Alvin. Alvin can dive down to about 3,600 m (about 12,000 ft), and is equipped with underwater lights, cameras, a television system, and a mechanical manipulator to collect samples from the bottom of the sea. There are also unmanned robot submarines capable of descending to depths of as much as 6,000 m (20,000 ft). In 1985 an unmanned submersible called Argo was used to find the wreck of the *Titanic*. A smaller robot, Jason, was then used to explore the wreck.

Did you know?

In space travel and weapons systems, automatic pilots and automated guidance and control systems are used to carry out some operations much more efficiently and more quickly than humans could.

Benefits and limitations

Whenever you consider commercial or industrial information technology systems, you need a balanced view. This means understanding both their benefits and their limitations. For example, a software house might come up with a system that lets you buy music as you hear it on the radio, without knowing the record, singer, group or even radio station. The system just listens to the track, compares it with an online music database, orders your choice and debits your account.

One of this system's benefits would be efficiency – you wouldn't need to know any information or do anything apart from press the Buy Button. Another benefit would be cost – with a people-less order processing system, it would be cheaper than buying from shops. On the other hand it might have limitations such as not being completely accurate. It might, for example, send you a collection of traditional Norwegian folk music ballads instead of your favourite band's latest album.

Below is an overview of the main benefits and limitations you should consider when examining any commercial or industrial system:

Benefits	Limitations
Accuracy	Costs
Cost	Security and related problems
Speed and efficiency	Health and safety considerations
Impact on the environment	Negative impact on the environment

Accuracy benefits

After any initial bugs have been ironed out, accuracy is one of information technology systems' greatest benefits. Commercial and industrial systems don't make mistakes – as long as the user enters the right data or information. For example, commercial systems such as business accounts packages never make maths mistakes. Industrial systems such as

robots producing electronic circuit boards always put the right components in the right position. In contrast to humans, information systems also:

- never get tired
- never get bored
- never get lost in daydreams
- always pay attention
- never ask for a pay-rise.

Consequently they are 100% reliable with the data they have. You will be demonstrating this accuracy when you work with spreadsheet packages in Element 2.3 and process control in Element 2.4.

Cost benefits

Information technology systems have been used to improve or lower the cost of many existing products, such as kitchen appliances, televisions, radios and high-fidelity equipment. Lowering costs means making goods cheaper for manufacturers to produce and for commercial organisations to buy and sell. In mass production, for example, a manufacturer may need to assemble 500,000 washing-machine units. The cost of a custom-built assembly robot might be around £7,000 while the price of human labour might be double, around £14,000. The £7,000 cost benefit can then be used to boost the company's profits or, in some cases, lower the retail price to the customer.

Did you know?

The main reason that computer-aided manufacturing (CAM) was introduced into the automobile manufacturing industry was to increase productivity and so reduce costs. The average modern car would cost over seven times the price, if mechanical robots controlled by computer systems didn't perform many routine assembly tasks.

Speed and efficiency benefits

Efficiency, just to remind you, means producing something effectively with the minimum of waste, expense or unnecessary effort. Telecommunications are a clear example of how IT has dramatically increased speed and efficiency: if you had to get a message to a friend on the other side of town without using IT, how could you do it? Whatever the method – pigeon, bike or missile – it would have to be transferred physically. Telecommunications can transfer your voice or words or pictures or even music to the other side of the world in a few seconds.

IT systems not only make ordinary life more efficient but they also make themselves more efficient. In Element 1.4 you will be using and developing *macros*. A macro is a single instruction in programming language that results in a series of instructions in machine language. For example, with a single keystroke you can start a series of letters, such as a word. Then rather than retyping a word you often use such as your name, you just type, for example, *Alt* plus the first letter of your name. Macros can speed up any sort of data entry and are particularly useful for databases.

Beneficial impact on the environment

Apart from helping us to understand and look after our environment generally, IT systems can have a direct beneficial impact. For example, they have reduced the amount of paper we need to use and the amount of pollution we create.

The better-quality companies provide their documentation on recyclable paper. IT systems have made it possible to go one step further – they can remove the need for any paper at all. The 'paperless office' is rare because it is necessary to keep back-up hard copies of some documents, such as signed contracts or hand-produced artwork. Nonetheless, most offices contain a great deal less paper than before IT systems became commonplace.

Did you know?

Local area networks (LANs) link information systems in the same room, office or building. Wide area networks (WANs) link information systems, usually by telephone, at much greater distances. They extend electronic links between people in the office to workers at home or in satellite offices. This capability has led to a sharp increase in telecommuting or people working from home.

Telecommuting reduces the need to drive to work so there is less traffic congestion and fewer harmful fumes. It reduces the number of people coming into and working in towns and cities and that reduces the level of noise pollution. As well as having environmental benefits, telecommuting has cost benefits to companies (they no longer need to rent so much expensive office space). It also has efficiency benefits because people

who no longer spend hours travelling from home to office increase their productivity.

Did you know?

As well as being used extensively in environmental monitoring, IT systems have been applied in the automotive field for diagnostics and pollution control: catalytic converters are the part of a vehicle's exhaust system that reduces the pollutants in the exhaust gases to environmentally harmless levels.

Cost limitations

Many larger organisations either modify commercially available systems to suit their needs or develop their own systems. The research and development budgets of these companies allow them to invest in engineers, consultants and specialist manufacturers to develop more efficient systems. For the small company, commercially available software and hardware costs alone represent a significant investment and can be a barrier to entering a market. For example, a small television production company could not afford the special effects systems used by the BBC.

Nor could they afford the cost of training staff in system use. This is an equally important limitation to the use of ordinary office software. It would not be realistic to pay for staff training in a system that was only used once a month.

Did you know?

Cost limitations of small-scale, industrial processing systems can be extended by *flexible manufacturing systems* (FMSs). FMSs extend automation to companies where small production runs economically limit full automation. A computer is used to monitor and control the entire operation of the factory, from scheduling each step of the production process to keeping track of parts inventories and tool use.

Security and related problems

Problems occur with both information and the system that stores and manipulates it. The main problems are data corruption and loss, the loss of confidentiality and data theft, contravention of copyright, equipment theft and software theft. You may well have experienced some of these yourself.

If a disk is damaged in any way, data usually becomes corrupted and inaccessible. It is also easy to lose data before it's saved, perhaps by accidentally overloading a system's memory and freezing it. When that happens, it is too late to save whatever you are doing. All you can do is to reboot the system. This is obviously a disaster (but not an excuse) if you are doing your homework. If a network fails, for example because of a voltage overload or spike, everyone loses unsaved work. So the message is simple – save regularly.

Activity

Most modern systems have an *AutoSave* setting. This allows you to specify how frequently the file you are working on is saved automatically by the computer. Ask you tutor how this feature works on the computers you use in your school or college. Then, change the setting to one minute, watch to see that it works, and change it back to the original setting.

Information can be priceless. Although you may not be dealing with exclusive or highly sensitive information at this point in your career, any information is potentially valuable to an

organisation's competitors. Unauthorised access to a company's systems such as its databases is only possible if staff do not follow security and confidentiality procedures properly.

Different computer systems allow different confidentiality procedures. Among the most common computer systems are passwords, time-restricted access and back-ups. Passwords may be changed daily or weekly and be available at different clearance levels. Time-restricted access systems limit the time that you have to find the information you want. If you do not know the procedures, you are unlikely to retrieve the information you want within the given period. Storing copies of data on disks or digital tape is usually carried out at the end of every day.

You are probably familiar with copyright warnings at the beginning of rental videos. This is the same for most published text or graphics, where it says something along the lines of 'All rights reserved. No part of this publication may be reproduced or transmitted, in any form or by any means, without the prior permission of the publisher'. Check for the symbol ©, followed by a date and name, as at the beginning of this book. This indicates that a work is copyright.

Both data disks and software are usually kept in disaster-proof safes. Less valuable data or software may be kept in locked filing cabinets. Some organisations bolt filing cabinets and computer hardware to the floor to avoid theft.

Health and safety considerations

Your school or college and tutors care about your health and safety. The business you work for may not. Many young people continue to be hurt or disabled by accidents at work which are the result of irresponsible employers. There is no job that is good enough to risk your health and safety for. Know the Health and Safety at Work Act. This Act was passed in 1974 to put a legal responsibility on employers and employees to observe health and safety procedures. Under the Act, employers must provide:

- A safe means of entry to and exit from the workplace.
- A working environment that is safe and has adequate facilities and arrangements for welfare at work.
- Equipment and systems of work that are safe.
- Arrangements that ensure the safe handling, transport, storage and use of articles and substances.

- Information, instruction, training and supervision of employees.
- Accident investigation.

Employees must:

- take reasonable care of their own health and safety;
- take reasonable care of the health and safety of others who might be affected by their actions; and
- co-operate with anyone carrying out their obligations under the Act.

Activity

Make a list all the risks to health and safety in an IT working environment you can think of – for example, cables that people might trip over. When you finish, discuss your ideas with your tutor and the rest of the class.

Negative impact on the environment

On the whole, IT systems contribute to a cleaner, healthier environment. Their negative impact on the environment can be in by-products such as the virtually indestructible polystyrene that is often used as packing material, and in social costs such as unemployment.

Robots are specifically designed to replace people. Many traditional employers such as the automotive, mining and manufacturing industries have moved over to robotics. This means that their workers are either made redundant or have the opportunity to learn new skills for new jobs. Some people criticise IT for taking people's jobs, but they ignore the new jobs it has created.

Activity

1   List all the IT-related jobs you can think of that didn't exist when your parents were your age. When you have finished, discuss these with your tutor.
2   It would be a good idea to visit local organisations and research the benefits and limitations of two commercial and two industrial systems. When you visit you must get as many details as possible because you will need this information for your evidence assignment. You will also be presenting your findings to the class.

Before you go, prepare a research sheet for each system you will see. Write out the name of each organisation and system, together with a brief description of what they do. Then make headings for all the benefits and limitations you have considered above. Under each heading make notes on the sort of information you want to find out. Check your research sheet with your tutor.

When you get back, write up your findings as fully as possible and keep this work for your project. Then, list the most important benefits and limitations of the systems and use your lists to practise giving a system presentation to a partner. Be ready to give one or more of your presentations to the whole class when your tutor asks you to.

Features

To understand any system better, you need to explore its different features. The main features to look at are data, hardware, software, people, processing activities, effectiveness and purpose.

Data

Data means *information,* any information. It can be a specific item of information such as a telephone number, a group of such items such as a telephone directory on CD-ROM or computer instructions such as the contents of a program. Although data means any information, most people in IT distinguish between program files and data files. For example, your digitised photograph would be a data file in a graphics package such as Adobe Photoshop.

Figure 1.4 Some travel agents use commercial systems on CD-ROM showing videos of holidays they offer

Commercial and industrial systems are designed to deal with different types of data. For example, some travel agents use commercial systems that allow people to see photographs and even videos of the places they offer as holidays. Some industrial systems such as CAD packages are designed specifically for architects. To know whether a system will be useful or not you need to know exactly what data it is designed to store and manipulate.

Did you know?

Data communication, the process of transmitting data in digital form by wire or radio, is the fastest growing area of information technology.

Hardware

The data in an information system is digitised, stored and manipulated by system hardware and software. Hardware devices include the computers, terminals (devices that transmit and receive information) and peripheral equipment such as printers that you will be studying in the next element. Whenever you examine a commercial or industrial system make a list of all the different pieces of hardware that are needed for it to be up and working.

Processing activities and software

The processing activities of any information system are what it does and the software is the program that makes these functions possible. For example, many airlines have systems that connect terminals at the desks of travel or ticket agents to a central, host computer. The processing activities of the system are to transmit data such as flight information or to receive data from the host computer. To do this, many travel agents use a software program called Galileo.

Each time you explore a software system and its processing activities, write the main functions into a list for future reference. Although you can find software with very specific processing activities available commercially, some companies may have software specially designed for them. Most car makers, for example, have their own CAD programs. They may also have their own in-car programs such as suspension balance control, air-bag release, fuel consumption and other driver information.

Activity

You have already found out the names of some popular commercial and industrial system software. Choose one package, go back to your sources and find out what that software does, what its main processing activities are. Write your findings into a short paragraph or a list, then discuss this with your tutor and compare it with your class.

People

People are the most important part of any information technology system. Although we might talk about artificial intelligence, or label terminals as 'dumb,' 'smart' or 'intelligent', this is misleading. It encourages people to think that computers have minds or brains like humans. They don't and never will. It's people that supply the intelligence to make computers work. If you supply a computer with nonsense rather than intelligence, you'll get nonsense back. Remember: garbage in, garbage out.

Each system, whether commercial or industrial, needs a set of people to operate it. Systems with basic operational requirements, such as a commercial system that works with data entry and a few simple codes, usually only require operators. In many cases these operators will make routine use of the system as part of their job. For example, the checkout clerk at the supermarket is using part of an information technology system to add up your bill.

Complex systems often use specialist operators and are backed up by software engineering support staff. For example, the system used at airports to control air traffic is very sophisticated. With flights taking off and landing every 30 seconds, it takes a highly trained team of operators and support staff to make sure the system runs smoothly, always.

For each system, however simple or complicated, find out how many people are needed to run it, whether they are needed full time or part time, and what they are required to do.

Effectiveness and purpose

No matter how clever or impressive a system is, it has to be effective to be useful. If it doesn't save time, money or effort, there's no point in using it. An order processing system, for example, that only deals with two packages per day is a waste of space – it would be quicker to pick the packages off the shelf and give them a label.

This means that in assessing the need for a new system, an upgrade or the value of an existing system, you must look at its purpose. Specify the amount of processing it is used for and the amount of work necessary to run it.

Activity

It would be useful to visit one or two local organisations and research industrial and commercial systems, this time focusing on all their features. When you visit you must get as many details as possible because you will need this information for your evidence assignment. You will also be presenting your findings to the class.

Before you go, prepare your research sheets. Write out the details of the organisation and the system and make headings for all the different features. Under each heading make notes on the sort of information you want to find out. Check your research sheet with your tutor.

When you get back, write up your findings as fully as possible and keep this work for your project. Then, list the most important features of the systems and use your lists to practise giving a system presentation to a partner. Be ready to give one or both your presentations to the whole class when your tutor asks you to.

Evidence assignment

Create a directory for Unit 1 and save all your work for this unit in the appropriate directory.

This project has been designed to cover all the evidence indicators related to Element 1.1. It may be completed at appropriate points in your studies or as one project at the end of the element.

Scenario

At the end of this course, when you are looking for a job, you will have to demonstrate your knowledge and ability to prospective employers. This means giving clear, well organised explanations about different areas of IT such as commercial and industrial systems. As well as contributing to your success in obtaining the IT GNVQ, your evidence assignments are ideal opportunities to practise the skills you need to get and keep a good job. For example, you have heard of a possible opening at a firm called Computer Consultants Ltd and have written to the manager. Figure 1.5 shows the reply.

COMPUTER CONSULTANTS LTD
108 King Street, Anytown AT2 3RJ
Tel 0132/549261
Fax 0132/319734

Dear _____,

Thank you for your application.

As a successful and prestigious firm, we receive many applications. To make more accurate assessments of potential new staff, we ask that you prepare and send a report prior to your interview. This report will form the basis of the interview discussion and should cover

1 the benefits and limitations of two commercial systems of your choice;

2 the benefits and limitations of two industrial systems of your choice; and

3 an explanation of all the features of one commercial and one industrial information technology system.

We look forward to receiving your report and then to meeting you.

Yours sincerely

Paul Goss

Paul Goss
Manager

Figure 1.5 The letter from Computer Consultants Ltd

1 Write the report requested by Computer Consultants Ltd. See the Core Skills chapter on Communication if you need help with writing or presentation skills. Remember to include suitable images or graphics in your report – clipart may be useful.

2 Write the covering letter, addressed to Paul Goss, to go with your report. Your letter should mention your continuing interest in working for Computer Consultants Ltd, and say that you hope to meet Mr Goss to discuss any possible openings.

Revision test

Name the following

1 Four uses of commercial systems.

2 Three uses of industrial systems.

3 Three payroll processing packages.

4 Three uses of process production control systems.

5 Three advantages that robot systems have over humans.

Complete the blanks

6 E_____ f_____ t_____ is a way of paying by paperless money.

7 P_____ o_____ s_____ is the place where a sale takes place.

8 The main benefits of commercial and industrial systems are a_____, c_____, s_____ and e_____, and impact on the e_____ .

9 The main limitations of commercial and industrial systems are c_____, s_____ and related problems, h_____ and s_____ considerations, and negative impact on the e_____ .

10 When trying to understand any system, the seven most important features to look at are: d_____, h_____, s_____, people, p_____ activities, e_____ and p_____ .

11 CAD stands for c_____ a_____ d_____ and CAM stands for c_____ a_____ m_____ .

Examine the components of a stand-alone computer system

This element develops your knowledge of the hardware and software that make up a stand-alone computer system. The first part illustrates and describes the physical components of a computer and explains what they do. The second part describes the main types of software and explains what they are used for.

After studying this chapter you should be able to:

1 identify *hardware components* of a stand-alone computer system
2 describe *purposes of the hardware components* in a stand-alone computer system
3 explain the *purposes of types of software*
4 describe the *hardware components* required for *types of software.*

Hardware components

We talk about our computers in the same way as we talk about our cars. A friend might tell you they have a P5-133 processor with a 1.62 GB hard drive, 16 MB RAM and a 64-bit graphics accelerator. Change the subject, and they will say they have a 1800 GTI with a 16-valve, four-cylinder engine and a twin OHCs.

This is the jargon. In fact it is simply terms that describe components. Once you know what the different components are, what they look like and what they do, you can easily understand and use the jargon.

Activity

As you've chosen to study IT you may already know quite a lot about hardware. So what would you do in this situation? You've just won a phone-in radio competition for the computer system of your choice. The presenter asks you for your hardware spec. What components would you ask for? List as many as you can and choose the best. File your list for comparison at the end of this section.

You can't tell much about a computer just by looking at it. Some, like cars, have badges. You've probably seen, for example, labels indicating Intel Inside, or

Pentium (type of processor), Quad Speed (the CD-ROM drive) or Super VGA (graphics card and monitor). To set up and get the best from a computer, you need to examine its physical components and appreciate their features. These are the input devices that get data into the computer, the main processor unit that manipulates the data, the output devices that display the data in electronic or hard copy, and the storage devices.

Activity

As you work through the following section of this element, you may be surprised at the number and variety of hardware components. Look at your own computer and the computers you use at school or college and list the components they have.

Input devices

Input devices enable you to enter data, commands and programs into the computer's central processing unit (CPU), its brain. The most common input device is the keyboard. Other input devices include:

- joystick
- mouse
- light pen
- scanner
- microphone
- sensor.

Did you know?

The word *input*, when you are talking about computers, means information. An input device is a hardware component that allows you to feed information into the computer. There are three main types – keyboard, mouse and sensor.

Keyboard

Check the keyboard(s) you use against Figure 1.6. Almost all keyboards follow the standard IBM layout and design. IBM call this their 'enhanced keyboard'

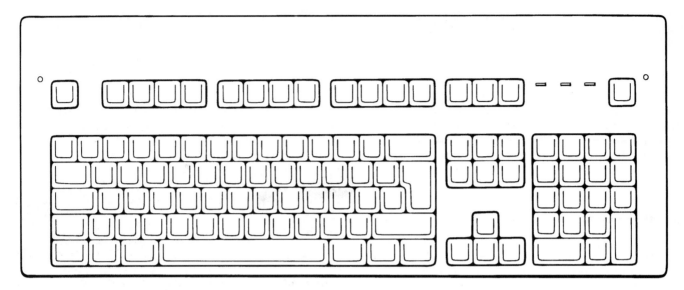

Figure 1.6 Standard keyboard

and it is very similar to Apple's 'extended keyboard'. Any computer keyboard is basically the same as an ordinary typewriter keyboard but has added keys for specialised functions. Computer keyboards are divided into four main areas (see Figure 1.6):

■ Function keys across the top.
■ Letter keys in the main section.
■ A numeric keypad on the right.
■ Cursor movement and editing keys between the main section and the numeric keypad.

Touching or pressing a key sends an electronic signal to the computer which it interprets as a character or function.

Did you know?

The standard layout of most typewriters and keyboards is called the QWERTY layout. The name comes from the first six keys on the top row of alphabetic characters. Have a look the next time you use a keyboard. The original design was based on mechanical considerations rather than on efficiency: the letters you would use most often were put as far apart as possible so that the old typewriter hammers (that swung up and hit the print ribbon) did not stick together. The Dvorak keyboard is easier to use but everyone is used to QWERTY and it is far more common.

Activity

Go back to Figure 1.6, take a copy of it and label:

■ nine of the letter keys;
■ the numbers on the numeric keypad (in the correct position); and
■ the cursor movement keys.

Mouse

A mouse (computer mouse) is a pointing device. Like the joysticks you've used in arcades or at home, a mouse translates the physical motion of your hand and fingers into motion on a computer screen. By moving the mouse around on a surface such as a desk, you can control the on-screen cursor. To select

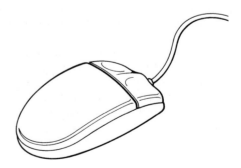

Figure 1.7 A mouse

items such as words, numbers or icons, you press one of the mouse's buttons. This produces a 'mouse click'.

The basic features of a mouse are the casing, buttons and base. The casing is designed to be held by the fingers and thumb of one hand, with the bottom of your palm resting on a mat or other surface. The top has one, two or three buttons, each clicked for different functions. The bottom is flat and has a 'multidirectional detection device', usually a ball. A cable connects the mouse to the computer.

Did you know?

The mouse has become a standard hardware component now that most commercial software is operated through a GUI (graphical user interface – pronounced 'gooey'). A GUI is a screen display that lets you start programs, choose commands and other options by using the mouse to click icons and lists of menu items. Although you can still use the keyboard for most commands, a mouse makes things much easier.

Sensors

A sensor is a device that reacts to certain physical conditions such as light, sound or movement. For example, buildings in California and Japan are equipped with sensors to detect earthquake tremors. Computers detect light and sound from input sensors. The main computer sensor devices are light pens, scanners and computer microphones.

A *light pen* is another type of pointing device. You hold it up to the screen or move it over an electronic

pad, like a wand. To select icons, commands or other items you press the light pen against the surface of the screen or click a clip on the side of the pen. When you make your selection the light pen sends a signal to the computer through its light sensors.

Scanners are another type of light sensor. They 'read' words, symbols or other graphics from a printed page and 'translate' the pattern of light and dark or colour into a digital signal that the computer can manipulate and store.

Figure 1.9 Design work can be carried out on screen

The commonest types of scanner are hand-held and flat-bed. Hand-held scanners are usually only a few centimetres wide and so this limits the amount of information you can scan to small areas. You use a hand-held scanner simply by moving it across the document to be scanned.

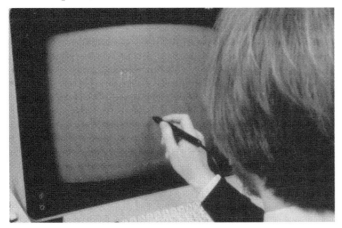

Figure 1.8 Light pen

Figure 1.10 Flat-bed scanner

A flat-bed scanner looks like a printer and works in a similar way to a photocopier. You put the document face down on a flat bed of glass and close the lid. The sensor moves across (scans) underneath the glass reading the information very like the operation of a photocopier.

Microphones are sensors that detect sound. The microphones used with computers are basically the same as any other. At present they're mostly used with voice recognition modules that take spoken words and translate them into digital signals for the computer. This makes it possible to operate a computer without using your hands.

Did you know?

IBM have developed a Personal Dictation System. You simply have to speak into the microphone, one word at a time, and whatever you say is typed out on the screen.

Central processing unit (CPU)

The central processing unit – or *microprocessor* – is the computer's brain. It is the component that interprets and executes the instructions you give the computer through the input devices. It fetches, decodes and executes instructions and transfers information to and from other components. The commonest examples are Intel's 80486 and 80586 (or Pentium) processors.

Did you know?

Microprocessors are built on to a single piece of silicon, called a wafer or chip. These chips are usually around 0.5 cm (0.2 in) long and 0.05 cm (0.02 in) thick.

Compare Intel's first microprocessor and their latest Pentium chip: the first microprocessor had 2,300 transistors on it and could execute what at the time seemed an amazing 60,000 instructions a second. The Pentium chip contains 3.3 million transistors and can process more than 100 million instructions per second. How much faster is the Pentium than Intel's original microprocessor? No idea? Well, a mathematician worked it out as 300 times faster than the original.

Output devices

There's no point in inputting data and processing it if you can't see the end result. An output device lets you see the results of the computer's operations – its data manipulations or calculations. The commonest output devices are video display units (VDUs), printers, speakers and modems.

VDUs

A VDU is a computer video display and its housing. Together they are usually referred to as a monitor. VDUs display images (characters or graphics) generated by the computer's video adapter. Common types of adapter are monochrome display adapter (MDA), colour/graphics adapter (CGA), enhanced graphics adapter (EGA) and super video graphics adapter (SVGA).

Did you know?

The sharpness or clarity of the image on a VDU (or on a printer) is determined by its *resolution*. Resolution is measured in *pixels* (short for picture elements; pix-els). If you look at your computer monitor closely, you will see that the image is made up of tiny dots. Each dot is called a pixel. The more pixels per square centimetre of screen the better the resolution. For example, an EGA can produce a higher resolution (640 pixels across by 350 pixels down) than a CGA (640 pixels across but only 200 pixels down). Compare your TV screen resolution with your computer screen – which is best?

Activity

Find the answers to these questions about VDUs then check them with your tutor and compare with your class:

1 What sort of video adapter does the computer you use have?
2 What resolution is it capable of?
3 What is the best resolution you know of and on what sort of monitor?
4 How much would you expect to pay for such a monitor?
5 What resolution does your TV set have?

Did you know?

Like television sets, most VDUs use a cathode-ray tube (CRT). At one end there is an electron gun (pointing at you as you look at the screen – think about that!). The gun fires a beam of electrons against the luminescent screen at the opposite end of the tube, where you are. A bright spot of light appears wherever the electrons strike the screen. A collection of bright spots forms an image.

Printers

You don't just want to see your information on a screen. Because you sometimes need a hard copy to send to people or look at away from a computer, you need a printer. At first, the commonest PC printers were daisy-wheel. They received that name because of the shape of their print head. Their quality of print was about the same as a typewriter's but they were slow, noisy and could only deal with text rather than text and graphics. Today most PCs use dot-matrix, ink-jet or laser printers.

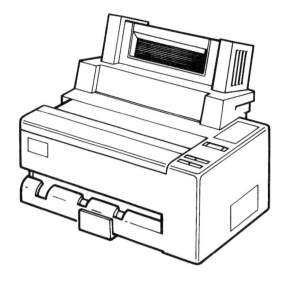

Figure 1.12 Ink-jet printer

Ink-jet printers provide high resolution and quiet operation. It can be difficult to tell the difference between a printout from a good-quality ink-jet and a standard laser printer.

Laser printers are based on the technology used by photocopiers. They have a high resolution, can reproduce complex graphics, are almost silent and operate at a reasonably high speed.

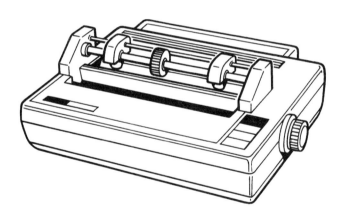

Figure 1.11 Dot-matrix printer

A *dot-matrix* printer produces characters made up of dots using a 9, 18 or 24 pin print head. The pins hit the paper through a ribbon making patterns of dots in the shape of letters and numbers. They can do this in different fonts and type sizes. The print quality depends mostly on the number of dots in the matrix. This could be low enough to show individual dots or high enough to look almost like fully formed characters.

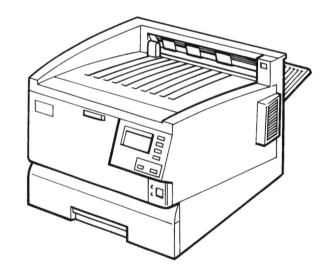

Figure 1.13 Laser-jet printer

Did you know?

The following is how a laser-jet printer works:

1 The laser beam, together with a rotating mirror, draws an image on a photosensitive drum.
2 The image is then converted to an electrostatic charge (the sort you sometimes get from hairbrushes or car doors).
3 The charge attracts and holds the toner.
4 Electrostatically charged paper is rolled against the drum.
5 This pulls the toner off the drum and on to the paper.
6 Heat then melts or fuses the ink on to the paper (which is why it is hot when you get your printout).

Activity

If it is possible to do so at your school or college, obtain a printout of the same image or text from each of the three different types of printer. Compare the different printouts for quality and clarity.

Did you know?

Printer resolution is measured in dots per inch (dpi). It ranges from about 125 dpi on a low-quality dot-matrix printer to about 600 dpi on a typical laser printer. Just to compare, the sort of professional typesetting equipment used for magazines, prints at resolutions of more than 1,000 dpi.

Plotters

A less common type of printer is a plotter. This is an output device that draws graphs or pictures, usually by moving a pen. It is also sometimes called a plotting board or plotting table. Plotters are mostly used by engineers, mappers and architects who need to print from CAD programs on to larger-sized sheets of paper such as A3.

Speakers

Most computers are fitted with a small internal speaker that will beep to draw your attention if, for example, the wrong keys are pressed. On MPCs (multimedia PCs) this speaker is either absent or is bypassed to external, stereo speakers that provide better-quality sound. The amplifier driving external speakers is built on to the sound card or into one of the speakers themselves.

Modems

A modem is a device that connects two or more computers and transmits data by telecommunications. You will find out more about these in Unit 4.

Storage devices

Once you've input data and spent time working on it, you don't want to lose it when your computer is switched off. To keep your work 'electronically alive', you can choose from a range of storage devices. Computer systems store information in internal memory or on external storage devices. A storage device is anything that can record data in a semi-permanent or permanent form. The RAM chips, floppy disks, hard disks, CD-ROMs and magnetic tape units described below are the commonest storage devices.

ROM and RAM

ROM and RAM are computer memory. ROM stands for 'read only memory' – a type of memory that can be read many times but cannot be changed. RAM stands for 'random access memory' – a type of memory that can be read and changed. Both ROM and RAM are connected to the CPU.

RAM chips are mounted directly into the computer's main circuit board or on peripheral chips that are plugged into the circuit board. Actually there are two types of RAM – *dynamic* and *static*. The DRAM you see in graphics accelerator specifications is dynamic RAM. It needs voltage applied at regular intervals of about two milliseconds or it loses its data. Static RAM holds its data as long as there is current flowing through it.

Activity

Which is which? Should RAM or ROM go at the beginning of these sentences?

_____ is like a book; its data has been printed on to each page.

_____ is like a piece of paper; you can write on it, rub out and use it again.

Did you know?

Pound for pound, RAM chips are more valuable than diamonds. Along with Pentium processors, they are now the main target of computer thieves. These criminals no longer bother to take the whole computer, they just take the lid off the main box, unplug the chip, put it in their pocket and walk out. Computer theft is one of the fastest-growing crimes. So far it has mainly been directed at organisations, but police advise you to protect your home computer.

Floppy disks

Floppy disks are round, flat, made of a substance called mylar and held in a protective plastic shell. Depending on their capacity, they can hold from a few hundred thousand to over one million bytes of data. The stronger and more convenient 3.5 inch floppies have taken over from the old 5.25 inch disks and become the standard.

Figure 1.14 3.5 inch floppy disk

Figure 1.15 5.25 inch floppy disk

Did you know?

On the Macintosh, a single-sided disk can hold 400 kilobytes (KB), a double-sided disk can hold 800 KB and a double-sided, high-density disk can hold 1.44 megabytes (MB). On IBM and compatible machines floppy disks can hold either 720 KB or 1.44 MB of information.

So how much is a byte or a megabyte? Just as a pixel is the smallest element that display or print hardware can manipulate in creating graphics, a bit is the smallest unit of information a computer can process. Eight bits make one byte, and one byte is roughly the amount of computer memory needed to store one character.

Hard disks

Hard disks are flat, round, rigid platters that provide faster access to data than floppy disks and are capable of storing much more information. Because they are rigid, they can be stacked so that one hard disk drive can access more than one platter (hard disk). Most hard disks have from two to eight platters.

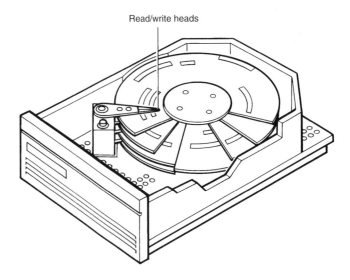

Read/write heads

Figure 1.16 Hard disk

Did you know?

The reason hard disks come in sealed units is to protect them from contaminants such as dust that might interfere with the close head-to-disk tolerances. The read/write heads you can see in Figure 1.16 ride over the surface of the disk on an air cushion 10 to 25 millionths of an inch deep.

CD-ROM disks

Rather than the magnetic means for reading data used with floppy and hard disks, CD-ROMs use laser optics. This is the same laser technology that is used to make audio CDs. In fact, you can play your music CDs on most MPCs.

CD-ROMs have a very high storage capacity – around 650 megabytes. One CD-ROM can hold roughly the same amount of data as 450 1.4 Mb floppy disks. Which would you rather carry around with you?

Figure 1.17 CD-ROM

Did you know?

The entire contents of a text-based encyclopaedia take up only 25% of one standard-sized CD-ROM. This has allowed publishers to fill up the other 75% with video sequences, animations, photographs, sound and interactive programs. The result is interactive multimedia encyclopaedias such as Microsoft's, Grolier's and Hutchinson's.

Tape back-up

Most organisations need to store large volumes of data. For example, a magazine needs to keep all its back issues and a college registry needs to keep all its student and other records. These require far greater storage capacity than is available on hard disk. The easiest solution is to back up data on to digital audio tape (DAT).

Activity

As a group, research three current tape back-up systems and note the following information for each. Then compare with another group and say which you think is best value for money.

Name of system _____

Maximum amount of uncompressed data _____

Maximum amount of compressed data _____

Transfer rate (in megabytes per minute) _____

High street price _____

Types of software

Software programs are sets of instructions that make hardware work. There are two main types – operating systems (system software) and applications. Operating systems control the usually invisible workings of the computer, such as file maintenance and screen management. Application software performs the different tasks that people use computers for, such as word processing and spreadsheet calculations.

The basic purposes of operating systems are to provide:

- system control
- routine file management and maintenance
- graphical user interfaces.

The basic purposes of applications are:

- processing (structured data, documents, graphics and numerical data)
- controlling
- modelling.

Activity

Before going any further, make two lists and keep them for comparison at the end of this element. On the first list write the names of all the operating systems you know of. On the second list, write the names of all the application software you know of.

The hardware specifications needed to run operating systems and applications vary with the different packages. For example, complex, sophisticated programs need more powerful CPUs, more hard disk storage space and more RAM. Although operating most programs is easier with a mouse, the minimum hardware components required for any type of software are:

- CPU
- monitor
- keyboard.

Operating systems

Operating systems (OS) are the software programs that control the use of hardware resources. For example, they control:

- central processing unit (CPU) time;
- the allocation and use of memory;
- the allocation and use of disk space; and
- the operation of peripheral devices such as printers.

This makes operating systems the foundation that application software, such as word processing and spreadsheet programs, are built on. The most common operating systems are MS-DOS, the Macintosh system – OS/2 – and systems that use windowing environments such as Windows '95.

Figure 1.18 Operating systems control many different functions

MS-DOS stands for Microsoft Disk Operating System. Like other operating systems, MS-DOS controls many internal computer functions – for example, the way programs are executed. You can use MS-DOS to tell your computer where you want it to start – what you will see on screen – when you turn it on. You may want it to start at the C:\> prompt or to go further and start Windows, or to go even further and to start in a particular application such as word processing.

MS-DOS has what is called a command-line interface – this means that you operate it by typing in command codes. For example, typing 'ver' at the C:\> (or command) prompt and pressing Enter will display the version number of MS-DOS.

Did you know?

How did the richest man in the world obtain his fortune? IBM were looking for an OS to make the microprocessor they got from Intel work as a computer. They went to a small business called Microsoft, run by a computer 'nerd' called Bill Gates. At their meeting, Mr Gates did not mention that he did not actually have an OS to sell. Instead he went out and bought one from another small business just down the road. He polished it up, renamed it MS-DOS and licensed it to IBM.

The OS/2 was originally developed as a joint project by Microsoft and IBM. It can run most MS-DOS and Windows-based applications, and can read all MS-DOS disks. The OS/2 includes two important subsystems – Presentation Manager, which provides a graphical user interface (GUI), and a Local Area Network (LAN) Manager, which provides networking facilities. You will find out more about LANs in Element 4.3.

Activity

Do you remember from the earlier part of this element what a GUI is? And how to pronounce it? Make a note of some of the features of a GUI, then check this with your tutor.

Windows is the popular name for Microsoft Windows. It is a user-friendly graphical face (GUI) built on to the user-unfriendly text face of MS-DOS. Windows has a standardised interface with screen windows, drop-down menus and a mouse or other input device such as voice. Programs have to be specially designed to take advantage of Windows features.

Did you know?

The name Windows comes from the computer term *windowing environment*. A windowing environment is an operating system that can divide the screen into independent areas called *windows*. Each window has its own frame that can usually be resized and moved around on the screen. Individual windows can contain different documents or messages, or even their own menus or other controls. In some programs, windows are opened side by side on the screen while in others, open windows overlap one another. In Microsoft Windows, the OS/2 Presentation Manager and the Apple Macintosh Finder are all windowing environments.

Activity

Using computer magazines, manuals or any other source, research, list and briefly explain three features of the latest version of MS Windows and one other OS. Discuss this with your tutor and compare it with your class.

Applications

Operating systems run a computer. Applications are programs designed to help people perform certain types of work by manipulating text, numbers and graphics, or all three together. Although there are many different software applications, the most popular systems are word processing, spreadsheet and database programs.

Word processing

Word processors manipulate text-based documents and range from the simple to the sophisticated.

Activity

As a class, list the names of any word processing packages you've heard of.

The simplest word processors make typing and basic editing tasks such as deleting and inserting easier. The more complex check your grammar, find synonyms, allow you to drop text, graphics or calculations created with another program into your text, display documents in multiple on-screen windows, and record macros that simplify difficult or repetitive operations (you will learn more about macros in Element 1.4). Word processing applications are ideal for presenting written assignment work. You will be finding out more about them in Element 2.1.

Activity

Make a list of all the tasks you know that word processors can perform. Use these headings: Editing (e.g. insert and delete), Formatting (e.g. fonts), Other (e.g. grammar checking). When you have finished, check your list with your tutor and compare it with your class.

Spreadsheets

Spreadsheet programs make financial tasks, such as calculating how much money you have, much easier.

Activity

As a class, list the names of any spreadsheet packages you've heard of.

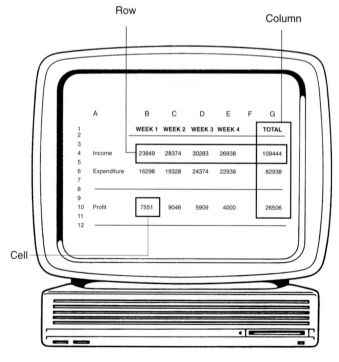

Figure 1.19 Spreadsheet screen

You might use a spreadsheet to work out how much spending money you'll have for your holiday: you can enter all the income you expect between now and July and also make deductions for your spending before July. You can then 'play around' and see what happens if you halve the money you plan to spend on clothes, or do two hours' overtime on five Saturdays, or work on Bank Holidays. You wouldn't have to do all the sums again because the spreadsheet would recalculate for you. A business might use a spreadsheet to calculate the difference between how much money it receives from sales, and how much it spends. The difference is the profit.

Did you know?

The basic element of a spreadsheet is a cell. A cell is the intersection of a row and a column – the place where they meet. Each row and column in a spreadsheet is unique so each cell can be uniquely identified rather like a map reference. For example, cell C6 is at the intersection of column C and row 6. Look at Figure 1.19 and locate cell C6. Each cell holds a number (or text). The number might just be a number you type in, or it might be a formula such as 'cell B4 + cell C4'. In Figure 1.19, what would cell B4 + cell C4 equal?

Sophisticated programs can link one spreadsheet to another so that when you change the numbers on one sheet the numbers in linked spreadsheets are updated automatically. For example, you might have one sheet showing the money you have saved and spent this month. When you get to next month you might want to carry the total over to a new sheet for the new month. You can use the program to link the two spreadsheets automatically. This means that if you change a number in one month, the next month will also change. Like word processing programs, spreadsheet programs usually include macro facilities.

Activity

In your group, make a list of all the tasks you know that spreadsheets can perform. Use the headings: Calculations (e.g. adding) and Other (e.g. bar charts). When you have finished your list, compare it with others in your class.

Databases

Have you ever done any of the following?

- Subscribed to a magazine.
- Opened a bank or building society account.
- Applied for a driving licence.
- Paid for goods or services with a debit card.
- Paid for goods or services with a credit card.
- Applied to a college.
- Joined a club or society.

If you have, then there is a database file about you that contains the information you gave.

Did you know?

If you ever wonder what 'they' know about you, the Data Protection Act 1984 gives individuals the legal right to know what personal data concerning them is held on computer (this is explained more fully in Element 3.4).

A database is any organised collection of data or information. It might not be very well organised, but your personal address or phone numbers book is a database. Card index systems or filing cabinets are also databases. The more phone numbers or other information you add to your database, the more space you need and the harder it is to find. Imagine the amount of information kept by government agencies such as MI5, the CIA or Interpol. Even a small business such as a local newspaper may need to store and access databases of information on subscribers, advertisers, writers and so on. A computer-based system can store vast amounts of data in memory, organised for easy access by authorised users.

Did you know?

Most unauthorised access of database systems is for international or corporate spying or sabotage. One of the biggest problems in corporate computer security is **hackers.** These people are either sacked or disgruntled staff wanting revenge, or they are paid by rival companies to plant viruses. If undetected, these viruses can totally destroy a database and all the time and effort it has taken to enter information and build it up.

Most commercially available databases are a type called *relational*. This means they store information in lists (rows and columns of data) and retrieve information by using data in one list to find information in another. The rows in a database are called records (collections of information about a particular item). The columns are called fields (particular details of a record). Relational databases access information by using the data in the columns of one table to find further data in another table.

For example, you might have one list with the names and addresses of all your friends in the school or college where you study now. You might have another list with the names and addresses of all the friends you studied with at a different school or college. If you have lots of friends and want to check whether any of them were at both schools or colleges with you, a relational database would relate the two lists to produce a third one containing the names you asked about.

Here's another example: your school or college probably uses a relational database. It may have one table with the fields *Student-ID, Last-name, First-name* and *Department,* and another table with the fields *Course, Student-ID* and *Assignment grades.* As a relational database, it could then match the *Student-ID* fields in the two tables to find such information as the names of all students with pass grades on specific courses, or names of all students joining courses in the IT department in 199– and so on.

Activity

1 As a class, list the names of any database packages you've heard of.
2 'Suites' are packages of integrated programs – for example, one package containing a word processing program, a spreadsheet program and a database program. Again as a class, name all the commercially available suites you've heard of. Your tutor will then allocate a suite to you and you should research what programs it contains and the minimum hardware needed to run it. Report your findings back to your tutor and class.

Evidence assignment

This project has been designed to cover all the evidence indicators related to Element 1.2. It is divided into three sections. Your tutor may ask you to complete the sections at appropriate points in your study. Alternatively, you may do the entire project at the end of the element.

Scenario

Your report on commercial and industrial systems was good, and so was your interview. You got the job and have been working with Computer Consultants Ltd for some time now. Although you have to work hard, you are well paid and involved with leading-edge hardware and software. Your latest assignment brief is to advise a new client on the potential benefits of computerisation – what hardware and software would best suit their requirements.

The client is a sports centre, 3L (Loose Limbs Leisure). Owing to a successful advertising campaign, the centre is seeing a steady increase in its membership. This is putting a strain on the old paper-based administration system.

You contact the centre and arrange a meeting with the manager, Chris Jones. When you arrive you wait briefly in the smart, modern reception area and then are taken on a tour of the equally smart centre facilities. When you get to the offices – total contrast: papers piled up everywhere, bulging filing cabinets. It's like something out of an old detective movie. At the manager's desk, you move a couple of files off the chair she indicates and sit down.

Manager - successful business person - wants to know exactly what she's getting for her money.
Prepared to invest in 2 stand alones with appropriate software (OS + apps.)
Wants quality but no unnecessary extras
Areas identified for poss. computerisation = standard letters
    wages/salaries
    notices (e.g. in reception for members)
    details of membership (names, addresses, tel. etc.)
    posters - basic stuff similar to notices
    petty cash accounts
    mail-shots
    membership fees
    letters
    class registers (aerobics, weights ... tennis, football)
    staff timetables
    adverts (for local newspapers and put up in centre etc.)
    storing records from previous years - lots of records (back-up?)
Heard about light pens and voice input and wants to know if these will help.
Thinks CD-ROM is essential.
Wants Computer Consults. to recommend different possibilities and she'll choose between them.

Figure 1.20 Your handwritten notes of the meeting

Back at Computer Consultants Ltd, you review your notes (see Figure 1.20).

As you consider your assignment, you plan your research approach. You are going to have to:

- go through current issues of computer magazines, such as *Windows, Windows User, CD-ROM Today,* and *PC Plus*;
- write to the software distributors and retailers for details of the packages;
- write to hardware distributors and retailers for details of their systems; and
- visit computer shops in your area, talk to the assistants and pick up any leaflets.

Stage 1 – software research

Arrange your notes on areas identified for computerisation into lists headed by the application you would recommend.

Using computer magazines and any other available sources, select and research some word processing, database, graphics and spreadsheet packages, available today, for the applications you have recommended. For each package you should:

1 prepare a description (150–200 words);
2 state which operating system(s) it runs under;
3 list the minimum hardware specifications required to run the application; and
4 specify the best high street price you can find.

As this involves a lot of work, you could assign different packages to different pairs in your class. Each pair should work together to obtain the information required and then report back to the rest of the class in the form of mini-presentations on your findings. When listening, make notes and ask questions to clarify any points. Finally, as a class, decide which ones to recommend to 3L.

Stage 2 – hardware research

Your software research has specified the minimum hardware requirements 3L will need. Now research and specify two hardware configurations that will easily run the applications. Remember that the manager will pay for a quality system, but not for anything she does not really need.

For all components in each configuration you should list:

1 the name
2 make

3 full specification
4 best high street price you can find.

Stage 3 – the report

You now have enough findings to put your report together. To help you, here are the headings you should include in your report:

- *Front page* Report title, whom it is prepared for, your name and company.
- *Contents list*
- *The brief* Explain what you were asked to do in a short paragraph.
- *Software* A choice of two packages for each application, including the OS and the minimum hardware requirements.
- *Hardware* A choice of two hardware configurations. Name the components, briefly explain what they do, give the specification.
- *Conclusions* Set out your personal recommendations (choice) of applications and hardware and why. You may mention software suites here if you think they are appropriate.

Write your report on a word processor, using graphics if possible or any pictures you have cut out of magazines. This will help you provide evidence of Core Skills in Communication.

Save your work systematically and make a back-up copy, as required for Information Technology Core Skills, Element 3.1 PC4 and Element 3.3 PC 6.

Put your finished report into a folder.

Revision test

Complete the blanks

1 The standard keyboard layout is called _____ .

2 What do these computer jargon initials stand for?

VDU _____

CRT _____

dpi _____

DAT _____

GUI _____

EGA _____

MPC _____

ROM _____

RAM _____

DRAM_____

CPU _____

SVGA _____

3 List six different input devices

_____

_____

_____

4 What's that? For each of the pictures below, write down the full name of the device.

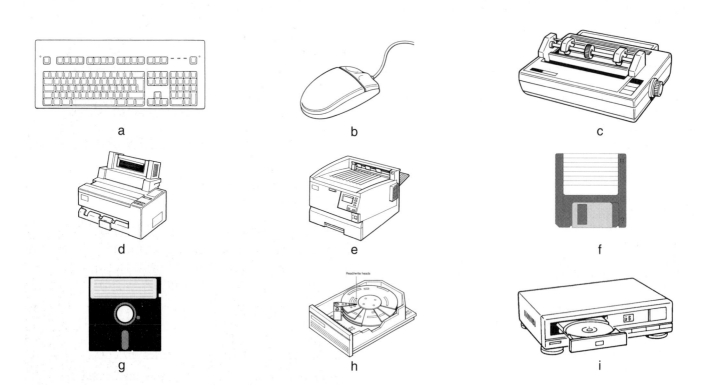

a

b

c

d

e

f

g

h

i

Write a short paragraph to show you clearly understand

5 the difference between an operating system and an application;

6 a windowing environment;

7 the basic uses of word processing applications;

8 the basic uses of spreadsheet applications; and

9 the basic uses of database applications.

Name the following

10 Three things that an operating system controls.

11 Three basic features of MS Windows.

12 Three popular word processing packages.

13 Two popular spreadsheet packages.

14 Two popular database packages.

Set up a stand-alone computer system to meet user requirements

Using actual examples and a detailed case study, this element shows you how to identify user requirements. It then uses the knowledge you gained in the previous elements to help you specify the right software and hardware to meet user requirements. The next part illustrates the hardware connections you are expected to perform and helps you develop a fail-safe routine. The final part explains the software installation procedures you should follow and helps you to develop a thorough testing procedure.

After studying this chapter you should be able to:

1 identify the *user requirements* for a stand-alone computer
2 identify the *hardware* and *software* needed to meet *user requirements*
3 connect *hardware* together
4 *install* applications software
5 *test* the computer system.

User requirements

As someone 'in the business', you will increasingly find people asking your advice on what sort of system they need. Your answer depends on three factors:

1 *Purpose* – what exactly they want the system for.
2 *Type of processing activity* – letter-writing, financial calculations and so on.
3 *Method of processing* – how they want to process their data.

Here are two typical illustrations. Paul Refahi runs a small accountancy firm with his brother, Chris. 'Most of our clients are local businesses – shops, cleaning contractors, a couple of restaurants, that sort of thing. We do their basic accounts for them, you know, payroll, tax, National Insurance, VAT returns. We've always worked the old way – by pen, paper and calculator. These days we're getting so busy, we're thinking of buying an old computer to help us out. You know about all this modern technology, which one should we get?'

Like most organisations, Adventure Tourism Ltd advertise their services to the public through their

brochure. Natalie Sutherland is their director: 'Adventure Tourism used to be for the few travellers rich, brave or mad enough to step into the unknown. Nowadays people read brochures and get a good idea of where they're going before they set off. We visit the locations, take photos and write up descriptions. When we get home, our text and graphics are scanned into the computer. After any editing, a graphic designer merges the material into a desk-top publishing layout and the printers produce the brochure.'

Both these users are explaining their requirements. Their purpose is what they want to do with the system, what they want it for. Their type of processing activity involves numbers, text, graphics and so on. Their method of processing depends on the way they convert their basic data into a finished item. Look at how their requirements can be analysed under these three factors.

Paul is an accountant. He wants a system that will help him do his accounts more quickly (*purpose*). He makes mathematical calculations (*type of processing activity*). His method is to use pen, paper and a calculator to draw up and present his accounts (*method of processing*). He would be better off using a spreadsheet or accountancy application.

Natalie is a tour operator. She produces a brochure to advertise her tours (*purpose*). She manipulates text and photographs into a brochure layout (*type of processing activity*). Her methods are word processing, scanning and desk-top publishing (DTP) (*method of processing*). So she uses a word processing, a graphics and a DTP package.

Activity

Read through the following case study carefully. Next, analyse and set out what each person says under the headings, *purposes* and *type of processing activity*. Then decide which software application types would best improve their *methods of processing*. When you have finished, file your analysis for the next activity.

Case study

Do you like video and cinema? Have you noticed how most of the film reviews you read are difficult to understand and don't tell you much anyway? So did four college leavers who decided to set up their own film magazine – *CineManiac*. The one who was always good at spelling is the editor. The art student is the graphic designer. The other two studied business administration and do the accounts and marketing.

After a struggle they got the magazine off the ground and are just about making ends meet. What they can't do by hand they pay someone else to do and that expense is stopping them from developing. They know a computer would help them enormously but none of them has much idea about IT. The editor has heard about your course, comes in to speak to someone and ends up offering to cut you into the business as part-time IT manager.

Your brief is to identify *CineManiac's* user requirements, and the hardware and software needed to meet those requirements. Your starting point is to ask each person what he or she sees as the purpose of having a computer, and what type of processing activities they are involved in. Here are their answers.

Editor 'Well, two things you should know first are that we can only afford one computer at the moment, and that we picked up a fax machine in a car-boot sale so we don't want a modem. This means you are dealing with a stand-alone system that is complete in itself and requires no other devices to operate satisfactorily.

'As for my work, I need something to make writing and editing easier. At the moment I write out the reviews on my electric typewriter, then do most of my rewrites, grammar, spell and style checks in red ink, directly on to the text. I do the same thing with other writers' articles and to save time I cut and paste a lot as well.'

Graphic designer 'Right, I do the artwork. Most of the drawings are my own and I sometimes use paint – gouache mainly. I worked with computers a bit at college but didn't really appreciate them until I started doing this work. Oh, and I take a lot of photographs as well, and cut them up until I get what I want. It takes me hours to get the look I'm after and even then it's pretty limited. Once I've finished the basics I put the art with the text. It looks pretty flat and obvious, but what else can I do?'

Accountant 'You should understand that financial control is the most important part of any business. And that's my role. In my book here, I set out all the income and all the expenses, month by month. That way I know where we stand. Let me tell you now, a computer would be a major expense that I will not be able to find the money for, unless I see significant advantages. By advantages I mean, for example, something that would automatically recalculate my totals each time I add or subtract an item.'

Marketer　'I don't really think a computer would make much difference to me – I'm out and about, places to go, people to see, deals to make. I'm a businessman, understand? The only thing that keeps me in the office is looking after my card index systems. I've got one for subscribers and one for advertisers, though some people subscribe and advertise, and that plays havoc with my system. Sorry, can you excuse me? I'll just take this call...'

Software requirements

Software companies are well aware that meeting user requirements sells programs. Consequently they spend millions of pounds every year researching those requirements in as much detail as the users can stand. They then design the software to do what the users want. If you look at this the other way round and start with the finished program, you can work backwards from knowing what a program does to knowing the range of user requirements it can meet.

Activity

Following your work in Element 1.2, you should be familiar with the different software applications on the current market. Using your analysis from the previous activity, specify which package would best suit each person and write 100 words explaining each choice.

CineManiac needs a complete stand-alone system. This means that you should also suggest an operating system and a user interface. Which OS and interface could cope with all the software applications you are suggesting, and why? Again, explain you choice in around 100 words. Refer back to Element 1.2 if necessary.

Hardware requirements

The ideal software application would be able to meet each one of every user's requirements. To meet as many user requirements as possible, developers are including multiple applications in single programs. Current word processing software, for example, is capable of basic spreadsheet calculations and a range of DTP features as well as word processing.

The problem is that as applications become more flexible and complicated they require more hardware power – faster processors and bigger memories. This means that for anyone intending to use computers in his or her professional life, the rule of thumb is to buy the best you can afford. When you are selecting or recommending a system, you should be able to specify a range of hardware power: the minimum requirements to run its applications and a configuration that would run the applications comfortably.

However, before choosing hardware power, you need to specify all the components that are needed to get the system up and running. Just to remind you, these are:

- input devices
- output devices
- main processor unit (type, memory, ports and hard disk)
- cables and connectors (for power, printer, mouse, monitor and keyboard).

Activity

Specify the minimum hardware requirements to run the software you are recommending for *CineManiac*. To do this,

divide your page into three columns. In the first column, list all the necessary hardware components. In the second, specify the minimum requirements to run the software you suggested in the previous activity. In the third, write your own specification recommendations to run the software comfortably.

Connections

Whenever you set up or move a stand-alone system you have to use cables to connect up all the components. This is relatively straightforward as hardware connections on desk-top and tower cases, and on portables, are all standard. Newer computers even have easily recognisable symbols for some connections, on the back of the case. For example, the mouse symbol shows you where to plug in the mouse. Once you have learnt the system, you only need to check the connector type and the right way up for fitting it into the socket.

Did you know?

When you are looking at connectors, check their gender. Most are classified as male or female. A male connector has one or more exposed pins whereas a female connector has one or more receptacles, designed to accept the pins on the male connector.

Activity

Take a look at the back of your home or school/college computer and draw a plan showing where each of the cables and connectors goes.

To avoid damaging a computer, never plug in or unplug a cable when the system power is on. To avoid *death,* never handle a live connector. Connect all the power cables to the rear of the system unit before plugging them into the wall outlet or power strip.

Connect up your basic cables and make sure the system powers up and runs properly before connecting any accessories such as printers or scanners and so on. This keeps things simple so if there are any problems they will be easier to isolate and deal with.

Did you know?

Electrical surges and voltage spikes can cause serious damage to computer systems. Surges and spikes are momentary overvoltages of up to several thousand volts and lasting a few millionths of a second. They may be caused by the switching of large loads such as air conditioning or lifts, hydropower adjustments or lightning storms. If any device is not connected to a surge protector, a surge can enter and damage the whole system through that one unprotected device.

No surge protectors are much help against lightning. If the weather is severe or if there is any threat of an electrical storm, disconnect the entire system from the power supply. If you are working with a system that has a modem, lightning can ride in on the phone line connected to the modem, destroy it and then the system connected to it. So, always disconnect systems from telephone lines before a storm starts.

Activity

The easiest and most efficient way of connecting up a system is to develop your own routine. To help you do this, number and list all the checks and each step you would take to connect up a keyboard, mouse, monitor and printer to the main system. When you have finished, check this with your tutor and compare it with your class to make sure you have the most logical list. File the final version of your routine to help you with your evidence assignment project.

Installation

Once you have the basic system connected, powered up and running smoothly, you are ready to install the software and prepare the system for use. Almost all systems come with the operating system preinstalled and configured. From this point, you may have to install drivers for the display, the printer and any other peripherals, as well as the application software. Once those are functioning correctly, you are ready to set up data directories ready for the user.

Drivers

Device drivers are programs that enable a computer system to communicate with a device. A printer driver, for example, translates computer data into a form that is understood by the specific type of printer you have connected. In most cases, device drivers also manipulate the hardware involved in sending data to the device.

D:\setup

The installation procedure for device drivers and for applications software under most operating systems is very similar. Once activated, the software walks you through the rest of the process. Here are the initial steps you follow in the two operating systems you are most likely to use – DOS and Windows:

- In *DOS*, insert the first disk into the floppy or CD-ROM drive
- At the C:\> prompt, type the letter of the drive where you have put the software followed by a colon (usually A: or D:)
- At the appropriate prompt, type: setup
- Press: Enter
- Follow the instruction on screen
- In *Windows*, insert the first disk into the floppy or CD-ROM drive
- Select the Run command
- Type the letter of the drive where you have put the software followed by a colon (i.e. usually A: or D:)
- At the appropriate prompt, type: setup
- Press: Enter
- Follow the instruction on screen

On-screen instructions vary according to software and the capabilities of the operating system. Here are a few of the commoner and more important messages:

- 'Type your product ID number in the box below.' Make sure you have this number otherwise you will have to terminate the installation before it has even begun.
- 'Standard or customised installation?' Choose standard (or normal); you can always customise it later if necessary.
- 'Select directory.' The program will usually suggest a directory and name which you should accept unless you have a specific reason not to.
- 'Restart (Windows)?' You must restart your computer to allow the changes to take effect. Remember to restart with the reset button rather than turning the computer off.

Data directories

When you are installing new application software, the program setup usually asks if you would like it to create a new directory (or folder) to store the new program in. It also suggests a name and shows the path. For example, if the program is called Gamer, it might suggest C:\Gamer.

Did you know?

Normally C:\ is the topmost or 'root directory' on a stand-alone PC, and each program has its own subdirectory of C:\. On a network it is often F:\. The program files in each subdirectory are thus kept separate from each other and are easier to organise.

It is also a good idea to keep datafiles separate from program files by creating subdirectories specifically for them. This results in the user's datafiles being all in one place and so easy to locate, edit, view and manage. There is also less likelihood of accidentally deleting program files.

The procedure for setting up data directories in *DOS* is to start at the C:\> prompt and type md (for make directory), space, then the name you want to give it. For example:

C:\>md<space>Andrew

To remove a directory in DOS, you type rd, space, then the name. For example:

C:\>rd<space>Andrew

31

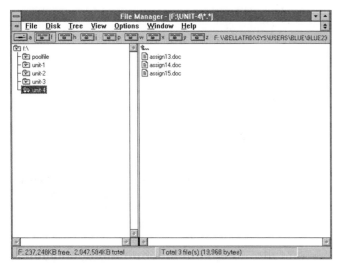

Figure 1.21 A file manager screen with directory tree

In *Windows* you access the C: drive through the File Manager or Explorer, choose File then Create Directory (or Folder), then type the name you want to give it.

Activity

Using the procedure above, create a DOS data directory with your first name, then a Windows data directory with your family name.

Testing

Your installation and setup are only successful once you have tested them thoroughly. Testing means being able to perform each of the following actions without any problems:

■ powering up
■ accessing applications software
■ entering, saving, retrieving and printing data.

Complete the activities in this section on a word processor. They have been designed to help you develop a setup test form that you will be able to use both for your evidence assignment and in the future.

Powering up

When you power up you should hear the hard disk beginning to spin and see the monitor flicker into life. If nothing happens, check the power cables to make sure they are still plugged in securely. If you are using a surge protector, make sure it is switched on. If you can hear the power supply fan whirring, but nothing shows up on the monitor, make sure the monitor is turned on. You may also need to check and adjust the monitor brightness control.

Did you know?

Keeping a system in good shape has a lot to do with the way you power up and down. Here's the advice of top systems suppliers:

■ Power up the monitor first, then each of the accessories before you switch the system on – this causes fewer devices to pull on the same power source simultaneously.
■ Avoid frequently turning the system on and off.
■ Never turn the system off when the hard drive indicator light is on.
■ Once you have shut the system down, do not turn it back on again until the hard drive has come to a complete halt.
■ Whenever you restart the system, use the reset button rather than the power button.
■ Always exit whatever programs you are using and wait for the C:\> prompt before you power the system down.
■ If you use a power strip, never turn the system on and off from the power strip switch.

Activity

Prepare heading information for your test form such as its name, a date and time field, and a field for you initials. Then draw up the first section – powering up. List each of the items to check and insert a check box next to them. The first few have been done to get you started.

ITEM	CHECK
All cables are plugged in securely	☐
Power strip switch is set to on	☐
Monitor powers up	☐

Application access

You can access applications software in different ways depending on the operating system. Here are the commonest:

- In *GUI* environments, click the program icon or name, or select Run ... then type the program command line (e.g. `D:\Setup`).
- In *DOS*, starting from the `C:\>` prompt, change to the program directory (e.g. type `cd<space>Gamer<Enter>`). Then type the program execution command line (e.g. `C:\Gamer>Gamer.exe<Enter>`).

Activity

On page two of your form, draw up the second section – accessing applications software. Use the whole page, leaving a blank space for the application name, followed by enough space for three access routes, followed by the check boxes. Here is a completed example:

APPLICATION	ACCESS	CHECK
Gamer	Icon	☐
	DOS	☐
	Run...	☐
		☐
		☐
		☐

Application function

To ensure that each application is functioning correctly there are four tests: entering data, saving it, retrieving it and then printing it out. Here is a standard 11-point procedure that you can follow for each application:

1 Open the program.
2 Open a new file.
3 Type `<Test-3>`, your initials and the date.
4 Save the file as `<Test3>` with any appropriate extension.
5 Exit the program.
6 Open the program.
7 Open the file.
8 Type `<Check>` at the end.
9 Select print.
10 Save and close the file.
11 Exit the program.

Activity

Draw up the final section of your test form. List each of the applications to test followed by each of the tests and check boxes. For example:

APPLICATION	ENTER	SAVE	RETRIEVE	PRINT
	☐	☐	☐	☐
	☐	☐	☐	☐
	☐	☐	☐	☐
	☐	☐	☐	☐

Save and print out you full setup test form. Compare it with others in your group, amend it if you wish, then file it for later use.

Evidence assignment

This project has been designed to cover all the evidence indicators related to Element 1.3. Your tutor may ask you to complete different parts of the project at appropriate points in your studies. Alternatively, you may do the entire project at the end of the element.

This project is divided into three sections. In the first you are going to formalise the work you have done on the *CineManiac* case study into a user requirement specification including the appropriate software and hardware. The second is entirely practical and requires you to connect a range of hardware. The third is also practical and requires you to set up and test a stand-alone computer system together with its applications software.

Section 1 – CineManiac *report*

To complete this section you will need the work you prepared in the activities of the *CineManiac* case study. Here is the structure that your report should follow:

- *Executive summary*   Briefly explain the objective and the outline recommendations of your report.
- *Requirements*   Describe *CineManiac's* user requirements. To fulfil the requirements of Information Technology Core Skills, Elements 2.4 and 3.4, you need to compare the use of manual methods and justify the use of IT.
- *Software specification*   Set out the software you recommend to meet their user requirements and why.
- *Hardware specification*   Set out the hardware needed to run your software recommendations.
- *Conclusion*   Briefly explain how your report has met its objectives.

Section 2 – connecting hardware items

In this section you will be observed connecting a keyboard, mouse, VDU, main processor unit and printer, with the appropriate cables and connectors.

Your tutor will give you a selection of cables and equipment to work with. You must identify and select the correct items for the task, then connect them up.

Section 3 – operational systems

In this section you are going to install printer drivers and applications software on a stand-alone computer. You will then test your installation to ensure it is fully operational.

Your tutor will give you the appropriate disks. Use and complete the test setup form you have devised and *hand it in when you have finished.*

Revision test

Name the following

1 The three things would you need to know before advising someone on what sort of system he or she should buy.

2 The four groups of hardware components needed to get a system up and running.

3 The processor type and speed, and the hard drive and RAM sizes you would recommend to run Win95.

4 Five hardware connections you would expect to see on the back of a computer case.

5 Each step you would take when connecting up a keyboard, mouse, monitor and printer to a main system.

Write a short paragraph to show you clearly understand

6 Your own user requirements from your school or college computer systems. (Follow the three factors you identified in question 1.)

7 Why the software package you use most often suits your requirements.

8 What drivers are.

9 How to install software under Windows.

Complete the blanks

10 Testing your system setup means being able to p_____ up, access a_____ software, e_____, s_____, r_____ and p_____ data without any problems.

Produce an applications software macro to meet user requirements

This element explains application software macros and how to create them. After exploring the different types, you will practise creating common examples of each. You will then go over the steps to agree a seven-point user specification – a specification you can use for all the macros that you create, test and review. The knowledge and skills you gain in this element will also enable you to suggest further possible uses of application software macros to users.

After studying this chapter you should be able to:

1 describe the *purposes* of using applications software macros
2 describe the *uses* for applications software macros
3 agree a *user specification* for an applications software macro
4 create and test an applications software macro
5 review macro and suggest possible further uses of macros to the user.

Macros

A macro is a sequence of commands that is activated by a single keystroke or click. For example, instead of saving, then printing, then closing a file, one click can set off a sequence that performs all three actions.

Macros save time and make everyday tasks easier. They reduce the possibility of making input errors, speed up processing, standardise procedures and generally make computer operation more convenient. If you use a computer for work or study, you can use macros to make your life easier.

Did you know?

Macros are a common feature of most applications software. Whenever you select a spell checking function, you are activating a powerful, repetitive keystroke sequence macro. Each time you open a new document or worksheet and begin to type, the same size and type of font appears. This is a default macro. Each time you start a new document you can choose from a ready-made selection of document types. These are template macros. Whenever

you click the sum $\sum$ button to add up a column of numbers in a spreadsheet, you are using a calculation macro.

Macros can also be created by the user. If you have to repeat the same sequence of keystrokes or perform the same calculations over and over again, record them into a macro. It doesn't matter how complicated your keystroke sequence or calculations are, the procedure for recording them into a macro is simple: you open the macro recorder, give your sequence a name, and assign it to a menu item, toolbar button or short-cut key. You then record the sequence (i.e. carry it out) and save it. After that, running the macro is as simple as clicking the button or menu item, or pressing the short-cut keys. This makes the macro as convenient to use as a built-in command.

Activity

Think about the types of word processing activity you carry out as part of your course – writing assignments such as letters or reports and so on. List a step-by-step sequence of three commands or instructions that you repeatedly perform. For example, to write a letter you might:

- open a new document
- type your address and phone number
- block them
- right align them
- then left align the cursor.

All this is before you begin to type the recipient's name and address.

Check your sequences then file them until later in this element, when you will find out how to assign them to a macro and make your life easier.

Did you know?

Most applications software now comes with a selection of pre-recorded macros. These are based on the type of macros that many users commonly create. For example:

- Rather than making a back-up copy each time you save a file and storing it in a different location, you can create the back-up automatically and get a prompt that asks you where you would like to save it.
- You no longer have to use drawing tools to prepare a chart that shows how an organisation is structured – from the boss down to the cleaners. A macro will build the chart (called an *organigram*) and all you have to do is fill in the jobs and names.

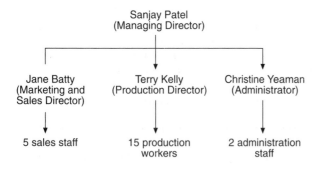

Figure 1.22 An organigram

In software suites such as Microsoft Office or Lotus SmartSuite there are macros that copy active documents from one application to another. For instance, you can copy numbers or a graph from a spreadsheet into a word processing document, then the word processing document into a presentation.

Purposes

The general purpose of macros is to make using software applications convenient, easier and more effective. They do this in three specific ways:

1 by reducing input errors
2 by speeding up processing
3 and by standardising routine procedures.

All three save time by replacing often-used, sometimes lengthy series of keystrokes with shorter versions. This eliminates frequent retyping, and reduces your typing errors. It also enables users who are unfamiliar with a program to play back sets of instructions pre-recorded by someone more adept with the application.

Reducing input error

Is your handwriting slowing down the progress of computer science? Because handwriting recognition programs have such difficulty with some people's writing, manual input is still one of the commonest methods of inputting data. It is also the most subject to typing error. Macros can help reduce these errors when data is transferred across applications or programs. At the same time, macros can eliminate errors that occur when the same information has to be retyped many times – for example, in standard letters.

Because databases are often shared, a single input error can quickly multiply. Then, however simple the error, it becomes very complicated to track down and amend each instance. Data transfer macros allow organisations to download from networks of shared databases and merge data from other programs and files. For example, a list of names and addresses can be created on one program then used in most other applications.

Did you know?

If input error results in your name being spelt wrongly on official documents, you would probably feel irritated. How do you think you would feel if it resulted in your being arrested, bundled into the back of a police car and thrown into the cells for the night? That is exactly what happened to Joe G. when he was working in a foreign country. A data entry clerk mistyped his name and his records were confused with a known petty criminal.

Beyond letter templates, standard paragraphs are essential for organisations that correspond with large numbers of people. A college, for example, deals with thousands of applicants for its courses. Some are rejected immediately and some get through the full application and interview process and finally join a class. At each stage of the process, the college has to send out letters telling applicants about the status of their application. You have probably received this type of 'We regret to inform you ...' or 'We are delighted to inform you ...' letter.

Letter templates help reduce errors, but when only one or two paragraphs are different, it is easier to use paragraph macros than prepare different templates. To do this different standard paragraphs are prewritten then assigned to buttons or keystrokes. The appropriate paragraph is then simply inserted into a basic letter template to produce the right letter.

Speeding up processing

Templates and standard paragraphs also to help speed up processing. Whenever a routine is involved, macros can usually make it faster. Every time you send someone a formal letter, you have to write out their address on the letter and on the envelope. Sending out circulars or form letters is a common way to advertise new products and services. If you had to send out form letters to hundreds or even thousands of people, you could spend hours and hours just copying out addresses. One of the commonest uses of macros in any office environment is to speed up form letter processing through mail-merge macros.

To create form letters, envelopes or mailing lists, you merge a main document with a data source. The main document is the standard letter containing the text, graphics, punctuation, spaces and any other information you want to be the same in each letter. The data source is the information that varies in each version of the letter, such as the names, addresses and phone numbers of the recipients. Using a macro you can automatically insert, position, then print names and addresses on the envelopes. You can also set up and print mailing labels in the same way.

Did you know?

Macros can help you fill forms out faster. Instead of using the tab or arrow keys to move to the next section or question, a box exit macro can be set up to take you there automatically.

Standardising procedures

Macros are often designed and implemented by professionals so that standard procedures can be followed simply and accurately by less expert users. For example, marketing departments design prompt lists to make sure their sales people ask all the right questions, and don't forget essential details like phone numbers and addresses. You may have noticed that most organisations use the same font on all their documents – this is part of what is called house style. House styles are based on template macros.

When an organisation receives a high number of inquiries and needs to keep a log of calls, staff have to obtain exactly the same basic information from each caller. This is then used to process caller requests more efficiently. It is also an important type of market research. For example, a private training company may offer courses in a range of business software applications including WordPerfect. Some customers will want WordPerfect but others may prefer Lotus. If there are enough inquiries for Lotus, that course will be developed and added to the range.

Macros can help organisations to process inquiries efficiently and collect valuable research by standardising inquiry procedures: staff who take calls follow screen prompts to ask for information and they complete forms. Each time a particular box is checked, a macro adds that information to a total. At the end of each week the macro will have totalled the number of times a specific request has been made.

Did you know?

Computer company answer-machine macros try to standardise the procedure for every possible inquiry type. The macros are set up to play different messages according to the telephone keypad number you press.

- for software press 1
- for hardware press 2
- for portables press 3
- for a pizza and coke press 17
- for extra pepperoni press 24
- for a quick check on how much money you've got press 43
- if you can't remember what to press, press 71

Template macros have become the foundation of many organisations' house style or printed image. A standardised company image creates an impression of consistency and reliability. Consequently, most organisations are careful to use the same style on all their documents. If you have received different letters from the same organisation, compare the layout. You will notice that, although they may be written by different people and on different machines, they all have the addresses, dates and references in the same position and all use the same font.

Marketing departments make sure their style is adhered to by designing a standard letter template that everyone in the organisation uses whenever they write a letter. A template is a blueprint for the text, graphics and formatting in a document. A fax template, for example, contains the company name, a date field, and placeholders to indicate where to type the recipient's name, address, fax and phone numbers, the number of pages and the message text.

Uses

Macros are used to replace repetitive keystrokes, to produce templates, set defaults and make calculations. After a detailed look at each of these uses and an outline of the steps involved in creating them, you are going to write your own example macros.

Repetitive keystroke sequences

The basic use of macros is to save time by replacing often-used, sometimes lengthy series of keystrokes with shorter versions. When you want to automate a repetitive task you can assign a macro to run when a particular key combination is pressed (a keyboard short-cut), or when you click a particular graphic object, menu item or toolbar button. For example, a secretary using a word processing package might always use the same signature block for her boss:

Yours sincerely,

Chris Huntley

Systems Engineer

This takes 52 keystrokes. If she assigned the block to a macro she would only need one.

Creating macros in most applications software is easy. You start the macro recorder then record a sequence of actions. You can then run the macro whenever you need to perform that same sequence. Although the way that macros are recorded in different applications varies, the general procedure is the same. The following is a typical outline for recording a macro:

1 Open the application's Record Macro dialogue box.
2 Type a name for the macro (or use the name that the application suggests).
3 Type a brief description of the macro (for future reference).
4 Assign the macro to short-cut keys, a menu item or a toolbar button.
5 Begin the recording process.
6 Perform the actions you want to include in your macro.
7 Finish the recording process.
8 Save your macro.

Activity

You are now going to record a word processing macro. Open the word processing program you use most, go to the Help menu and find the instructions for recording a macro. They will look something like the typical outline above. Write out the instructions, step by step.

Follow the instructions you have copied out to create the address sequence you looked at earlier in this element. These were:

- open a new document
- type your address and phone number
- block them
- right align them
- then left align the cursor.

When you have finished, test and review your macro: press the key or click the button to activate it and see how it works. You may need several tries before you get it exactly right. If you make a mistake while recording or if you forget a step, just stop recording. You can then either delete the macro and start again, or edit it.

- *Loan Manager* Work out the interest you save by paying back part of the loan.
- *Purchase Order* Prepare a purchase order.
- *Personal Budgeter* Itemise family income and expenses.
- *Car Lease Manager* Compare car-lease options.
- *Expense Statement* Itemise work-related expenses.
- *Business Planner* Analyse projected income, expenses and other company finance.
- *Sales Quote* Prepare price estimates for goods and services.
- *Timecard* Track hours studied by students or worked by employees.

Once this macro is working perfectly, record the sequence you set out yourself. Test and review it to make sure it works the way you want, and make any modifications or improvements. Demonstrate your macro to your tutor.

Activity

Research the range of templates and their uses that are available in the programs used on your system. Report your findings to your tutor and the rest of your class. Note and file this information for possible later use in your evidence assignment project.

Templates

One of the most commonly used types of macro are templates. Templates are standardised document types such as letters, fax cover sheets or invoices. Selecting a specific template activates the sequence of layout and formatting commands that results in the saved document type.

Template macro sequences are often quite complex. For example, an organisation's standard letter template might typically hold the following:

- *Standard data* Such as the company logo, address, telephone, fax and e-mail numbers.
- *Input data locations* Such as the position for the recipient's name and address, the date, references and greetings.
- *Style data* Such as font type and size.

Did you know?

While most applications software comes with basic templates, more sophisticated packages include wide ranges of document types. The following is an example from a spreadsheet program, showing some of its template types and example uses:

- *Invoice* Prepare an invoice.

Even when a program offers different styles of the same document type, many users still prefer to create their own document templates. They may want to develop and use a company 'house style' or to personalise their documents. There are two starting points to creating your own templates: you either base the new template on an existing document, or you base it on an existing template.

Here is an outline procedure for creating a new template:

1 Open the document or template you are going to use as your basis.
2 Select: Save As.
3 Type a name for the new template.
4 Select the appropriate extension code (e.g. .dot) or select the templates directory.
5 Select: OK.
6 If the program you are working with has closed your template, reopen it.
7 Add the text and graphics you want to appear in all new documents that you base on the template, and delete any items you don't want to appear.
8 Make the changes you want to the margin settings, page size and orientation, styles and other formats.
9 Select: the Save option.
10 Select: Close.

Activity

You are now going to create your own fax template by modifying an existing template. Use the above outline procedure, but research and follow the specific options of the program you are using. When you have finished, print out a copy of the original template and a copy of your personalised version. Show your work to your tutor, then file both printouts for later reference.

Did you know?

To obtain even greater efficiency and control, form templates often include their own macros. If a macro has been saved in a form template, it runs automatically when the insertion point enters or exits a form field. An entry macro, for example, is activated when the user selects the CC or To: placeholder on a memo or fax. Also, an entry macro might bring up a standard distribution list (i.e. a list of colleagues who usually receive copies). The user then selects names to receive the memo. An exit macro, for example, is when the user selects a Mrs checkbox, and other related fields, such as Maiden Name or Name of Spouse, are activated.

Set defaults

A default macro is the choice made by a program if the user does not specify an alternative. Default macros are built into programs if some value or option needs to be assumed in order for the program to work. For example, when you enter a word processing program it might default to normal page style, regular 12-point Times New Roman font, single-spaced paragraphs and tab stops every 0.5 inch. It does this to present a recognisable format, a starting point, until the user specifies otherwise.

Most applications software include set default options that appear whenever you enter a feature that can be changed by the user. The following is an example outline of how to reset the default font:

1 Select the font list.
2 Choose the font you want to use.
3 Select the Set Default option (at this point, most programs will check that you want all new documents based on the current template to use the font you have chosen).
4 Select the Yes or OK option.

Activity

If you haven't done so already, look through the different fonts available in your program, choose the one you like most, then set it as a default. If you are going to use this font for your coursework, bear in mind that clarity helps you achieve better marks.

Find out how to change the following defaults, write them out as a numbered sequence of instructions and check with your tutor. If you change any defaults, don't forget to change them back again to their original settings:

■ Change the default unit of measure from inches to centimetres.
■ Change the default language used to check spelling from English (UK) to English (USA). When you do this, type 'colour' and check its spelling to make sure it is corrected to 'color'.
■ Change the spacing between default tab stops.

Calculations

The problem with most calculations is that if you don't use them often, you forget how to. On the other hand, if you use them all the time they soon become very boring. Either way, calculation macros can help you. You only need to make the calculation once, record it in a macro and then it's always available (and always correct) at the click of a button.

All organisations have to keep accounts. Basic accounts are usually repetitive and time-consuming. A calculator can make it easier, but you still have to perform each step. A formula in a spreadsheet is often sufficient and will automatically update results when new data is entered. A macro will complete the whole calculation, no matter how complicated it may be – from preparing a bill and calculating VAT to working out an engineering design.

Activity

Easyway Insurance Company has recently upgraded its software, and you think that the programs could be made easier to use (especially for staff who are novices) by taking advantage of some of the shortcuts which are possible through using macros. The office manager has suggested you arrange some training for the staff.

1 To prepare the training session, enter the data shown in Figure 1.23 into a spreadsheet, **using formulae to calculate the totals,** and save as **ei-sales.**

	A	B	C	D	E	F	G	H
2				Sales This Month				
3	Region	Area	Agent	Life Ins.	Health Ins.	Contents	Buildings	Total
4	South	01	Smith	2000	997	3298	10259	16554
5		02	Patel	1843	1064	2997	111225	117129
6		03	Brown	2009	864	2003	3472	8348
7		04	Aolad	3211	500	3421	3218	10350
8			Total	9063	3425	11719	128174	152381
9								
10	Midlands	05	Shimizu	1875	887	2765	4094	9621
11		06	Williams	2359	453	2876	3980	9668
12		07	Ling	2399	1290	2974	3217	9880
13		08	Evans	1988	211	3096	2994	8289
14			Total	8621	2841	11711	14285	37458
15								
16	North	09	Davis	3008	438	2544	3056	9046
17		10	Dimitri	1453	785	2681	3865	8784
18		11	Wong	2265	996	3892	2994	10147
19		12	Thomson	1876	566	1135	10777	14354
20			Total	8602	2785	10252	20692	42331
21		Grand Total		26286	9051	33682	163151	232170

EI-SALES

Figure 1.23 Spreadsheet ei-sales

2 Each month agents earn 1.5% commission on their total sales. Create another spreadsheet, either in a separate file or on a separate sheet, as shown, and save as **ei-comm** (see Figure 1.24).

You should be able to **copy** the area reference and agents' names, from ei-sales into ei-comm. You can **link** the total sales in ei-sales to ei-comm, so that the data is automatically updated when new figures are entered each month.

Link the files by using the = and the cell reference for ei-sales. For example:

■ in the ei-comm file, place the cursor in cell **C5** and type =
■ switch to the ei-sales spreadsheet and select cell **H4** and press enter.

You should find the total automatically transferred. Repeat this process for the other totals.

In cell **D5** create a formula to calculate the commission. Please note that you must use **absolute cell references** when referring to the rate of commission which is always going to be in cell **B1**. (This is important if you wish to achieve IT Core Skills at Level 3, as absolute cell references are required for Element 3.2, PC3.) Copy the formula down to **D16**.

3 Each month the sales manager needs a printout of agents' sales in order of ranking from highest to lowest.

Create a macro to sort the ranking and assign a macro button to do this task automatically in future.

Please note: You cannot simply sort the rows in ei-comm, because the linked cells will no longer be in the correct place. You must **COPY cells A5: C16** to another part of the spreadsheet and then sort them into ranking highest to lowest following the instructions for the software you are using.

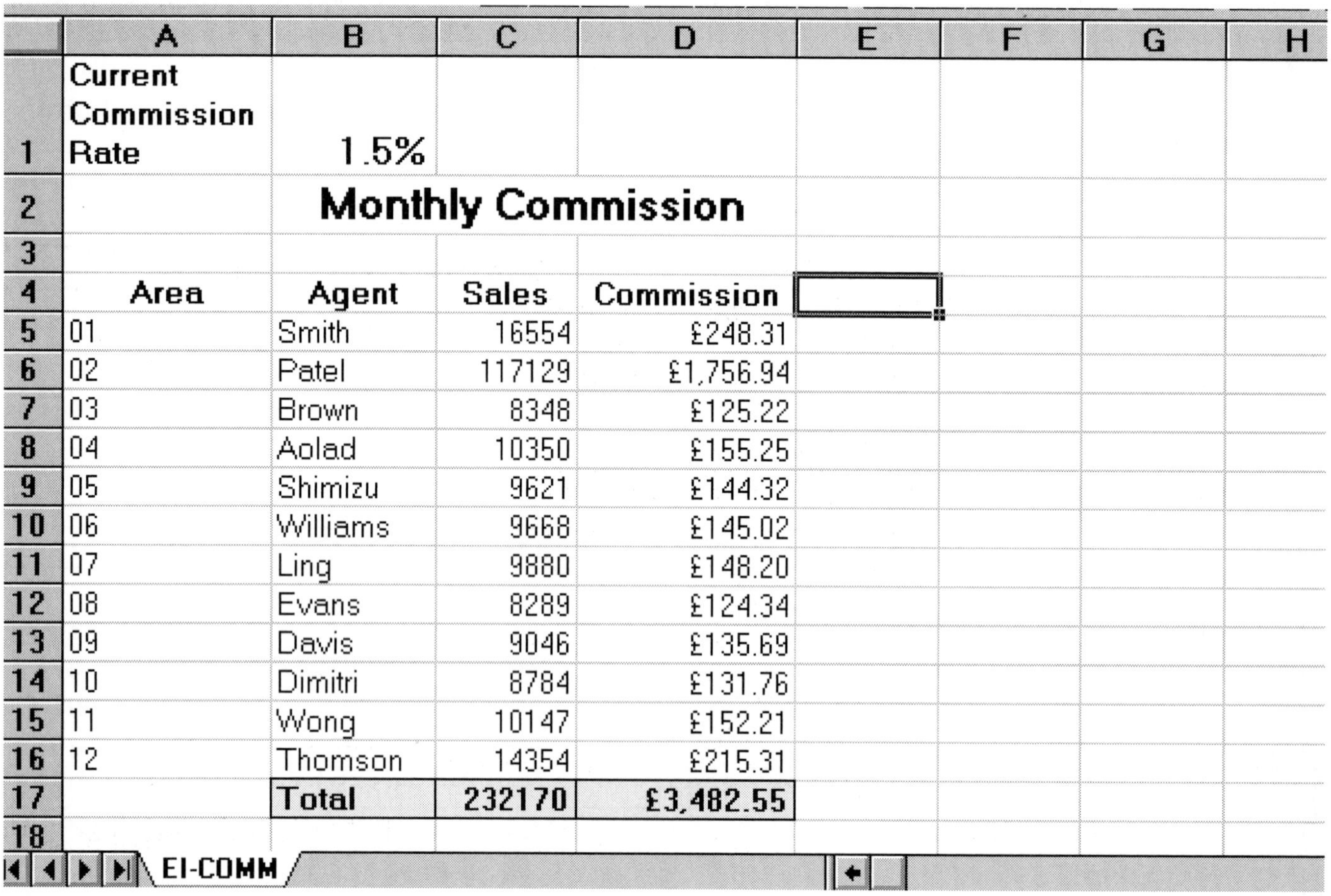

	A	B	C	D	E	F	G	H
1	Current Commission Rate	1.5%						
2		**Monthly Commission**						
3								
4	Area	Agent	Sales	Commission				
5	01	Smith	16554	£248.31				
6	02	Patel	117129	£1,756.94				
7	03	Brown	8348	£125.22				
8	04	Aolad	10350	£155.25				
9	05	Shimizu	9621	£144.32				
10	06	Williams	9668	£145.02				
11	07	Ling	9880	£148.20				
12	08	Evans	8289	£124.34				
13	09	Davis	9046	£135.69				
14	10	Dimitri	8784	£131.76				
15	11	Wong	10147	£152.21				
16	12	Thomson	14354	£215.31				
17		Total	232170	£3,482.55				
18								

EI-COMM

Figure 1.24 Spreadsheet ei-comm

4 If the spreadsheet program has this facility, assign a macro button to place on the toolbar to run the macro recording.

5 **Change** the figures for Buildings in the file **ei-sales** as follows:

Area	Buildings	Area	Buildings	Area	Buildings
01	2796	05	8321	09	2116
02	9845	06	4356	10	6357
03	6357	07	5321	11	8321
04	4789	08	764	12	4789

If you have linked the files, you should find the totals in ei-comm automatically updated.

6 Run the macro or click on the macro button to show the new ranking.

If you are using Excel 5 spreadsheet, the instructions for creating a macro are as follows:

1 Start from the file **ei-comm** and select **Tools, Record Macro, Record New Macro.**

2 Type the name **Ranking** in the Macro Name Box and Click on **OK.**

3 Press **CTRL HOME** (to ensure you start in cell A1).

4 Highlight **Cells A5–C16** – select **Edit, Copy.**

5 Move to Cell **F5.**

6 Select **Edit, Paste Special** and click on **Values** (under the Paste list) and **OK.**

7 Press **Esc.**

8 Click on cell **H5** and highlight from **H5** back to **F16.**

9 Select **Data, Sort** – make sure you sort by **Column H.**

10 Select **Descending Order** and **OK.** (The agents should be listed in order of highest to lowest sales.)

11 Click on any cell (removes highlight).

	B	C	D	E
1	0.015			
2				
3				
4	Agent	Sales	Commission	
5	Smith	='C:\A1\[EI-SALES.XL	=C5*B1	
6	Patel	='C:\A1\[EI-SALES.XL	=C6*B1	
7	Brown	='C:\A1\[EI-SALES.XL	=C7*B1	
8	Aolad	='C:\A1\[EI-SALES.XL	=C8*B1	
9	Shimizu	='C:\A1\[EI-SALES.XL	=C9*B1	
10	Williams	='C:\A1\[EI-SALES.XL	=C10*B1	
11	Ling	='C:\A1\[EI-SALES.XL	=C11*B1	
12	Evans	='C:\A1\[EI-SALES.XL	=C12*B1	
13	Davis	='C:\A1\[EI-SALES.XL	=C13*B1	
14	Dimitri	='C:\A1\[EI-SALES.XL	=C14*B1	
15	Wong	='C:\A1\[EI-SALES.XL	=C15*B1	
16	Thomson	='C:\A1\[EI-SALES.XL	=C16*B1	
17	Total	=SUM(C5:C16)	=SUM(D5:D16)	
18				

EI-COMM

Figure 1.25 A spreadsheet on screen showing formulae

12 Press **CTRL Home.**
13 Select **Tools, Record Macro** and **Stop Recorder.**

Instructions for assigning a macro button are as follows:

1 Select **View, Toolbars, Customise** and **Custom** (under Categories).
2 Choose the **Yellow Smiling Face** for your macro button and drag the button on to the toolbar.
3 A Dialogue Box opens – select **Ranking** Macro and **OK** and **Close.**

User specification

With practice you will find that setting up powerful and sometimes complicated macros is just a question of logic and time. The measure of a macro's quality is how convenient it is to the user.

Before setting up a macro you should arrange to meet and speak to the user at his or her computer. This will give you an idea of how the user works with his or her applications. It will provide an opportunity for users to show you what they mean, and for you to show users what you mean. It will also allow you to check details that users often do not know, such as the program release number. At your meeting, go through the following seven-point user specification and obtain detailed answers:

1 Applications software to be used

Note down the program name in full and ensure you check and include the version number. Some macros may already be available on certain versions and the user is simply unaware of them. Also, procedures for creating macros are almost always updated with new software versions – if the user has an older version you may need to refresh your memory.

2 Purposes of using a macro

Understanding why the user wants the macro will help you obtain a general picture of the macro you are going to create. It will then be easier to refine the picture with the subsequent points in your specification. Remember that there are three basic purposes: to reduce input error, to speed up processing and to standardise procedures. The user may be interested in only one or a mixture of all three. Ask questions and take notes until you are both completely clear about the purpose.

3 Uses of a macro

Now that you have the general picture, what specific uses will be made of the macro? Will it be used for repetitive keystroke sequences, to set or reset defaults, for templates or calculations?

4 Method of executing a macro

Explain the different methods of execution that are available to the user and help him or her to decide which is the most convenient and simplest to use. Remember that the macro will probably be used by several different people, and some may be unfamiliar with the program or even with the idea of macros.

5 Data to be embedded in a macro

Your role is to create the macro and ensure it works satisfactorily. The user should supply any data such as company logos, prewritten paragraphs and so on to be embedded in the macro. If the user is able to give you the full and complete data he or she wants embedded, you will be able to produce a macro that requires the minimum reviewing and amendment. However, users are often unclear about their precise requirements until they see a working model. If necessary explain to the user that you will need example data before you can prepare a model.

6 Layout styles

When the user needs a template you should concentrate on asking all the questions you need to get the macro right first time – standard data, format data, style data and so on. Some of these may be modified after the user has seen the macro, but the starting point is always the user's full initial layout specification.

7 Tests to be applied

Even when you are completely familiar with the method for recording macros in a particular program, you may need to rerecord or edit it several times before it performs exactly to the specification. Once you have created and recorded a macro you should test it as many times as is necessary against each of the criteria in the user specification you have agreed. Your macro must meet all the criteria listed under points 2–6 before you present it to the user.

Activity

Choose an appropriate program and draw up a fully detailed seven-point specification checklist form of your own. Your aim is to be able to use your form for any user specification you may be asked for. To cover all the possibilities, look back through this element and include checkboxes and spaces for notes for every detail you may need to ask about.

When you have completed your specification, show it to your tutor and compare it with your class. If you have forgotten anything or if they give you any good ideas, revise it. Print out a copy of the final version and save it to help you with your evidence assignment.

Evidence assignment

This project has been designed to cover all the evidence indicators related to Element 1.4. It is divided into four sections. Your tutor may ask you to complete different parts of the project at appropriate points in your studies. Alternatively, you may do the entire project at the end of the element.

Scenario

As part of Computer Consultants Ltd's ongoing customer support service, you return to 3L (Loose Limbs Leisure) to find out how they are getting on with the systems you have installed. Now that they have become familiar and comfortable with the software they are delighted with the benefits of increased efficiency. You have meetings with two of the main users – the marketing manager and the accountant.

The marketing manager is particularly pleased with the new applications as it allows him to establish a house style for staff to follow and a more professional image. The accountant is also moving beyond basic record keeping to save time by standardising data entry. You notice that in both their word processing and spreadsheet applications they are following repetitive sets of commands to achieve these standardised documents and calculations.

You point out that they can become even more efficient by using macros. They don't really understand what macros are or what they are for, so you agree to:

■ give a brief presentation on the purposes and uses of applications software macros;
■ create a user specification; and
■ create an applications software macro.

Section 1 – purposes and uses presentation

Your presentation may be videoed and should take no more than 10 minutes. To make it as clear as possible base everything you say on examples of macros that could be used by 3L. Use the following structure:

■ *Introduction* Brief explanation of what you are going to talk about; definition of a macro; example of a macro. You can use the example created for the Activity on page 40.
■ *Purposes* Explain the main purposes and give one example of each.
■ *Uses* Explain the main uses and give one example of each.
■ *Conclusion* Offer to answer any questions or explain further.

Section 2 – creating a user specification

To complete stage two you will be working in pairs. Your first assignment is to meet the 3L marketing manager. The manager wants a standardised letter format and style that includes:

■ headings such as the centre logo, address, fax and so on;
■ placeholders for addressee information, date, references and greetings; and
■ standardised font, tab and line spacing.

1 Design and print out an example letter.
2 Take it in turns to role play the marketing manager and yourself, the computer consultant. When you are the consultant, remember to take your seven-point user specification to the meeting.

Section 3 – creating the macro

Now that you have all the necessary information you can create the macro:

1 Prepare by checking and familiarising yourself with the macro creation routine on the specified program.
2 Create and record the macro.

Section 4 – test and review the macro

Run the macro you have created and see how it functions. If there are any obvious errors, edit and correct them. When you have finished, go back to the user specification, rerun the macro as many times as necessary and tick off each of the criteria that were specified.

Revision test

Name the following

1 The three main purposes of macros.
2 Three ways that macros achieve these purposes.
3 Three macros that are common features of most word processing applications.
4 Two macros that are common features of most spreadsheet applications.
5 The seven points you would cover in a user specification.

Complete the blanks

6 A macro is a sequence of c _____ that is a _____ by a single keystroke or click.

7 The procedure for recording a macro is simple: You open the macro r _____ , give your s _____ a name, and assign it to a m_____ item, t _____ button or s _____ key. You then record the sequence and s _____ it.

8 Macros are often designed and i _____ by professionals so that standard p _____ can be followed simply and accurately by less expert users.

Write a short paragraph to show you clearly understand

9 Templates – what they are and what they're used for.

10 Default macros.

Process commercial documents

This element gives you the opportunity to gain the practical skills involved in processing commercial documents. We begin by describing the purpose of different commercial documents and researching examples. Next, we will study the main attributes and layouts, and practise creating them in your own layout reference document – a style sheet. You then combine your understanding of document types and formats by developing a template to specification. After studying file names and editing, you will develop your understanding of security checks and the practical skills to put them in place.

After studying this chapter you should be able to:

1 describe *commercial documents*
2 create templates with appropriate *page attributes* and *layouts*
3 enter *data* and *edit documents*
4 *find* and combine data from different sources
5 save using appropriate *file names* and apply *accuracy* and *security checks*
6 produce documents and suggest *improvements*.

Commercial documents

It doesn't matter whom you work for, commercial documents are recognisable in all organisations because they share standard features. Since they are standard and everyone is used to them, they simplify business communication. The commonest commercial documents and the ones you are required to process are agendas, business letters, invoices, memoranda, minutes, newsletters and reports.

Activity

The following are definitions of everyday commercial documents, together with their most important features. See how many you already know (or can guess). When you have finished, check your answers with your tutor or lecturer.

1 A brief document used to communicate with colleagues in the same office or organisation. Features:

- To . .
- From . .
- Date . .
- Subject . .
- Copies to . . (other colleagues)
- the content or message.

2 A publication providing general information to staff. Features:

- headlines
- photographs
- articles
- column layout.

3 A formal, written communication from one company to another. Features:

- sender's logo, address, phone and fax numbers
- addressee's name and address
- reference number(s)
- date
- greeting (Dear . .)
- content
- salutation (Yours sincerely or faithfully).

4 A list of subjects for discussion at a meeting. Features:

- date and time of meeting
- location (where the meeting will be held)
- list of people attending the meeting
- name of chairperson
- name of minute-taker or secretary
- list of topics to be discussed.

5 Detailed description of an investigation and its results. Features:

- summary
- contents list (main headings)
- information under each heading
- conclusions or recommendations of writer.

6 A statement of how much money is owed for goods or for services. Features:

- sender's logo, address, phone and fax numbers
- addressee's details
- references such as an order number
- date
- item (description of goods or service)
- amount of money owed for each item

- total amount owed.

7 The details of what was said at a meeting. Features:

- date of meeting
- list of people who attended the meeting
- description of what was said and who said it.

Did you know?

The plural of memorandum is memoranda. So you can write one memorandum or several memoranda. Informally, it is commoner to use the short form, memo, and its ordinary plural, memos.

Activity

Work in groups. Divide the different commercial documents between you. Using libraries or any other source, find two examples of each document and circle or make a note next to each of the features. Back in groups, show your examples to the others, pointing out their different features.

Templates

As you will remember from your introduction to templates as macros in Element 1.4, templates save time. Instead of having to produce the same layout each time you want to write a memo, for example, you can use a memo template and just get on with writing it. This element requires you to extend your practical skills by applying page attributes and page layouts – the basic constituents of templates – to the range of commercial documents.

Page attributes

Page attributes are a page's orientation and the size of paper it will fill. Orientation can be either portrait or landscape. To remember which is which, just think of which way up a portrait, such as a passport photo, usually is. Although portrait is used for most documents, landscape can be very useful for graphics and for spreadsheets with more columns than rows (Figure 2.1).

The paper size you print to depends on the capabilities of your printer. These are the standard sizes used on most office and home printers:

Portrait orientation of A4   Landscape orientation of A4

Figure 2.1 Page attributes

- Letter   8.5   ×   11 inches
- Legal   8.5   ×   14 inches
- A4   210 ×   297 mm
- B4   257 ×   364 mm

Did you know?

In most industry standard software, you will find the commands for selecting both page orientation and page attributes under Page Setup in the File menu.

Page layout

Page layout means the format or the basic appearance of the page – for example, the width of the margins or the amount of space between the lines. The following is an illustrated explanation of all the layout features you will be using in your document templates. As you work through it you will be preparing a layout reference document – a style sheet – that will help you with your evidence assignment project.

There are three basic types of *column layouts*: newspaper columns, positioned columns and columns in tables.

Desk-top publishing (DTP) packages and some word processing packages enable you to arrange all or part of your document in newspaper columns. The text flows from the bottom of one column to the top of the next. You can also place lines between the columns. When you use column formatting, ensure that you specify the section that you want in columns before executing the command. Otherwise you may put your entire document into columns.

Did you know?

When you need to *adjust the amount of space* between your columns, or the width of a selected column, drag the column marker (the line separating the columns) to a new position.

A positioned column is when a graphic or a heading text takes up the first narrower column and the main text takes up the other wider column. Positioned columns are useful for positioning company logos, CV headings and for making circulars more interesting.

To place a graphic exactly where you want it on the page, it is easier in most programs to put it into a *frame* and then move the frame. This is because a frame moves text out of its way to one or more sides, whereas a graphic just lies on top of text.

Another common way to present text or graphics side by side is in *tables.* Tables are made up of rows and columns of cells that you can fill with data. When you are typing in a cell and reach the end of a line, the text wraps on to the next line in the same way as it does between ordinary margins.

Activity

Try this for yourself. Open a new file and type the main heading 'Style Sheet'. Access Help and find out how to make newspaper columns. Type the subheading 'Columns', and write the instructions you find into a paragraph. Then convert your paragraph to three newspaper columns. Next, do the same thing for tables, except that you should produce only two columns. Then save the file and print a copy to check the columns have come out as you specified.

Fonts

You can use formatting to apply different fonts and font sizes to any amount of selected text, and even to single characters. In commercial documents, your choice of font and font size should be guided by *clarity.* When the font is easy to read, the message gets across. No matter how interesting or attractive you think a particular font is, always ask yourself if it is easy to read. The same rule applies to the range of fonts – limit yourself to as few as possible:

How ^{easy} $_{do}$ υοθ find it **to read** this sentence?

And how easy is this sentence?

As well as font types and sizes, most programs offer a choice of font *styles* and font *effects*. The most common styles are regular, *italic*, **bold**, ***bold italic*** and underline. The most common effects are:

- ~~Strikethrough~~
- SMALL CAPS
- Superscript
- Subscript
- ALL CAPS.

Activity

Try this. Open your Style Sheet file, go to the end of the document using the Page Down key and enter the next subheading, 'Fonts'. Find out how to change font type, size, style and effects. Type out and illustrate what you have learnt using different fonts. For example:

To change font type	Select:
To change font size	
To …	
To …	

When you have finished, save the file and print a copy to check the fonts have come out as you specified.

Headers and footers

A document header is the zone at the top of a page, before the first line. It is used to repeat text information such as a document or chapter title, or to repeat graphics such as a company logo. A document footer is the zone at the bottom of the page after the last line. It is usually used to show information such as page numbers and copyright © data, and might also show the date and author. Look at the header and footer zones of this page and notice what they are used for.

Did you know?

Headers and footers can be printed on the first page, all pages, or every even or odd page. You can format headers and footers in the same way as you format any other text, and centre or align them with the left or right margin.

Activity

Open your Style Sheet file, use Page Down until you are at the end of the document then enter the next subheading, 'Headers and Footers'. Find out how to insert headers and footers. Insert the header 'Style Sheet' on all pages except page one, and put it into a different font from your main text. In the footer, insert a copyright symbol, the month and year and *'Your name Publications'*. Use the same font as in your header. Then save the file and print a copy to check the header and footer have come out as you specified.

Indents

There are three types of paragraph indent, all of which can be increased or decreased in width. Figure 2.2 is an illustration of each:

First line indent   Negative indent   Hanging indent

Figure 2.2 Paragraph indents

First line indent. Used to create a handwriting paragraph style.

Negative indent. Used to stretch text into either the right or left margin.

Hanging indent. Used to hang text after the first line. Hanging indents are common in numbered lists and glossaries (see page 55 of this book for an example of a hanging indent).

Did you know?

A lot of people confuse indents with margins. They are not the same. Left and right margin settings specify the distance

between the text and the edges of the page. An indent specifies the distance between the text and the margins.

Activity

Open your Style Sheet file, go to the end of the document and enter the next subheading, 'Indents'. Look up how to indent paragraphs and copy out the instructions into two paragraphs. Put a first line indent into the first paragraph and a hanging indent into the second. Save, print and check the indents have come out as specified.

Justification

Justifying text means changing the distances between words so that each line ends at the right margin in the same way as it starts at the left. This paragraph, for example, is justified to the right, whereas the next paragraph is not. The resulting effect is a more formal, block appearance.

Left align, right align and centring are similar features to justification, but can be applied to text, numbers and graphics. Left align means that data insertion starts on the left, right align means that it starts on the right. Centring, not surprisingly, means that it starts in the centre.

Activity

Open your Style Sheet file, go to the end and enter the next subheading, 'Justification and Alignment'. Look up how to justify, left align, right align and centre text. Copy the instructions into four separate paragraphs and apply the relevant layout to each. Save, print and check they have come out as specified.

Line spacing

Line spacing is the amount of vertical space between each line of text. The standard line spacing options are single, 1.5 and double. Single-line spacing accommodates the largest font in the line, plus a small amount of extra space. Line spacing at 1.5 is one-and-a-half times the size of single-line spacing. Double-line spacing is twice that of single-line spacing. Most text-based software defaults to single line.

Did you know?

DTP software and some word processing programs offer advanced line-spacing facilities. For example, you can adjust spacing by percentage points, or to accommodate larger font sizes or graphics that would not otherwise fit within the specified spacing.

You can also fix the line spacing so that no automatic adjustments are made by the program and all lines are evenly spaced.

Activity

Try this for yourself. Open your Style Sheet file, hold down Ctrl and press End to get to the end of the document. Enter the new subheading, 'Line Spacing'.

Find out how, copy it out then adjust the line spacing to give a clear illustration of single, 1.5 and double. Save, print and check.

Margins

As you have already noted under indents, margins specify the distance between the text and the edges of the page. In most industry standard programs you adjust margins by dragging the margin boundaries on the ruler.

When you are binding several pages together, for example, in a report, brochure or booklet, use *gutter* and *mirror* margins. Gutter margins run down the centre of an open booklet. They add extra space to the centre or inside margin so that it is still easy to read the end of the lines in the middle. When you print documents on both sides of the page, mirror margins ensure that the margins mirror each other by having the same width.

Activity

Open Style Sheet, hold down Ctrl and press End to get to the end of the document. Enter the subheading, 'Margins'.

Find out how to adjust the left and right margins, copy the instructions then adjust them **only on your margin text.** In other words, select the text you are going to adjust first, otherwise you will change your entire document. Save, print and check.

Page numbering

You would think that page numbering was a simple matter of inserting a number instruction in the footer zone, then right aligning it. In fact, there are many options: you can place numbers in the header or footer zones, left, centre or right align them, and change their fonts.

You can also include text with page numbers, for example 'Page 3', and start numbering on a page other than the first page of your document. You might also want to change the page number format so that different sections of a document, such as the introduction, main content and appendix, are numbered differently.

Activity

Open Style Sheet, hold down Ctrl and press End. Type 'Page Numbering'. Look through the options available on the program you are using and copy out the procedure for ordinary numbering and for a more advanced numbering feature. Then place numbers in the right-hand corner of your footer zone, together with the advanced feature you have selected. Save, print and check.

Tabulations

Tabulations, better known as *tab stops* or just *tabs*, are standardised distances across the page, usually every $\frac{1}{2}$ inch, where you can insert text. Using tabs ensures that text inserted at different points across the page all lines up correctly. In most programs you set tabs on the horizontal ruler, specifying whether you want them left, centre or right aligned.

A special type of tab, useful for directing the reader's eye across the page in a contents list, is a leader character. This is a solid, dotted or dashed line that takes the place of a tab character. For example:

Element 2.1 _ _ _ _ _ _ Process commercial documents

Activity

1 Open Style Sheet, go to the end of the document and type 'Tabulations'. Find out how to set tabs in the program you are using. Copy out the instructions. Go back to the beginning of your style sheet and set out a contents list using tabs. Change the setting half-way through so that you can see the difference clearly. Save, print and check. Then write any improvements to the layout that you would like to make, by hand, into the margins. Copy the contents list with your handwritten notes and give this to your tutor.

2 Your final task is to create a commercial document template according to specification. First check that you know how to save a document as a template. Then open a new document, and save it as a template using your initials followed by 'plate'. Reopen then modify it according to this specification:

Orientation	landscape
Paper size	210 × 297 mm
Columns	two, newspaper, separated by a line
Font	Arial, 11-point
Header	Element 2.1 – Template *(centred)*
Footer	copyright, your initials, month and year *(left aligned)*
Justification	yes
Line spacing	1.5
Margins	standard
Page numbering	bottom right, Arial 9-point
Tabulations	set default at 0.6 inch, left aligned

Save, and check your finished work with your tutor.

Note: You will be using this template later.

File names and editing

Three fundamental procedures in processing any document are saving, editing and applying accuracy checks. All documents should be saved using file names that are both meaningful and appropriate to the system. Knowing the different editing techniques for basic functions allows you to work in your own style. Checking accuracy as a matter of habit saves time and leads to better results.

Saving then finding files

Have you ever lost or mislaid a file then tried searching through the different directories? On a typical stand-alone computer there are hundreds, even thousands, of files. As long as you know the right directory (to refresh you memory on directories, refer back to 'Data directories' in Element 1.3), file names are the key to saving then finding

files. A file name is the set of letters, numbers or symbols that you assign to a file to distinguish it from all other files in a directory.

Whenever you save a file, ensure the file name you choose is as meaningful and easily identified as possible. Some programs such as MS-DOS or Windows up to version 3.11 restrict you to eight characters long. Macintosh computers accept file names up to 31 characters. Win95 also accepts long file names, including spaces.

Did you know?

Programs and data have sets of characters added to a file name, known as *extensions*. Extensions further define the type or purpose of the file. In MS-DOS, for example, an eight-character file name may be followed by a stop (.) and an extension of up to three letters. You can chose the extension yourself, for example MYFILE.JOE, or it can be assigned by a program. When a program assigns an extension it has a specific interpretation. For example, .EXE means an *ex*ecutable program that MS-DOS can load and run.

Activity

Investigate the programs in your computer system and identify each of the file extensions. Make a list and report your findings back to each other. Be prepared to report to the class if your tutor asks you to.

Editing

Most programs offer several different ways to perform the same editing functions. You can achieve the same result by using menus, buttons or the keyboard. Knowing the different options allows you to work in the way that is most convenient to you personally. Here are some of the most popular procedures.

To move or copy text or graphics within the same document, first highlight your selection. Then either drag it into position or copy it to the clipboard, move to the insertion point and paste it in. To copy or move text or graphics to another program you must use the clipboard method. To delete text or graphics, highlight the selection then press the delete key or click the delete button.

Did you know?

When you have drawn a graphic object or imported one into a document, you may need to *rotate* it. Graphics packages usually include rotation and flip features. You highlight the object and select the degree of rotation you require. Rotating 180° is the same as turning the object upside down, which you can usually do with a Flip command.

Figure 2.3 Rotating 180° is the same as using the Flip command

When you insert a graphic object such as a piece of clipart, it is normally out of proportion with the rest of the document. Sizing the object brings it into proportion. The small squares or circles on the line that surrounds a graphic object are called *handles*. By clicking and dragging these handles you can size the object. Sizing is also important in tables. As with table columns in the layout section above, to size a column (or row), drag the cell border in the direction you require.

Activity

Open a new document, go to the clipart directory, flick through the options and select an object. Note its file name and extension. Import the object into your document and type out its file name and extension underneath. Copy it further down the page. Make one copy a different size from the other and flip it over if that command is available. Next, insert a table of 3 columns by 3 rows. Make the first row and the first column half the size of the others. In column 1 type: 'Sizing columns'. In column 2 type: 'This column is twice the size of column 1 and equal to column 3'. In column 3 type the instructions for sizing columns. Save, print and file your work.

Accuracy checks

Good working habits mean that you no longer have to think about routine operations because you carry them out on automatic pilot. One essential habit is to save documents frequently while you are working on them. Another habit to develop is accuracy checking. The main check is *proof-reading* – frequently looking over a document to ensure that the content and layout of text and the positioning of tables and graphics is correct.

Most programs offer a range of *proofing tools* – spelling, grammar and hyphenation checks, for example. Although these are helpful, the final decision is yours – you have to check that the checking tools have got it right. If you wait until a document is completed before you apply program checks or your own checks, you are less likely to see all the errors. As with saving, you should frequently check for accuracy as you work on a document.

Security checks

Working in the computer industry means dealing with highly valuable equipment and data. This requires the skills to use security techniques that protect computer systems from accidental or intentional damage. This damage includes theft of hardware and software, the loss of data, breach of confidentiality and breach of copyright (see Element 3.4 for more information).

The techniques to avoid or limit this damage are:

- anti-theft procedures
- regular saving, back-ups and retaining source documents
- non-disclosure of confidential information such as passwords
- adhering to data and software copyright.

Anti-theft procedures

The risk of theft depends on the environment of the system. In public places, basic anti-theft procedures include building hardware into casing, bolting it to desks and locking up equipment. Make a point of finding out about the organisational security procedures wherever you are, and following them carefully.

Saving and backing up

There are always people with stories about how they lost hours or even days of work because of a system failure. No sympathy. If you back work up regularly, you never lose more than a few minutes' worth. As well as the regular saving procedure, most industry standard software has advanced settings.

To avoid the consequences of power failure or other problems, you can set up a program that will automatically save the document you are working on at regular intervals. Although you can choose how often the automatic save takes place, the default is normally every 10 minutes. As you know from your work with macros, you can also set up a program to save a back-up version each time you save a document. You will learn more about this in Element 3.4.

Activity

In groups, each choose a different program. Using the Help menu, find out how to change the automatic save default setting. To check your understanding, make a note of what it is currently set at (e.g. every 10 minutes), change it to every 2 minutes, then change it back again. Teach the other people in your group how to do this for the program you investigated. Is it the same or different for each program?

Saving also refers to retaining *source documents*. When valuable data or any data that is not easily replaced is transferred on to disk, the source documents must be retained in a filing cabinet or safe.

To avoid the damage done by viruses or other system-wide disasters, it is not enough to back up files into a different directory in the same computer. Files should be regularly backed up on to other storage mediums, such as tape drives or floppy disks, or another computer on a network (see Element 3.4 for more information).

Activity

Work with a software program that includes a back-up program. Check if you are unsure. Find out how to use the back-up program and type it out step by step. Save, print and use the document to help you back up all the course files you have created so far on to floppy disk.

Non-disclosure

Sophisticated methods for restricting people's access to data and programs include identification numbers and password, and encoded user cards. These procedures can apply to the system as a whole or to specific information banks or programs. Many organisations rank data files according to their degree of confidentiality.

Data and software copyright

Copyright protects the work of authors, artists and composers from being reproduced by anyone without permission. The only person who can reproduce a copyright-protected work is the owner. This means that you cannot make multiple copies of software without the necessary licence. Copying without a licence, whether it is program or data files, is a criminal offence.

Did you know?

Although copyright becomes effective when a work is created, all publicly distributed copies must contain a copyright notice, otherwise it is lost. A copyright notice is either the word 'Copyright' or the abbreviation 'Copr.' or the symbol © together with the name of the owner and the year of first publication. Most software has the copyright notice under About on the menu bar. Check this to see.

Evidence assignment

Create a directory for Unit 2 and save all your work for this unit in the appropriate directory.

This evidence assignment has been designed to cover all the evidence indicators related to Element 2.1. It has two sections.

Scenario

The directors of Computer Consultants Ltd believe that their competitive edge over other providers is their high level of customer service. Following the success of their 'Toll-free technical support' and 'Next business day response on-site service', they are introducing a document processing service. 3L (Loose Limbs Leisure) is one of the first customers to express an interest in the new service, and has completed and returned the requirements and specifications form.

Section 1

Your assignment is to produce example, template-based documents according to the following specification, including the production of data. Make sure you print one copy of the blank template for each of the four templates to be produced, and another printout *after* data has been entered into the template. This will provide evidence for IT Core Skills Elements 2.1.4 and 2.2.2.

1 Business letter

Orientation	portrait
Paper size	8.5 × 11 inches
Tables	one – 2 columns by 6 rows
Font	Times New Roman, 12-point
Header	logo
Footer	company registration no. 3627361832, centred, 10-point
Justification	yes
Line spacing	single
Margins	standard
Page numbering	none
Tabulations	0.5 inch, left aligned
Data	Standard letter to customers, telling them about next month's activities. Use the following:
Introduction	We are writing to let you know about the Centre's main activities for next month. Here is a table that shows which sports sessions are available at which times of day:
Table	*(Make up a table showing two activities in the morning, two in the afternoon and two in the evenings, for a six-day week. The same activities should take place every other day.)*
Final paragraph	Remember, all these activities are very popular and places fill up on a first come, first served basis. So, avoid disappointment and register today.

2 Memorandum

Orientation	portrait
Paper size	210 × 297 mm
Columns	none
Font	Arial, 10-point
Header	none
Footer	day, month and year – right aligned, 9-point
Justification	no
Line spacing	single
Margins	standard
Page numbering	none
Tabulations	set default at 0.6 inch, left aligned
Data	Memo from Marketing Manager informing staff that the new logo has been developed, and asking for their feedback. Use the following:
Introduction	3L (Loose Limbs Leisure) is proud to unveil the prototype of our new logo:
Clipart	*(Select a sports clipart object, or object you have drawn, as the logo.)*
Final sentence	Your opinion is important to us – please pop into my office and let me know what you think.

3 Invoice

Orientation	landscape
Paper size	210 × 297 mm
Columns	three × 1 row in centre of page
Font	Courier New, 12-point
Header	'Invoice' Impact 16-point, company name and address – centred
Footer	company registration no. 3627361832, centred, 9-point
Justification	none
Line spacing	1.5
Margins	standard
Page numbering	none
Tabulations	default at 0.5 inch, left aligned
Data	Use the column headings Date, Item, Amount. Then enter today's date and think of three items of sports equipment to list under Item. Put the current prices next to each item and under Amount. Calculate the subtotal, VAT and total. Refer to the Application of Number unit if necessary.

4 Newsletter

Orientation	landscape
Paper size	210 × 297 mm
Columns	Page 1 – three, newspaper, separated by a line
	Page 2 – four, newspaper (no line separation)
	Page 3 – two, newspaper (no line separation)
Font	use four types including italics or bold and different sizes
Header	3Ls Newsletter, month and year
Footer	page number
Justification	yes
Line spacing	1.5
Margins	standard
Page numbering	centred
Tabulations	set default at 0.5 inch, left aligned
Data	Make up a name for the newsletter, headlines and headings for news items (you do not have to write articles, just put xxxxxxxxxxx). You should also include at least two items of clipart or objects you have drawn on each page.

Section 2

Print out each of your documents, assess them against the specification and write a paragraph (50 words) commenting on how successful they are and offering your suggestions for improvement.

Revision test

Name the following

1 The four standard paper sizes.

2 The three basic types of column layout.

3 The three types of paragraph indent.

4 The four types of equipment and data security check.

Complete the blanks

5 Page attributes are a page's o_____ and the s _____ of paper it will fit. Orientation can be either p _____ or l _____ .

6 Page layout means the f_____ or the basic a_____ of the page.

7 Justifying text means changing the d _____ between words so that each line ends at the right m _____ in the same way as it starts at the left.

8 Line spacing is the amount of v _____ space between each l _____ of text. The standard line spacing options are s _____ , 1.5 and d _____ .

9 File names are the key to s _____ then finding files. A file name is the set of l _____ , n _____ or s _____ that you assign to a file to distinguish it from other files in a directory.

Write a short paragraph to show you clearly understand

10 Fonts.

11 Headers and footers.

12 Tab stops.

Element 2.2

Process graphic designs

In this element we are going to focus on the practical skills required to produce graphic designs according to specification. We start by examining the different types of image and example applications, then research current programs. As we explore and practise with image attributes and graphic components, you will develop your own graphics style sheet. After a brief review of page attributes, you will have a range of design specifications to analyse. This will equip you with the knowledge and practical skills to produce high-quality work for your evidence assignment project.

After studying this chapter you should be able to:

1 identify *graphic design software* and give examples
2 identify the *graphic components* required to meet given *design specifications*
3 set *image* and *page attributes*
4 produce and *edit* graphics to meet given *design specifications*
5 save and output graphic images
6 compare graphics with the specification and make recommendations for *improvements.*

Activity

In groups, tell each other about any graphic design programs you know of and what they do. Make a list of these programs and file it for later comparison.

Types of graphic design software

There are two basic approaches to generating images – *bit map* and *vector*. A bit map graphic is a pattern made up of dots. A vector graphic is made up of unconnected elements such as lines, curves, circles and squares.

Graphical user interfaces (GUIs) and *paint programs* are typical bit map applications. *Technical drawing software, computer aided design* (CAD) and *illustration packages* are typical vector applications. Charts and slide show presentations use both.

Bit map graphics

Bit mapped graphics treat images as collections of dots *(pixels)* rather than as shapes. Each bit in a bit image corresponds to one pixel (short for picture element, as you will recall from Element 1.2) on the screen. Because computer screens have high resolutions, it can be difficult to see the way an image is constructed from pixels. However, if you can zoom your screen view to at least 200% you should just be able to make out the bits in a character's font.

You can see the individual pixels in a bit mapped image more easily on a television screen, particularly in the way online information service graphics, like Teletext and Ceefax, are constructed. When you begin to work with them, you will find clearly constructed pixel images in Paint programs – they usually include a facility that allows you to change a paint pattern or a small section of a drawing, pixel by pixel.

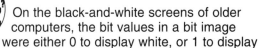

Did you know?

On the black-and-white screens of older computers, the bit values in a bit image were either 0 to display white, or 1 to display black. The pattern of the 0s and 1s that made up the bit image specified the pattern of black-and-white dots that made up the screen graphic. To display shades of grey or colour images, two or more bits are required – for example, two bits for 4 colours, four bits for 16 colours and sixteen bits for the standard 256 colour display on today's screens.

Vector graphics

In vector graphics, often called object-orientated graphics, objects are treated as collections of lines rather than as patterns of individual dots. You manipulate an object as a complete unit. For example, you can change the length of a line or enlarge a circle (or a block of text) as an independent screen element.

Vector images are described mathematically as sets of instructions to create the objects in the image – for example, the position, length and direction in which lines are to be drawn. This makes it much easier to magnify, rotate and layer object-orientated graphics than bit map graphics.

Charts and slide shows

Bit map and vector graphics are frequently combined in two of the most common graphic design applications – charts and slide shows. Charts (area, bar, column, pie, line and so on) are used to illustrate and compare statistical information. Their lines are created with vectors while their colour fills are usually bit maps.

For example, the bar chart in Figure 2.4 has a Y axis showing percentages and an X axis showing processor types (you learn about Y and X axes in the application of number unit). The axes are vector images. The shapes in different shades that distinguish the different brands are bit map images.

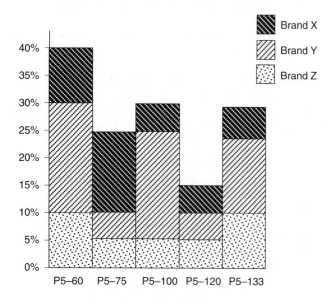

Figure 2.4 Bar chart showing processor sales

Activity

■ What percentage of P5-60s is Brand Y selling?
■ What percentage of P5-100s is Brand X selling?
■ What percentage of P5-133s is Brand Z selling?

Slide show software is a computer-based version of overhead projector (OHP) transparencies, used for giving presentations. You deliver your presentation by connecting the computer to a video display unit, or by simply printing your slides as transparencies. The individual slides are the pages of your presentation. Their structure is created with vector graphics. The contents (titles, text, charts, clipart and other drawn objects) can be either vector or bit mapped, but are usually a combination of both.

Activity

Work in groups. Divide this activity into parts and assign each part to different people or pairs. Your group objective is to draw up a reference sheet showing types, program names and descriptions of current graphic design software. You will need to research recent copies of computer magazines, go to computer software shops and investigate any other source that might help. Ensure that your sheet includes paint, drawing, charting and presentation programs, and the name of everyone in your group. Save your work at regular intervals in the right directory, using a suitable file name and make a back-up copy. Print out a hard copy and give it to your tutor or lecturer.

Graphics

Like any other application, graphics software is best learnt by experimenting. As you work through the explanations and activities in this section you will be preparing another style sheet. Your graphics style sheet will help you in your evidence assignment project and in your future work practice.

When you open a graphic design program it typically displays a screen area for the design and several sets of tools. These tools are the graphic components required to meet given graphic design specifications. The basic tools are line, shape, text, brush and a colour palette. Further tools allow you to specify the attributes of each graphic component and of the entire image. Attributes include fills, styles, line thicknesses, colours and shades, height and width.

You also have access to manipulation tools such as size and move, and to standard editing tools such as copy, cut and paste. Before examining and experimenting with different graphic components, you need to acquire a clearer understanding of the basic image attributes that you will be using.

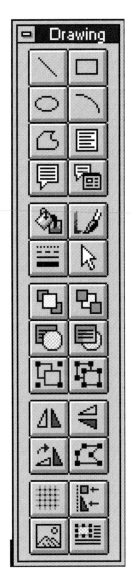

Figure 2.5 Drawing tool icons

Image attributes

Most programs enable you to choose image attributes before, during or after you have created the different components. The main attributes you will be working with are colours and sizes.

Colours

Colours (and shades) are available in the colour palette which is usually a separate toolbox. They can be used for text, single lines, outline shapes and for filling backgrounds and shapes.

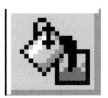 You can colour shapes and backgrounds with solid or shaded colours, patterns and even textures. To fill an area or object with colour, the standard procedure is to select the fill icon (shown here), choose a colour, then click in the area or object you want to fill.

Did you know?

Most programs include a custom colours option. To use it, select the colour you want to customise, then choose Edit Colours. You will then see a chart where you define the colour you want by moving the cross-hair shape around. There are two models: RGB (red, green, blue) and HLS (hue, luminescence and saturation). When you have achieved the colour you want, save it to the custom palette.

Sizing

You can usually manipulate and reshape an image or any of its components by dragging its resize handles. Resize handles appear when you reselect an image by clicking on it. To resize the height, drag the handles on the top or bottom of the frame. To resize the width, drag the handles at the sides of the frame.

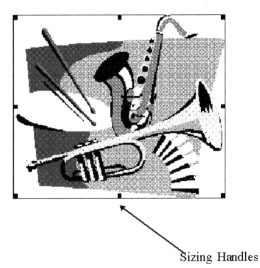

Sizing Handles

Figure 2.6 Using a sizing frame

Resizing in this way has a fair-ground mirror effect of altering proportion. To resize an object while maintaining its aspect ratio, drag from a corner of the frame.

To change the size of your entire image, select attributes, then click on the unit of measurement you want to use for the width and height. Then set the image scale in x and y planes using the mouse or keyboard, and your picture will be resized.

Did you know?

Design specifications for manufacturing state *tolerances.* Tolerances refer to the maximum errors in size that a manufactured article may have, or the size of the graphic image that is required.

To move an entire image, avoid the handles and click on the border. Then drag the image to the position you want.

Graphics tools

The main tools you will be working with to construct graphic components are the text, line, shape and brush tools. As you create images with these tools you will also be applying the above attributes.

The text tool

The text tool is used to type and format text. The standard procedure for using it is to select the icon and create a text frame by dragging the mouse pointer diagonally. Next, choose the font, size and style that you want to use. Then, click inside the text frame and type the necessary text.

Once you have entered your text you may want to move or enlarge the text frame as necessary, or to change the colour of the text.

To write text on a coloured background, select the foreground icon from the colour palette, then choose your colour. By selecting the background icon, then a colour, you can change the background colour.

Activity

Open a new file in a graphics program. Use the text tool to write the heading, 'Graphics Style Sheet'. Choose an appropriate heading font, style and size. Move or enlarge the text as necessary for a main heading. Next, write the subheading 'Text Tool'. Put it into a different font, style and size from the main heading, then into a custom colour. Save your work at regular intervals in the right directory, using a suitable file name and make a back-up copy. Print out a hard copy and check the text has come out as you specified.

The line tool

The line tool draws straight lines from the point you click as the start, to wherever you drag the mouse and click again to finish. The standard way to use the line tool is to select the icon, choose how wide and what colour your line will be, then draw it. In many programs you can add arrow heads and make a line dotted, dashed or a lighter shade.

Activity

Try this for yourself. Open your Graphics Style Sheet, enter the text 'Lines' and draw three lines. One should be separate and the other two joined at right angles. All three should be different colours. Save your work at regular intervals in the right directory, using a suitable file name and make a back-up copy. Print out a hard copy and check the lines have come out as you specified.

The shape tools

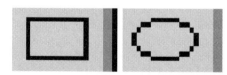

Basic shapes are constructed with the Rectangle, Circle and Polygon tools. They are created in the same way. Select the shape tool icon from the toolbox. Choose the thickness of the outline, its style and a colour. Then, to draw the shape, drag the mouse pointer diagonally in the direction you want.

Rectangle tools usually offer a choice of a square-cornered or a round-cornered shape. To draw a perfect square, in most programs you press and hold down the Shift key while you are dragging the mouse pointer. An ellipse is an elongated circle, like a rugby ball. To draw an ellipse, select the ellipse tool, then follow the standard shape procedure. For a perfect circle, follow the square procedure.

Did you know?

Poly means many. So *poly*gamy means having many husbands or wives. A *poly*glot is someone who speaks many languages, and a *poly*gon is not a dead parrot but a shape with many sides!

In most graphics programs you can draw a polygon with the specific polygon tool or with a Freeform – a freehand drawing tool. If you use the freeform you can add text then group them so that they move, rotate, flip and resize together. In either case, start by following the same procedure as for the other shapes.

If you want to fill any of these shapes with colour, choose the colour, select fill, then click inside the shape.

Activity

Experiment. Find out how to draw shapes. Open your Graphics Style Sheet and type 'Shapes'. Then:

- produce at least one rectangle, square, circle, ellipse and polygon;
- use different outline colours, thicknesses and styles; and
- use different fills and two (labelled) custom colours.

Next:

- copy, paste and resize two of your shapes underneath their originals; and
- save your work at regular intervals in the right directory, using a suitable file name.

When you have a drawing that illustrates each shape and attribute clearly, make a back-up copy and print out a hard copy to check your work.

The brush tool

Use the brush tool to create a range of different sized and shaped brush strokes. To paint with a brush, select the brush tool, then choose the size and shape you want and the colour. To paint, just drag the mouse pointer.

Did you know?

Most graphics programs include an airbrush effect with adaptable spray areas. Its effects are very similar to using a spray-can at different ranges, and so it is particularly good for graffiti. The procedure for spraying is the same as for brush strokes.

Activity

Try it for yourself. Open your Graphics Style Sheet. Type 'Brushes' and produce a drawing that clearly illustrates different-style brush strokes and the effects you can achieve with the airbrush. Save your work at regular intervals in the right directory, using a suitable file name. Print out a hard copy of your completed sheet.

Compare the result with the specifications given in this series of activities and consider where you could make improvements. Write out the improvements by hand, directly on to your sheet, then go back into the file and make them. Save your work at regular intervals in the right directory, using a suitable file name. When you have finished, make a back-up copy and print a hard copy. Give both the hard copy and the original sheet, with your handwritten improvements notes, to your tutor.

Page attributes

You are already familiar with page attributes from your work with commercial documents in Element 2.1. As a review of orientation and paper sizes, try this activity.

Activity

1   Which is which? Label the orientation of these pages:

2 Match the paper size (letter, legal, A4, B4) to each of these measurements:

- 8.5 × 14 inches
- 257 × 364 mm
- 210 × 297 mm
- 8.5 × 11 inches

3 Margin or indent? What should the correct word be at the beginning of these sentences?

_____ settings specify the distance between the text and the edges of the page.

_____ settings specify the distance between the text and the margins.

4 Horizontal or vertical? What is the correct word for the gaps?

To adjust the margins at the top or bottom of the page, display the rulers and point to a margin boundary on the _____ ruler. Then drag the margin boundary.

To adjust the margins at the side of the page, display the rulers and point to a margin boundary on the _____ ruler. Then drag the margin boundary.

Design specifications

Activity

The following are a selection of graphic design specifications. For each:

i state its purpose;

ii identify the graphic type(s);

iii identify all the graphic components, including attributes, required to meet the specification;

iv identify the page attribute; and

v write a paragraph suggesting any improvements you can think of.

1 A new version of *Campbell's Tomato Soup.* Show basic ellipse and rectangle shapes with different line styles and thicknesses. Three shades. Specification of text font, style and size on label. Background fill in light shade and different colour. Graffiti-style slogan 'Campbell's – the art of soup'. Specify margin sizes all round and show orientation. Something on the lines shown in Figure 2.7.

2 *Bar chart* illustrating time spent on different programs in a college self-access centre. Indicate colours for

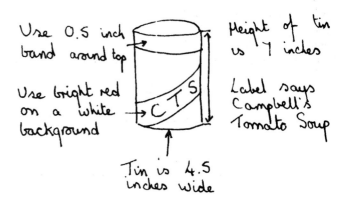

Figure 2.7 Campbell's Tomato Soup

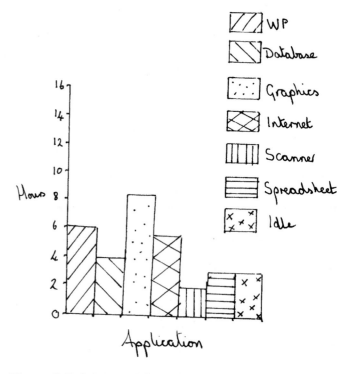

Figure 2.8 Average daily computer use

applications, text styles and sizes, height and width of chart, units of measurement and tolerances (see Figure 2.8).

3 *Slide presentation* for new mountain bike design. Slide title, 'Cougar FX – Mountain Lion':

- text size and style
- customised colour
- shading

- background graded fill

Object: basic illustration of bike:

- lines and shapes (wheel, cross-bars, handle bars, etc.)
- dimensions (wheels, height of cross-bar from ground)
- different thicknesses of wheels and other lines
- colours of bike
- colours of background
- image height, width and tolerances
- page attributes: orientation – landscape; margins; transparency size – A4.

Evidence assignment

This evidence assignment project has been designed to cover all the evidence indicators related to Element 2.2. It has three sections. Use the graphics style sheet you prepared, to help you complete them.

Scenario

CineManiac are selling more magazines than ever before and enjoying the work-rate gains their computer has brought them. Although you stopped working with them when you got the job at Computer Consultants Ltd, you still keep in touch and receive a copy. Yesterday evening the editor phoned and told you that the graphic designer left the magazine last week, in sudden and mysterious circumstances.

He also said that they need two special graphic designs and have heard about your work on document processing. The first design is a chart that shows the breakdown of film types reviewed over the past two years. The second is an ad for a film that will go in the magazine, and be used in a presentation. He asked if you would be interested in the opportunity of a freelance contract. Although you don't have much free time these days, you accepted.

Section 1

Before going to CineManiac, you make some initial preparations to save time. One is to send a list of all types of graphic design software, with an example of each. You ask CineManiac what they are using.

Set out a two-column list showing types of graphic design software and one example of each.

Section 2

1 State the purpose, then prepare a list identifying the appropriate graphic components required to meet the following design specification:

- 2D pie chart
- film types in percentages:
  - horror 22%
  - romance 9%
  - murder mystery 11%
  - psychological thriller 17%
  - music videos 18%
  - comedy 11%
  - science fiction 12%
- graphic components
  - specify slice fill colours including one custom
  - text size and style
- dimensions (height and width)
- orientation – landscape
- paper size – A4.

2 Prepare the graphic according to the specification (refer to the Application of Number unit if you need to check on pie charts). Ensure that you set image and page attributes, produce and edit the image to meet the design specification, save your graphic at regular intervals in the right directory, and use a suitable file name.

When you have finished, make a back-up copy, print out a hard copy and compare it with the specification. Write a memo to the editor recommending improvements to the graphic and to the specification.

Section 3

1 Prepare a list identifying the appropriate graphic components required to meet the following design specification:

- presentation slide – title, text and object
- components
  - text sizes, styles and colours
  - background fills
  - lines (style, width)
  - shapes (circles, polygons, rectangles)
  - spray (graffiti)
- image attributes – height and width, and tolerances

- page attributes – portrait, A4, $\frac{1}{2}$ inch side margins, 1 inch top/bottom margins.

2 Research the style of film ads in newspapers and magazines. Then, choose any film you like and have seen, and design your own ad according to the specification. Make sure that you set image and page attributes, and that you produce and edit the image to meet the design specification. Save your work at regular intervals in the right directory, using a suitable file name.

When you have finished, make a back-up copy, print out a hard copy and compare the result with the specification. Write a memo to the editor recommending improvements to the graphic and to the specification.

Revision test

Name the following

1 Five basic tools in a graphics package.

2 Five attribute tools in a graphics package.

3 The three basic shape tools.

Complete the blanks

4 You can colour shapes and background colours with s_____ or sh _____ colours, p _____ , and even t _____ .

5 The text tool is used to t _____ and f _____ text.

6 The line tool in most graphics programs allows you to add a _____ heads and make a line do_____ , da_____ or a lighter s_____ .

Write a short paragraph to show you clearly understand

7 The difference between bit map and vector images.

8 The use of image resize handles.

9 The brush tool.

Process and model numerical data

In this element we are going to explore a way of using numbers to predict the future – modelling. Models are constructed from data, calculations and layouts, and usually based on spreadsheets. We will be taking a detailed practical look at each of these in turn and using them to construct different models. You will make predictions yourself. At the same time, you'll have the opportunity to develop a numerical modelling style sheet for future use. In the final part of this element, we will look at the purpose of 'what if' queries and use your modelling skills to practise their application.

After studying this chapter you should be able to:

1 identify types of *models* and give examples
2 identify the *data* in a given numerical processing activity
3 define the *calculations* required to produce a model of the activity
4 construct *layout* of model and enter *data*
5 undertake 'what if' queries of the model
6 save the file, back up regularly and produce required output.

Models

If you drive or plan to drive a car or any other motor vehicle, you need an insurance policy. When you're looking for a quotation, insurance companies ask all sorts of questions about your age, where you live, what sort of car you have, the size of the engine, where you park and so on. Your answers are used to calculate how much of a risk you are.

For example, insurance company statistics show that the more experience you have the lower the risk you are. They also show that certain types of car are more often involved in accidents than others. This information allows the company to create a chart to help weigh up the risk and so decide the premium (Figure 2.9).

In the past, your insurance agent would look up each of your answers on a chart, manually note the risk factor, then add all the factors together to find your premium. Today, commercial programs do all that automatically. They have also allowed insurance companies to put a lot more questions and answers

Risk factor out of 10	10	9	8	7	6	5	4
Years' experience	1	2	3	4-5	5-10	10-20	20+
Type of car	A	B	C	D	E	F	G
Part of town	East		South		North		West

Figure 2.9   Insurance risks

into the balance. Even your choice of colour can make a difference – black is the most expensive, because black cars are more often stolen or broken into!

All the questions, answers and risk factors are put into a model. The model is a kind of formula that calculates the chances of an accident occurring in a certain period, based on the number of risks involved and the law of averages. This is how insurance models determine the amount of premium you have to pay.

Did you know?

Insurance is rather like gambling – putting money on a game of chance. The insurance company is betting that you won't have an accident. The difference between insurance and gambling is that an insurance policyholder must be someone who would suffer a material loss if the event takes place. In other words:

■ You can insure your own car because if there were an accident you would suffer the loss of your car.
■ You cannot insure a stranger's car because in the event of an accident you would not suffer any loss – it isn't your car.
■ At a race meeting you can put your money on a stranger's car – maybe Damon Hill's – and gamble that he would not have an accident.

Insurance quotations and games of chance (whether for money or not) illustrate two of the most important models that use numerical data. These are *prediction* and *gaming*. Predictive models can forecast information such as how much profit an investment can make. Gaming models can demonstrate the results of changes in the rules.

Predictive models

How would you react to the following business proposition? A friend has come up with a neat idea for a new computer game and thinks she can make a lot of money. She says she has spent £100 on equipment to design the game and now needs another £100 to buy floppy disks to copy and sell it. You agree that if the game is offered at £10, it might sell as many as 100 copies. Anyway, you like the idea and are pretty sure it would sell at least 50 copies. You wouldn't really mind if it didn't make any money, but you are not prepared to lose your £100. How would you decide whether to invest or not?

Your decision would be based on a financial model for predicting her break-even point. This is the point at which there is no loss and no profit. You break even when you sell enough copies to get the costs back (your £100 and her £100), but before you start making a profit. Although this deal does not represent a huge sum of money, the investment calculation is basically the same as an entrepreneur would make when investing millions. (Note that you will be coming back to construct this investment model later in the element.)

Calculating break-even points is a typical example of how predictive models are used in financial forecasting. You construct a model to forecast the financial future, in this case when you are going to break even. Another everyday use of predictive models in financial forecasting is budgeting. Budgets show predicted amounts of income and expenditure. Figure 2.10 is an outline extract from CineManiac's budget.

	April	May	June	July	August	September
Income						
Subscriptions	277	283	284	299	301	314
Advertising	500	350	700	200	540	620
Subtotal	777	633	984	499	841	934
Expenses						
Salaries	400	400	400	450	450	450
Printing	200	200	200	200	210	210
Consultant	0	0	250	0	0	0
Subtotal	600	600	850	650	660	660
Total	177	33	134	−151	181	274

Figure 2.10 CineManiac's budget (extract)

By preparing this budget, the accountant can predict how an increase or decrease in income or expenses would affect the bottom line. He or she can then use this information to make decisions such as whether to increase salaries or hire a computer consultant.

Activity

Like a budget, most predictive models in financial forecasting are set out and calculated with spreadsheet programs. In pairs, remind each other about spreadsheets and write a list of everything you remember about them from Elements 1.2 and 1.4. When you have finished, check with your tutor and the rest of your class. Then, using a spreadsheet program, copy out CineManiac's budget. Don't copy the subtotals and totals lines; use formulae. Once your copy of CineManiac's budget model is complete, play about with the numbers to see how the bottom line changes. Try, for example, increasing and decreasing advertising, increasing salaries, using a computer consultant in July as well as June and so on.

mph	kph
10	16.09
20	32.19
30	48.28
40	64.37
50	80.47
60	96.56
70	112.65
80	128.75
90	144.84
100	160.93

Figure 2.11 Mph to kph conversion table

Other examples of predictive models are conversion tables for mathematical functions that are used over and over again (Figure 2.11). You will see in the application of number unit that it is quicker to create a table showing conversions from miles per hour to kilometres per hour, for example, than to make new calculations each time.

Spreadsheets are the easiest way of calculating tables for reference. To convert miles per hour to kilometres per hour, you have to multiply the number of miles/hour by 1.609344. So in the kph box, put a formula that says 10×1.609344. Then use the same formula (but changing the mph of course) in all the other kph boxes. Then you have your complete table.

Gaming models

How do you learn new video games? Do you study the objectives and rules, then apply them, or watch someone else to get the general idea, or just have a go and get wiped out?

Most people learn games by playing them. After a while, as they become proficient, they begin to notice a 'system'. If you have played a lot of video games, you may have noticed that they all have a system and the better you understand it, the higher your level and scores. The system is a gaming model. When analysed it shows the consequences of changing the rules. In car-driving games or games where the player makes repeated decisions to look for treasure, or to meet a fictitious person, for example, once you have learnt Level 1, you go to Level 2. At Level 2 a new set of rules change the game and make it more difficult.

To understand or develop a game model, you have to understand the definition of a game. For most people, it is a conflict that a given number of players participate in. The conflict is resolved through a list of rules. The rules stipulate how the game begins, the possible legal 'moves' at each stage of play and the outcome at the end of the game.

Mathematical analysis of a game, analysing its system, can show the best choices to make in different situations to reach your objective. A gaming model sets out all these choices and conditions and so identifies the possible outcomes.

Because of the enormous numbers of strategies involved in even the simplest games, models can be extremely complicated. However, the basic idea is as easy to understand as a flow chart. How many choices do you have to make in Figure 2.12, in this simple outline example, if your objective is no. 5?

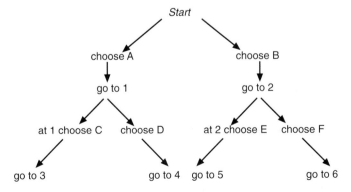

Figure 2.12 How many choices?

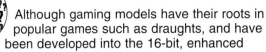

Did you know?

Although gaming models have their roots in popular games such as draughts, and have been developed into the 16-bit, enhanced graphics video games of Nintendo and Sega, they are also used to study more serious conflicts. In the Second World War, for example, military strategists working in submarine warfare, logistics and air defence used ideas that were developed in gaming models.

Gaming models can also be used to understand political and economic situations – for instance, markets for different goods where demand and supply keep changing. In this respect gaming models are similar to predictive financial models: they both help in understanding what might happen in the future. Knowing these possibilities helps organisations to decide the best way to use resources and maximise profits.

Construction

Models are constructed from three main elements: *data* – the information that the model manipulates; *calculations* – the way the data is manipulated; and *layout* – the presentation of the model.

Numerical models, like any other system, need a *blueprint* before they can be put together for the first time. A blueprint is a plan or design that you have worked out beforehand and that warns you of any likely problems. A blueprint helps you to identify, for example, all the different data that you will need to construct the model.

Data

There are four types of data you need to enter into a model. These are characters, numbers, dates and formulae. The following is an explanation of what a spreadsheet program or other numerical processing package understands by these terms. Numbers are usually classified as any of these, in any combination:

$$0\ 1\ 2\ 3\ 4\ 5\ 6\ 7\ 8\ 9\ +\ -\ ()\ /\ £\ \%$$

Any other combination of numbers and non-numeric characters is treated as text.

Did you know?

To distinguish between a number and a formula, numbers are classified as *constants*. A constant is a data entry that does not start with an equals sign. For example, today's date, a value such as 40 and a word are all constants. A formula, or a value that is the result of a formula, is not a constant.

Dates (and times) are usually treated as numbers unless you format the way they are displayed. For example, if you enter a date using numbers only (e.g. 07/08 for 7 August) and do not apply a date format to the cell, it will be treated as a fraction. Consequently the program will divide 7 by 8 and display 0.88. It is usually best to format your complete date column as you are setting up your model. Choose from the range of date formats available.

Dates can be added, subtracted and included in other calculations. The way to calculate a date in most programs is to enter it in a formula, enclosed by quotation marks. For example, if you want to know how many days there are left between now and the end of term, enter ='end of term date'–'today's date'.

Characters or text are mostly entered to describe items. It is important to keep any numbers separate from text, otherwise they cannot be used for calculations. For example, the information '7 soundcards' should be in two different cells. Like numbers, text and characters can have different font, size and styles applied to them.

Because the numbers that can be used to make calculations must be clearly defined, text is classified as any combination of numbers, spaces and non-numeric characters. This means that 14-100, 14Z, 14<space>14, for example, as well as a, b, c, etc., are all classified as text.

Activity

Open a new spreadsheet file and

- in cell A1, enter 'Numerical Style Sheet' (don't worry that it goes over several cells, you will correct this later). Format the font in an appropriate style for a heading;
- in cell A3, enter 'dates';
- in cell B3, enter today's date (day/month) and notice the number displayed. Then copy the date into C3, D3, E3 and F3, and format each one differently;

- use Help to check how to calculate dates in your program, then, in cell A4, enter the formula to calculate the number of days remaining until the end of term; and
- in cell B4, enter 'days until the end of term'.

Save your work at regular intervals in the right directory, using a suitable file name. When you have finished, make a back-up copy and print out a hard copy to check the data has come out as you specified.

Calculations and formulae

Formulae enable you to make a wide range of automatic calculations that take place instantaneously. As long as you set them up correctly their results are never wrong, no matter how complicated. However, to decide which formula to use you first need to define them manually, in your blueprint.

A formula is a sequence of values (numbers), cell references (e.g. D4) or operators (e.g. addition or multiplication) that produces a new value from existing values. A formula always begins with an equals sign (=). To enter a formula in a worksheet cell, type a combination of these elements in the formula bar. Although formulae range from the easy to the very complicated, the basic formula types are used over and over again. It is worth getting to know some of these.

Formulae use *arithmetic* operators and *comparison* operators. This sounds complicated but it's quite straightforward: arithmetic operators perform basic mathematical operations such as addition, subtraction, division and so on. For example, where A4 and A7 are example cell references and 17.5% VAT is an example percentage, to

add	=A4+A7
subtract	=A4–A7
divide	=A4/A7
multiply	=A4*A7
percentage	=A4*17.5%
sum (total)	=sum(A4:A7)

Comparison operators compare two values and produce the logical value (see Element 3.3 for more on relational and logical operators). The following are examples of comparison operators:

=	equal to
>	greater than
<	less than

Did you know?

An *algorithm* is a method of solving a problem by using a simple calculation over and over again. Multiplication is a good example: 2 × 10 is the same as 2 added together 10 times. In computer programs, an algorithm is a method of solving a problem through a mechanical sequence of steps. These sequences are often displayed in flow charts to make them easier to follow.

Activity

Try to set up some formulae yourself. Open your numerical style sheet, and

- in cell A5, enter 'Formulae'
- in cell A6, enter 'add'
- in cell B6, enter your age
- in cell C6, enter the value 10
- in cell D6, enter the formula for addition, and check that the answer is correct
- in cells A7 to D7, do the same for subtracting
- then follow the same procedure for each of the formulae above.

Save your work at regular intervals in the right directory, using a suitable file name. When you have finished, make a back-up copy and print out a hard copy to check your formulae.

Layout

The format of rows, columns and cells is the main tool to help you to present your model clearly. There are two ways to adjust row height and column width on current industry-standard software. The easiest is to place the cursor on the dividing line between the cell heading numbers or letters until it changes into a double-arrow shape (e.g. ⇔). Then, just drag the row or column in the direction you want, to make it larger or smaller. Alternatively you can specify the height or width of a row in numbers, using the format menu.

Most numerical processing programs have the basic data formatting features that you find on a word processing package – for example, font, font size, font type. These can be applied to any cell data (text or number) and are particularly useful for emphasising headings and totals.

As well as fonts and date styles, you can usually format number type. The main types specify:

- number of decimal places, e.g. 0, –0, (0), then 0.00, 0.000, etc.
- percentages, e.g. 0%, –0% (0%), etc.
- commas to separate thousands, e.g. 1,000, 1,000,000, etc.
- currency symbols, e.g. £0, £–0, (£0), etc.
- scientific symbols, e.g. 111.1+02

The use of brackets around numbers is an accounting convention that means they are minus amounts. This is no different from putting a minus sign before the number. You can also change the colour to red, to indicate a minus number.

Activity

Open your style sheet, and

- reformat your column widths to accommodate your data comfortably and clearly
- in cell A9, enter number types
- in cell A10, enter decimals
- in cell B10, enter 1234.789, and in cell C10 enter 1234.9
- in cell A11, enter %s
- format cells B11 and C11 to show %s, then enter 17.5 in B11 and 100 in cell C11
- in cell A12, enter commas
- format cells B12 and C12 to show commas (if they do not already), then 1,234 in cell B12 and 1,234.9 in cell C12
- in cell A13, enter £s
- format cells B13 and C13 to show £s, then enter 100 in cell B13 and 1,234.9 in cell C13.

Save your work at regular intervals in the right directory, using a suitable file name. When you have finished, make a back-up copy of your style sheet and print out a hard copy to check the data has come out as you specified.

'What if' queries

If you have a job earning £12,000 a year and your boss gives you a 5% increase, you don't need a spreadsheet program to work out what it is worth and the new total. However, pay rises are often negotiated – you ask for 9%, your boss offers 3% and you meet somewhere in the middle. Here, 'what if' queries can help. Simply by changing a single variable (the %), 'what if' calculations can show you the value of the different percentages and the new totals at a glance.

even point for the number of seats on an aircraft flight which need to be sold at a given price to recover costs.

Break-even points are one of the most frequently asked 'what if' queries, and so one you should be entirely familiar with. Remember you friend's business proposition at the beginning of this element? You are now in a position to construct a break-even point model that analyses the investment, and to see what possibilities it offers.

Activity

Go back and reread the proposition (see page 66). Open a new spreadsheet file, and

- enter 'Break-even point analysis' in cell A1 and format it as a heading
- in cell A3 enter 'Item', in B3 enter 'Quantity', in C3 enter 'Cost', in D3 enter 'Total' and in E3 enter 'Profit'
- double the width of column A
- in cell A5 enter 'R&D' and in D5 enter £100.00
- in A6 enter 'Floppy disks', in B6 enter 100, in C6 enter £1.00 and in D6 enter the formula =B6*C6
- in D7 enter the formula =sum(D5:D6)
- in A9 enter 'Price/game' and in C9 enter £10.00
- in A10 enter 'Break-even' and in B10 enter the formula =D7/C9
- in A11 enter 'Sales', in B11 enter the value 50, in C11 enter the formula =B11*C9 and in D11 enter the formula =D11−D7

You have now constructed a break-even point model. The break-even point line shows that you need to sell 20 copies to recover your costs. Your model also tells you that if you sell the 50 copies you expect, the game will make £300 profit – a tidy investment.

Save your work at regular intervals in the right directory, using a suitable file name, and make a back-up copy. Then ask the following queries of your model and make a note of how the profit is affected. 'What if' it sold:

1. 100 copies?
2. 50 copies at a price of £12 each?
3. 100 copies at a price of £12 each?
4. 50 copies but the cost of the floppy disks went up to £1.20?
5. 50 copies but the R&D cost went up to £150?
6. 100 copies at a price of £12 each, and the R&D cost went up to £150?

Check your answers with your tutor.

Activity

Set up this example to see the 'what if' results for yourself:

- open a new file and enter 'What if' queries in cell A1 and format as a heading
- enter 'Salary' in cell A3 and £12,000 (correctly formatted) in cell B3
- enter 3% in cell A4 and the formula =B3*+A4 in cell B4
- enter 'New total' in cell A5 and the formula =B3+B4 in cell B5
- now try changing the percentage in cell A4 to see the results of better pay deals.

Save your work at regular intervals in the right directory, using a suitable file name, and make a back-up copy.

Calculating the effects of different percentage increases is just one use of 'What if' queries. They are a powerful financial tool with everyday applications in almost all organisations. The nature of each 'what if' query depends on the nature of the processing activity being resolved. In manufacturing, for example, they might be used to assess the effect on production costs of the quantity of goods being produced. In tourism, they could establish the break-

Evidence assignment

This project has been designed to cover all the evidence indicators related to Element 2.3. It has three sections.

Scenario

The manager of 3L (Loose Limbs Leisure) is working on a plan to build a new sports hall. There is a waiting list for aerobic classes, badminton and squash, and the current teams all want more time. From a business perspective, a second hall would allow more m,embers to use the club and so increase revenue and, it is hoped, profits.

This is a big investment and the manager wants to study it from all angles before presenting her ideas to the rest of the management team. She contacts you at Computer Consultants Ltd to see whether the systems you have installed can help her. When you mention 'what if' queries, she tells you she's hopeless at maths and asks you to set up a model for her.

Section 1

The following is the basic information the manager gives you. Use it to set up a clearly formatted break-even point model. Your model should show how many new members are needed for the project to break even:

Construction costs	£120,000
Equipment	£30,000
Average annual membership fee	£200

Projected new members

Year 1	200
Year 2	300
Year 3	300

When you have finished, save, print out and back up your file.

Section 2

Demonstrate the power of your model to answer the manager's queries about how the following factors would affect the break-even point. 'What if'

1 the building costs rose to £135,000?

2 the equipment costs were reduced to £25,000?
3 the building costs rose to £135,000 and the equipment costs reduced to £25,000?
4 the average annual membership fee was increased to £250?
5 the building costs rose to £135,000 and the membership fee was increased to £250?
6 250 new members joined in Year 1?
7 250 new members joined in Year 1 and equipment costs rose to £40,000?
8 the average annual membership fee was reduced to £170, a total of 250 new members joined in Year 1, 350 in Years 2 and 3, and equipment costs rose to £50,000?

Make a written note of the answers to these questions.

Section 3

The manager of 3L asks you to explain the principles of computer models to her. Write a report that identifies the types of models, and gives an example of each.

Include descriptions of at least two types of data used in numerical processing activities, and at least three types of calculations required to produce models.

Revision test

Name the following

1 Three common uses of predictive models.

2 Two uses of gaming models.

3 The three main elements used to construct models.

4 The four types of data you enter in a model.

5 The three main tools for laying a model out clearly.

Complete the blanks

6 The two most important models that use n _____ data are prediction and gaming. Predictive models can f_____ information such as how much profit an investment can make. Gaming models can d _____ the results of c _____ in the rules.

7 The difference between levels in most video games
is that when you progress, a new s _____ of
r _____ changes the game and make it more
d _____ .

8 A formula is a sequence of n _____ , c _____
r _____ (e.g. D4), or o _____ (e.g. addition or
multiplication), that produces a new value from
existing values. A formula always begins with an
e _____ s _____ .

9 The format of r _____ , co _____ and c _____ are
the main tools to present your model clearly.

*Write a short paragraph to show you clearly
understand*

10 Break-even point.

11 What if? queries.

Use information technology for process control

In this element you are going to explore process control systems and how to construct them. You will begin by looking at examples to find out what they are and what they are used for. With this overview, you will be able to understand the stages in process control and the different components that are required to make up a system. As you work you will develop a log that will help you to design and construct a system for your evidence assignment project.

After studying this chapter you should be able to:

1 describe *uses of process control systems*
2 identify *stages in a given process control system*
3 describe the *components* of process control systems
4 select and use *components* to construct a control system for a given *specification*
5 review the performance of the control system and suggest improvements to the *specification*.

Working quietly away, behind the scenes, process control systems *monitor* and *regulate* much of your waking and sleeping life. Heating and cooling systems control the temperature of your environment, while security systems such as smoke and intruder alarms keep it safe. Traffic lights control the journey to school or college and street lamps switch themselves on as it becomes dark. Washing machines control how your clothes are cleaned and cooking timers control how your food is cooked. If you go on holiday by plane it is most probably flown and landed by a control system called 'automatic pilot'.

Did you know?

With the help of computers, petrochemical plants and steel rolling mills use the same basic idea of process control as washing machines. In an oil refinery, for example, process control turns crude oil into petrol and other products as it continuously flows in and through the refinery. A central computer co-ordinates a set of microprocessors and the microprocessors operate groups of process control systems. The process control systems monitor and regulate the heaters, valves and other flow devices that prepare the petrol and other products.

Uses of process control systems

The number and type of process control systems that monitor and regulate everyday life, and that operate industrial equipment, are growing rapidly. This is because they have many applications within the same industry and also between different industries. The simplest way to explore and understand process control systems is through their most important uses. These are:

■ environmental control
■ process production control
■ quality control
■ security.

Did you know?

In the Canadian Rocky Mountains winter's temperatures fall as low as −37°C (when it's painful just to breathe), while in summer they can reach a high of 32°C. A computer scientist who lives in the mountains has built himself one of the most sensitive environmental control systems in the world. No matter what the temperature outside, the system in his house maintains the temperature at a precise 22.513°C. The system is so sensitive that it reacts to the warmth of his dog's body heat whenever it enters the room, and adjusts the temperature down a fraction to compensate.

Environmental control

Most homes, schools or colleges and other indoor environments are controlled by the same basic system as the house in the Rockies – *thermostats*. Thermostats automatically maintain a constant temperature or vary it over a specific range. Here's how they work.

In a typical central-heating thermostat, two strips of different metals are bonded together into one bimetallic strip. The strip is then fixed at one end. Because the metals are different, an increase in environmental temperature makes one strip expand (become longer than the other). This causes the whole strip to curve. The curving motion trips an electrical contact or relay switch that, in turn, operates the heating controls.

The purpose of thermostats in environments such as college or home is to maintain a comfortable temperature. You will also find thermostats playing a crucial role in many commercial and industrial environments. For example, in market gardening the precisely correct temperature of a greenhouse

determines the quality of fruit and vegetables, as well as their survival. Airlines prepare and package the meals they serve you a day or more before your flight. Keeping the food as fresh as possible means that it must be stored at the right temperature in a giant room-sized fridge. Although the temperature in the swimming pool always feels cold when you first get in, it is kept at a level that allows for the heat you generate as you swim up and down.

Process production control

In Element 1.1 you looked at CAD applications. Do you remember what CAD stands for? The combination of *computers* and *microprocessors* has also led to the development of CAM (computer-aided manufacturing) technology.

Activity

In CAM systems, such as the oil refinery example at the beginning of this element and in most other process control systems,

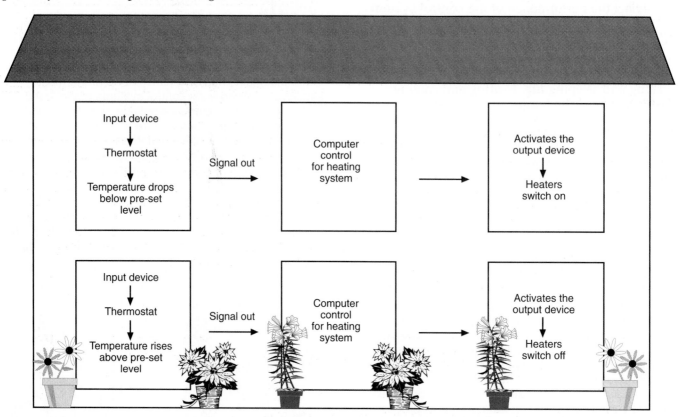

Figure 2.13 Specification diagram for a thermostatically controlled greenhouse

microprocessors are central. In pairs or small groups, tell each other everything you know about microprocessors and can remember from Element 1.2.

Microprocessors have two particular qualities that make the control of other machines or industrial processes one of their most important applications. One is that they can be programmed to handle many information processing tasks. The other is that they can be connected to external memories and other systems.

You can see these two qualities at work in a typical CAM system: a designer draws the component or part on a computer display screen and specifies its dimensions by using a light pen. When the draft is finished the computer produces a magnetic or punched tape. The tape then directs and controls the way that the machining device machines the component.

For example, a company might want to produce a new style of knife and fork for use in canteens. The designer would draw up the shapes on screen and specify their dimensions. This data allows the computer to prepare and generate the magnetic or punched tape. The tape directs how the machine tool cuts the shape from a piece of steel. It controls where the machining head is positioned, the direction and dimensions of the cut and so on.

Quality control

Quality control systems are used at home and at work. Rather than fiddling with a radio dial to find the best reception, most modern receivers tune in to the clearest wavelength automatically. Some types do this by 'listening' to the amount of interference (for example, the high pitch of crackling or white noise) then selecting the wavelength with the least interference.

An industrial use of quality control systems is in paper manufacture. Many different qualities of paper – from flimsy loose-leaf to company letterheaded paper to greeting cards – are used for different purposes. The factory making a particular paper type has to maintain a consistent quality. This is done by monitoring the amount of radiation that can pass through the paper. The higher the paper quality, the lower the amount of radiation that can pass through it. If the radiation sensor detects a change in quality, this information is used to adjust the machine that controls the pulp mix.

Security

Process control systems have become an essential part of domestic and industrial security. Timer systems that switch lights and TVs on and off when you're away on holiday give the impression that someone is at home. Video cameras are programmed to switch on when movement or body heat is sensed in a building. You may have come across these systems when walking up a path at night: lights suddenly switch on.

The different types of sensors used in alarm systems are heat, light, infra-red, movement, pressure pads or sound systems. In a heat sensor system, for example, a sensing element *(thermistor)* monitors the level of heat. The resistance of the thermistor goes down as the temperature goes up. In an electrical circuit, as temperature increases, the resistance of the thermistor goes down. This switches the circuit on or off depending on how it is configured (programmed).

Activity

Most shops and libraries have security control systems to stop people leaving with items they haven't paid for or checked out. In pairs, one of you should find out how a shop system works while the other finds out how a library system works. Then describe and explain the systems to each other. Be prepared to explain this to your class if your tutor or lecturer asks you to.

Figure 2.14 A CAM system could be used to produce knives and forks

Stages in a process control system

The three stages described above, sometimes called a *feedback loop,* are the fundamental principle of process control systems. Feedback allows a designer to build the capability for self-correction into a spacecraft or into any other machine.

A feedback loop starts with a device that senses and measures physical conditions, such as position, temperature, size or speed. The conditions are then compared with preset limits or tolerances. If there is any difference between the sensed condition and the preset limits, a preprogrammed action begins. This action takes whatever steps are necessary to correct and maintain the sensed physical conditions within the preset limits.

Besides controlling spacecraft, the stages in a process control system perform many everyday production tasks. In milling, for example, or refining and bottling, they enable machines to stop and start, work faster or slower, measure and compare, count, test and inspect. The next time you open a canned or bottled drink, remember that it was filled, measured and counted by a process control system.

Did you know?

Spacecraft use process control systems to steer automatically. They also use these systems to direct their cameras, radio antennae and solar panels. Making these movements requires three stages:

1 Sensing the conditions.
2 Comparing the conditions with preset limits.
3 Adjusting the output if necessary.

The conditions they sense are the direction of the sun and stars – just like traditional ship navigation. The preset limits are the intended directions set by space scientists when they prepared the spacecraft for its voyage. The output adjustment, if necessary, is the control of small jets that turn and orientate the spacecraft.

Activity

Before you begin this activity, open a process control log or notebook. Enter 'Process control systems – stages', then list the three stages. Next, choose your favourite soft drink and consider what probably happens to it at each stage of the bottling or canning process. Then, write these processes next to the correct stage. Below are examples of processes you may consider:

- count the number of cans
- add another can
- find 11 cans ready for a box of 12
- fill the bottle to the limit
- measure the amount of drink in a bottle
- know that more must be added

When you have finished, compare your answers with someone else in your group and with your tutor. Then, remaining in your pairs, select two example processes used in the control software available in your school or college. Choose one each, and identify its three stages. Explain the process stages you have identified to your partner, and write your analysis in your log.

Components

At each stage in a process control system, different components are at work. The key components are sensors, processors, control procedures, output devices and any interconnecting devices. In this section you are going to explore and then experiment with each.

Sensors

We have already looked in detail at different types of sensors in Element 1.2.

Activity

In pairs or groups, remind each other of what a sensor is and the different types you studied.

Process control systems use:

- contact
- heat
- light
- proximity (nearness)
- sound.

Look again at the Element 1.2, and tell each other which types might be used in process control.

Many keypads are based on contact sensors. Your calculator or computer keyboard probably uses the commonest type of contact sensor – the *micro-switch.* When you press on a key, the micro-switch contacts underneath it connect and send a signal to the processor. When you take your finger off the key, contact is broken and the signal stops.

Figure 2.15 Computer electronics

Activity

In pairs, remind each other how the heat sensor called a *thermistor* would work in a burglar alarm system.

Did you know?

Light, proximity and sound sensors are standard components on most modern cameras. Automatic focusing, for example, uses light or sound and proximity to adjust the focus.

The automatic focus feature is based on light or sound sensors. When you point the camera at your subject, and press the autofocus, it bounces an infra-red light beam or sound waves off the subject and back to the camera. This enables it to measure the distance between the camera and subject, and so set the focus to the best exposure level.

When there is insufficient sunlight, you need artificial light to illuminate the subject of your photographs. This is produced by the flash unit. However, the flash must be synchronised with the camera shutter (the bit that opens to 'take' the photo) so that the shutter opens at the split second that the flash lights up the subject. Automatic flash units use sensors called *photocells*. These sense and measure the intensity of the flash and automatically adjust its length for a particular scene.

Did you know?

A recent innovation in camera process control enables the camera to sense what sort of film it's using. By reading an electronic code printed on the side of the film cartridge, the camera senses the speed of a film (e.g. 100 for higher resolution or 200 for moving subjects), and how many exposures it has (usually 24 or 36).

Activity

Enter the heading 'Process control sensors' in your log and list the different sensors. Next, go back to the control software and find examples of processes using each type of sensor. Write brief descriptions in your log. Compare your findings with others in your group.

Processors

Automatic focus, automatic flash and the other electronic functions of modern cameras are controlled by *central processing units* (CPUs). Processors activate the light or sound, bounce it off the subject and use the distance measured by the sensor to adjust the focus. They also activate the flash and, using the measurement of intensity from the sensor, cut off the light when it reaches the best illumination. Processors are a common component in many other everyday devices.

Activity

You learnt about CPUs in Element 1.2. In pairs, refresh each other's memories.

While CPUs are the main processor unit of a microcomputer, special-purpose microprocessors may be used in cars and less complex devices such as dishwashers. These processors perform specific routine tasks – for example, washing your clothes at the correct temperature. You instruct the system by selecting a wash cycle. That cycle prescribes a certain temperature. A heat sensor measures the temperature of the water. If the temperature is below the prescribed level, the control system activates a heating element to bring the temperature up.

Activity

Look at how processors are used in your control software. In pairs, find one example each, then describe them together. Enter the heading 'Processors' in your log and write up both descriptions.

Control procedure

A control procedure program decides when a sensed input has reached the point where some action needs to be taken to adjust the output. For example, it could be the amount of water in the washing machine. When the washing machine starts and fills up with water, a control procedure decides when the water has reached the right level and it is time to close the tap and start the washing process.

Another example of control procedure is the number of cars necessary to change the traffic lights. Cars driving along the road towards the traffic lights pass through and break a light beam. When a specific number of cars has been counted by the beam, a processor changes the lights from red to green.

Activity

Identify two more examples of control procedures in your control software. Enter the heading 'Control procedure' in your log and briefly explain the examples you identified.

Output devices

Output devices are the components that process control systems monitor and regulate. The type of device depends entirely on the conditions that are being controlled or manipulated. For example, jets are the output device that affect the direction of the spacecraft, heaters are the output devices that affect temperature, traffic lights are the devices that affect traffic flow, and speakers affect the volume of sound.

Activity

Enter the heading 'Output devices' in your log. Look back through the examples of control procedures you have already written about. Identify the output devices and list them in your log together with their function. For example, you could write 'Cooling fan to reduce temperature'.

Interconnecting devices

As computers use digital (on/off) signals and many sensors detect analogue (continuous) signals (e.g. sound waves), interconnecting devices are needed to join the components in a process control system. A system that detects and reacts to sounds must have an *input/output* (I/O) port connecting it to the processor. This I/O interconnecting device would have an analogue-to-digital converter so that the analogue sound signals can be recognised and understood by the digital processor. The processor may then react to these signals and send a digital control message to the system. Because the system uses analogue signals, there has to be a digital-to-analogue interconnecting device between the processor and the output device.

Figure 2.16 illustrates how the sounds made by a burglar (footsteps, breathing and so on) are picked up by a sensor. The sensor sends the sound wave signals through an analogue-to-digital interconnecting device to a processor. The processor reacts to the message by sending a digital signal that closes the gates. It also sends a warning message through a digital-to-analogue interconnecting device.

Activity

Enter the heading 'Interconnecting devices' in your log. Construct a diagram that illustrates the components, including the interconnecting devices, needed for the control system in Figure 2.16. Label the diagram carefully and use arrows to show the direction of the signals. When you have finished, hand your completed log in for your tutor or lecturer to check it.

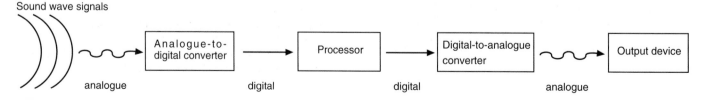

Sound wave signals — analogue — Analogue-to-digital converter — digital — Processor — digital — Digital-to-analogue converter — analogue — Output device

Figure 2.16 Sensors detect the sounds of footsteps, breathing and other noises made by a burglar

Constructing a process control system to specification

The *specifications* needed to design and construct a process control system are:

- purpose
- process control limits
- response time
- sensors
- type of feedback.

Purpose is the most important specification. All components, sensors, activators, interconnecting and other devices follow from the system's purpose. For example, a system intended to deter cat-burglars from entering a stately home might use body heat and movement sensors, a processor and floodlights.

As it is very difficult to predict and sense exact conditions, most systems have to function within *process control limits*. A system such as a thermostat to control temperature in the home might be set at 20°C. To allow for the room heating up and cooling

down, the system would accept a temperature between the limits of 17°C and 23°C before it turned the heater on.

Response times are particularly important in alarm systems and industrial processes. An alarm system that does not have fast response times may be too late to make any difference. In many industrial processes, a precise temperature has to be maintained so that a chemical reaction, for example, can take place. You can see this in a ice-cream making machine: if the cooling device doesn't cut in quickly enough, the ingredients turn to slush and may be ruined. Keeping systems simple is a key factor in any system design, especially in systems requiring quick response times.

Activity

You have already examined the main types of sensors. These are contact, heat, light, proximity and sound. List one example used for each type of sensor. Compare these with your tutor and the rest of the class.

Feedback is the process where part of an output is fed back into an input. It's a simple way of instructing a device to increase or to reduce the output. There are two types of feedback: *positive* feedback which results in increased output, and *negative* feedback which results in reduced output. In the thermostat example above, positive feedback would be a temperature below the limit (17°C) and negative feedback – too hot – would be a temperature above the limit (23°C).

Construction procedure

To help you with your evidence assignment, the following is an outline of the steps you should follow to construct a process control system:

1 Clearly establish the *purpose* of the system. Ask yourself what the purpose is and make sure you can explain it in one or two short sentences. Write it down.
2 Identify the stages in the system by drawing a *specification diagram* showing how it will work.
3 Select the appropriate *components* labelled on your diagram.
4 *Connect* the components into the system.
5 *Test* the system's *performance*.
6 *Review* the performance against the specification and look for possible *improvements*.

Evidence assignment

This project has been designed to cover all the evidence indicators related to Element 2.4. It has four sections.

Scenario

During one of your site visits to 3L (Loose Limbs Leisure), the manager mentions the difficulties they are having with ventilation in the changing rooms. The temperature is normally fine for the number of people who use the facilities, but when an entire team go in – an additional 11 or so people – the rooms become too hot and the steamy air cannot escape quickly enough. It also smells very, very unpleasant.

She is surprised to hear that you can help her with a computer-based control system. You offer to design the system and construct a working model. You also agree to outline other process control systems so that she can consider whether they could be used in the centre.

Section 1

Clearly state the purpose of the control system. Prepare a detailed specification diagram showing how it will work and the components that will be needed. Refer to Figure 2.13 for an example.

Section 2

Construct a working model of your system. Test and review its performance, and make notes of possible improvements to the specification.

Section 3

Present and demonstrate your model, explaining the possible improvements you identified.

Section 4

Write a brief report describing the following systems:

- process production control
- quality control
- security.

Revision test

Name the following

1 Five examples of the way process control systems monitor and regulate our everyday lives.

2 The four most important uses of process control systems.

3 The two particular qualities of microprocessors that make the control of other machines or industrial processes one of their most important applications.

4 Three examples of process control used in security systems.

5 The five specifications needed to design and construct a process control system.

Complete the blanks

6 The fundamental principle of process control systems is the f _____ l _____ . Its three stages are to s _____ conditions, c _____ conditions with p _____ -s _____ l _____ , and to a _____ o _____ if necessary.

7 The key components in a process control system are s _____ , p _____ , c _____ procedures, o _____ devices and any i _____ devices.

Write a short paragraph to show you clearly understand

8 Thermostats and their uses.

9 The ways process control may be used to help put Coke in cans.

10 How contact sensors work.

11 How light sensors focus cameras.

Examine the flow of information in organisations

This unit is concerned with business organisations and the impact information technology has on their functions (i.e. what they do); on the way businesses communicate internally (i.e. to their own departments and staff) or externally (i.e. to other organisations); and the types of information used and how the computer *handles* these tasks.

After studying this chapter you should be able to:

1 identify *types of organisations* and give examples
2 describe the internal and external *functions* of an organisation
3 describe the *types of information* used in an organisation
4 produce a diagram to show the flow of information between *functions*.

Types of organisations

If you walk along any high street or go to an out-of-town shopping centre, you will see a variety of shops and offices – but almost certainly they will all fall into the categories of *commercial* or *public service* organisations. *Industrial* organisations are more likely to be situated outside the town or city on an industrial estate or in an even more isolated situation. So what are the three types of organisations?

Figure 3.1 Alton Towers is a commercial organisation selling thrills

Commercial organisations

Commercial organisations exist to sell a product and make a profit, e.g. Marks and Spencer sell clothes (and many other things) and make a profit. However, the *product* that is sold does not have to be something you can see and hold.

- Alton Towers is a commercial organisation; it sells rides (and thrills).
- Price Waterhouse sells accounting services.
- Thomas Cook Travel is a worldwide travel agency which sells holidays and flights and exchanges English for foreign currency.

Industrial organisations

Industrial organisations exist:

- to process raw materials which are then used in manufacturing;

- to manufacture a product, which is usually sold to the public via a retail (commercial) outlet; or

- for construction (building) of houses, roads, bridges, etc.; and

- to make a profit.

Steel, one of the world's most important metals, is processed from iron and carbon. Ford Motor Co. manufactures cars. In some parts of the UK, coal is still mined from underground, but in Africa something more exciting is found – diamonds. British Petroleum (BP) extracts oil out of the North Sea and refines it for use as petrol or oil for cars. These are all examples of industrial organisations. We do see garages which are specifically Ford agents, or petrol stations selling just BP products, but these would be the retail or *commercial* side of the business, rather than the *industrial* side.

Public service organisations

Public service organisations exist to offer a service to the public. They are not profit-making organisations, and most of their income comes from the government, i.e. taxes. In this category would be included government organisations, both national and local. The national government uses the civil service to run the country, to provide services such as education. Local government provides services such as libraries, housing, swimming baths, and refuse collection. We might enjoy the swimming baths and think of that service as more important to us than refuse collection, but what a state we would be in if our rubbish was not collected every week!

Activity

1 List 10 commercial organisations in your local shopping centre and state what *product* they are selling. Include at least three examples where the product is a *service*. Add to your list three or four other commercial organisations you can think of, which are selling a less obvious product – such as Alton Towers with its rides and thrills.

2 Do you have any industrial organisations in your locality? If so list them and again describe what it is they manufacture. If you do not know of any near where you live, go to the local library and find at least six industrial organisations in the UK. The library should have a reference book called *Kompass – The Authority on British Industry*. The volume on *Company Information* lists businesses by county and town and most of the references have a subheading 'Nature of the Business'. This should help you identify which are commercial and which industrial organisations.

3 Create a table with headings like this:

List the following organisations under the appropriate category, explaining your choice, indicating what it is they have to offer and to whom (the general public, another organisation?):

British Home Stores plc, Anytown Parks Dept, British Telecom, Barclays Bank plc, British Gas, Ford Motor Co., British School of Motoring Ltd, Anytown Fire Brigade, Touche Ross Chartered Accountants, British Steel, Our Price Ltd, Anytown Police, Saatchi & Saatchi, Prudential Assurance Co. Ltd, Anytown Library, Pickfords Removals Ltd, The London Palladium, W.H. Smith Ltd, Anytown College, H. Samuel Ltd, Anytown Ambulance Service, Shell, Anytown Hospital, Heinemann Publishers Ltd, Anytown Job Centre.

(If you do not recognise any of the names, try to find out what the organisation does, which should then enable you to identify the category.)

4 Look in your local telephone directory and list the public services offered by the local authority where you live.

(The results of this activity can be retained and used as part of your evidence for this element.)

Functions of and types of information used in organisations

No matter how large or small an organisation is, there will be functions (activities) which occur *within* and functions (activities) which involve others *outside* the organisation. These are:

Commercial		Industrial		Public service	
Organisation	Reason for choice	Organisation	Reason for choice	Organisation	Reason for choice

- *internal* functions, without which the organisation would find it difficult to carry out its main business; and
- *external* functions, which in most cases will involve customers or clients.

Information is vital to every organisation; it is like the nervous system – if the brain sends the right messages, then the muscles respond correctly. If information flows smoothly between the various functions, then the business operates successfully.

In a small organisation with just a few staff, it is simple to pass on messages verbally: 'Customer X just phoned to increase the order from 40 to 50 units.' Even then documentation recording the order is essential, but the more employees there are, the less possible it is to use this kind of communication. In such a small organisation it is likely that everyone will be involved in a variety of functions, but the more employees there are and the larger the company, the more staff are likely to be involved in fewer functions and may well be grouped according to their function – i.e. the job they do. If there are hundreds or thousands of staff, then it is essential to have suitable systems and methods of recording information, so that each department is fully informed of what is happening in other areas of the organisation. Let's look at this in more detail.

Internal functions

Finance

Collecting the money and paying the bills – everyone knows what a headache that can be. It is just the same in business. All organisations have a variety of financial functions to consider and a large company will have an accounts department which deals specifically with financial matters such as:

- Paying for good/services received.
- Obtaining payment for goods/services sold.

- Paying staff salaries.

- Paying for gas, electricity, telephone, rates, rent.
- Keeping the company accounts.

Operations

In an industrial organisation the operation of the business relates to what is produced and how it is produced. A factory producing cars will purchase steel for the body of the car and a wide variety of other components – e.g. tyres, in-car audio systems, mirrors, glass, instrument panels, steering wheels, carpets – the list is endless. It is essential that the operations department ensures that all these components are available as needed, without having too much stock (stock being held has to be paid for and until goods are sold no money is received). It is equally vital that the right models are produced in suitable quantities. More of the inexpensive models are sold, so it would be foolish to make too many of the expensive models.

Figure 3.2 A car assembly line at Ford

These two will also involve paying VAT to the excise and claiming VAT refunds.

This will involve paying the income tax to the Inland Revenue, the national insurance contributions to the Department of Social Security, pension contributions to the pension fund, and the employee's salary to his or her bank account.

The general principle for all industrial organisations is to match what is made to the orders received and to ensure no delay in production because some components have run out, whilst large supplies of other components are held in stock. Products must be ready on time and should work correctly, so the operations department is also responsible for the quality of the product.

An industrial organisation must also consider designing new products or modifications to the existing ones. Why do you think car manufacturers continually change their models and add new features? They want to tempt us to buy a new car. Similarly the construction industry has to draw plans and write specifications of the materials to be used – e.g. the depth of footings required for a particular building. Design, planning and specifications are all aspects of the operations function of an industrial organisation.

Design → Specify → Produce → Sell → Make a profit

In a commercial organisation the operation relates to the provision of goods or a service. Many of the same considerations apply as in an industrial organisation. If you go to a clothes shop you would not expect them to sell only one size of jacket. The majority of people come within a certain range of sizes, so it is sensible to have more items in these sizes and fewer in the very small or very large category.

Similarly, in a commercial organisation offering a service rather than a product, it is important that the service matches the needs of the client. If you have booked a flight through a travel agency, you expect a seat to be available on the plane when you arrive at the airport. The operations staff should ensure that the information they are using is correct – i.e. there is space on the flight – and that your booking is recorded and your ticket issued.

Provide goods/service → Sell goods/service → Make a profit

The prime function of a public service organisation is the provision of that service, e.g. schools or colleges provide education, doctors or hospitals provide health care, the Inland Revenue or Customs and Excise collect taxes – the latter may not seem much of a service, but if taxes are not collected, then the other services cannot be provided.

In all three types of organisations the operations function might also include personnel, administration, computer services and frequently transport. To summarise, the operations function is concerned with the smooth running of the organisation, and to run smoothly each part of an organisation is very dependent on information received from or sent to other sections.

Purchasing

All organisations must *buy* goods and services from other organisations. This would include:

Goods
■ raw materials from which products are made
■ components
■ products bought in bulk and resold
■ goods needed simply to run the business (e.g. stationery, furniture, food for a staff canteen, etc.)

Services
■ cleaning
■ accountancy skills/auditing
■ legal advice
■ banking
■ decorating/repairs.

Sales

All organisations must *sell* goods or services to other organisations. In most cases you pay for the goods or services, but in some cases services are provided 'free'. If you go to an NHS hospital for an operation, you do not pay directly for the treatment, although you do pay indirectly through taxes. If an organisation cannot sell its goods or services, or no one wants them, then the organisation will go bankrupt/cease to trade.

External functions

Customers

Customers are simply the people/organisations who buy goods/services *from* you. It is important to treat customers well. If you do not, then you will lose that customer which is bad for business. If an organisation keeps accurate and correct records of its dealing with customers (see below), then it will be easier to do good business.

Suppliers

Suppliers are the people/organisations who supply goods/services *to* you. Similarly you expect to be treated well by your suppliers. If you receive poor service, the wrong goods arrive or are not on time, you will find another supplier. If, however, the supplier is efficient and courteous, you may even be prepared to pay more, which is good for their business.

All organisations will sometimes be the supplier, selling goods/services, and at other times the customer, buying the goods/services.

Activity

Think about the school or college where you are studying:

- What product is it selling?
- How would you describe the operations function of the school/college?
- How does the school/college finance its operations?
- In what circumstances does the school/college act as the supplier?
- In what circumstances is the school/college a customer?

Flow of information

Clearly all these various functions are very dependent on each other and for an organisation to be successful, the information must pass easily and efficiently from one department to another.

The Purchasing or Production Department will receive a delivery note when an item comes into stock, but they need to let the Sales Department know what is available. The sales staff receive orders from customers, but they need to inform the warehouse so that the items are delivered.

Purchase orders can be prepared and sent electronically to regular suppliers, but when the goods arrive, the Accounts Department needs to know so that bills are paid. Managers need to keep records of staff sickness, hours worked, and pass them on to the Wages/Salaries Department so that the payroll can be calculated.

By using the PC on one's desk, it is possible for all this information to be sent to the various people who need it instantly – without using any paper – the paperless office which is often mentioned. Do you think the *increased* use of computers has *reduced* the use of paper?

Let's look at an example of the flow of information between a manufacturer and a retailer.

Case study

Anytown Hi-Fi Ltd is low in stock of certain video recorders, so the purchasing department completes a purchase order form

---

Anytown Hi-Fi Ltd
12 Station Road
Anytown
AN1 7JP

Tel: 0132 444 7000

PURCHASE ORDER

VAT Reg No 414/62731/77

To: Video Manufacture plc
New Trading Estate
Bridgetown
BR2 8RC

Date: 17 July 199-

Order No: A129634

Please supply

QUANTITY	DESCRIPTION	REF. NO.	UNIT PRICE
10	Two-head video	VM2SP	205.00
10	Four-head video	VM4SP	239.00
5	NICAM video	VM4NV	313.00

Blue copy: file

Figure 3.3 A purchase order

(see Figure 3.3) for ten each of the two most popular models and five of the more expensive model. The purchase order, which will include a unique reference number so that staff can follow up the order, is placed with the supplier, Video Manufacture plc, quite probably by telephone or fax or sometimes directly by computer link, but the unique order number will be quoted and the order confirmed in writing.

When the goods are delivered a duplicate delivery/advice note is included to indicate what items should be supplied. The actual goods delivered are checked against the delivery/advice note (see Figure 3.4) and if all is correct the delivery note will remain in the showroom and the advice note is sent to the Accounts Department, which checks that the goods received match the original order. The supplier will send an invoice (see Figure 3.5) giving the same details as the order form plus the total cost and the amount of VAT. Accounts will also check that the invoice matches the order and payment will be made to the supplier.

Let's look at the same situation from the perspective of Video Manufacture plc. Orders are frequently received

Figure 3.4 A delivery note

Inside the delivery note figure:

Video Manufacture plc
New Trading Estate
Bridgetown
BS2 8RC
VAT Reg No: 325/61784/55

DELIVERY NOTE

To: Anytown Hi-Fi Ltd
12 Station Road
Anytown
AN1 7JP

Your order no.	Invoice date/tax point	Invoice no.	Despatch date
A129634	19 July 199–	6378	19 July 199–

Quantity	Description	Ref. No.
10	Two-head video	VM2SP
10	Four-head video	VM4SP
5	NICAM video	VM4NV

Received by _____   Date _____

White top copy: Stays at VM plc
Yellow advice note copy: Customer
Green copy: Return to accounts

Figure 3.5 An invoice

Inside the invoice figure:

Video Manufacture plc
New Trading Estate
Bridgetown
BS2 8RC

TEL: 0164 811 5050   VAT Reg No: 325/61784/55

INVOICE

To: Anytown Hi-Fi Ltd
12 Station Road
Anytown
AN1 7JP

Deliver to:

Your order no.	Invoice date/tax point	Invoice no.	Despatch date
A129634	19 July 199–	6378	19 July 199–

Quantity	Description	Cat. no.	Unit price	Total price	VAT rate	VAT amount
10	Two-head video	VM2SP	205	2,050	17.5%	358.75
10	Four-head video	VM4SP	239	2,390	17.5%	418.25
5	NICAM video	VM4NV	313	1,565	17.5%	273.88
	Delivery charge		00.00			1050.88
	Sub-total		6,005.00			
	VAT		1050.88			
	Total amount due		7055.88			

Terms:
E & OE

by telephone or fax, so the supplier needs its own *sales* order (see Figure 3.6) to record the details. The Sales Department will then enter the order into the computer – the electronic data-processing system – which checks electronically for stock. This generates a duplicate delivery/advice note (see Figure 3.4) for the warehouse which will arrange for the goods to be sent to Anytown Hi-Fi Ltd. The details of the order are transferred electronically into the customer's account. When the goods are delivered and receipt confirmed by the customer, the delivery note stays in the showroom, and the advice note is sent to the Accounts Department of Anytown Hi-Fi Ltd. To prove the goods were received, a duplicate copy of the delivery note is returned to Video Manufacture plc, whose Accounts Department sends the invoice (see Figure 3.5) to Anytown Hi-Fi Ltd just before payment is due (see Figure 3.7).

Did you know?

When organisations buy goods or services from other organisations, they do not usually pay for them straight away. If we go into a shop to buy goods, we expect to pay for it immediately, but suppliers send bills called *invoices* to their customers once a month. Organisations usually pay their bills on a set date once a month, or two months and sometimes even longer. These are known as the trading terms. So if Anytown Hi-Fi Ltd buy these goods on 17 July, and their trading terms are payment on the fifteenth of the month, they will not pay for the goods until 15 August.

Did you know?

Many large organisations send an invoice just to inform the customer of the amount due, but do not expect to receive a cheque in the post. Instead the customer signs an agreement – a direct debit – allowing the supplier to inform its bank how much is owed each month, and giving permission for the supplier's bank to debit the money directly from the

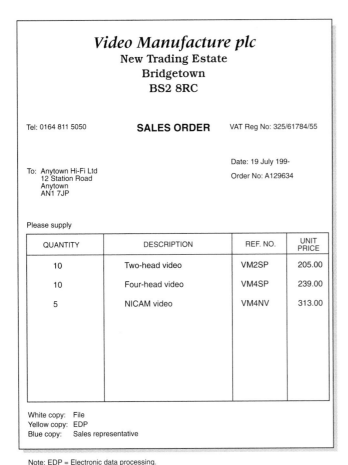

Video Manufacture plc
New Trading Estate
Bridgetown
BS2 8RC

Tel: 0164 811 5050   **SALES ORDER**   VAT Reg No: 325/61784/55

Date: 19 July 199-

To: Anytown Hi-Fi Ltd
12 Station Road
Anytown
AN1 7JP

Order No: A129634

Please supply

QUANTITY	DESCRIPTION	REF. NO.	UNIT PRICE
10	Two-head video	VM2SP	205.00
10	Four-head video	VM4SP	239.00
5	NICAM video	VM4NV	313.00

White copy: File
Yellow copy: EDP
Blue copy: Sales representative

Note: EDP = Electronic data processing.

Figure 3.6 A sales order

customer's bank account to the supplier's. The customer does not even write a cheque. Often the supplier gives a discount for this agreement, because it means they are more likely to receive what they are owed at the right time.

Did you know?

Domestic gas and electricity bills can now be paid by direct debit. This system is also frequently used when you pay the cost of expensive items, such as a washing machine, over an extended period – such as six or twelve months. Do you know anyone who has paid using a direct debit? Find out what they had to do. Did they receive any special discount?

Evidence assignment

Create a directory for Unit 3 and save all your work for this unit in the appropriate directory.

Scenario

Chris Jones, the Manager of 3L (Loose Limbs Leisure), is very pleased with the report you have produced for your employer, Computer Consultants Ltd (see Element 1.2), and has agreed to go ahead with the suggestions you have made to computerise their

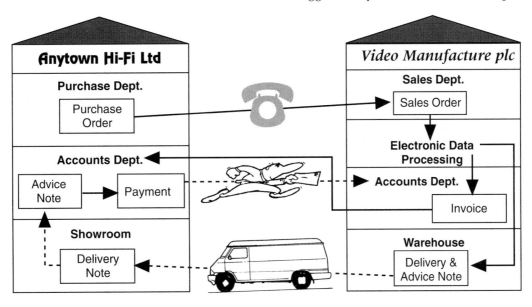

Figure 3.7 Diagram showing the flow of information between Anytown Hi-Fi Ltd and Video Manufacture plc

87

systems. You have been asked to deal with everything – ordering and installing the equipment and providing training for their staff. Your supplier for the hardware and software is PC Manufacturing Co. plc, Unit 24, The Industrial Estate, Anytown AN1 6HS.

1 We have looked at three types of organisations, commercial, industrial and public service. Classify each of the following and in each case explain your choice:

- Computer Consultants Ltd
- 3L
- PC Manufacturing Co. plc

Computer Consultants Ltd will also deal with many other organisations; suggest one example for each of the three types of organisations, again explaining your reasons.

2 Describe the internal and external functions you would expect to be required by Computer Consultants Ltd.

3 To help you understand the various documents used in business, complete the blank forms provided at the back of the book, but do remember in most modern offices this would all be computerised:

- Purchase order, detailing the hardware and software you identified for Element 1.2 – you will find suitable information from the computer magazines available at any bookstore or in the library.
- Invoice received from PC Manufacturing Co. plc showing the total cost and the amount of VAT.
- Invoice to be sent to 3L showing:
  - cost of the hardware
  - cost of the software
  - charge for installation of the system for three days at £350 per day plus VAT
  - charge for five days' training at £1,000 per day.

4 Produce a diagram showing the flow of information between the functions of Computer Consultants Ltd which you have identified in Task 2.

5 For Task 2 you described in words the internal and external functions of Computer Consultants Ltd, whereas for Task 4 you produced a diagram to show the flow of information between the functions. Compare the two methods of providing similar information and decide which you feel best meets the requirements of the task, explaining your reasons.

6 It is not essential, but you could recreate one of the invoices or purchase orders as a template, which would provide another opportunity for evidence for Element 1.4.

Revision test

True or false?

1 Public service organisations exist to make a profit.

2 Industrial organisations manufacture a product from raw materials, which is sold to a commercial organisation, which then sells the product to the public.

3 An invoice is a bill which is used by an organisation to inform its customers how much they owe.

4 The internal functions of an organisation are those which involve outside organisations.

Complete the blanks

5 A _____ organisation is one which exists to sell a product and make a profit.

6 The product sold does not have to be something tangible, like a television; the 'product' could also be a _____ , a _____ or a _____ .

7 A _____ _____ informs the supplier which items you wish to buy.

8 A _____ _____ informs the customer which items have been supplied.

Short answer questions

9 Examine the purchase order for Anytown Hi-Fi Ltd, and identify the two *unique* reference numbers.

10 Which of these numbers also appears on the delivery note and invoice from Video Manufacture plc?

11 The other unique reference number does not appear on these two documents. Why is that?

12 Why does the Purchasing Department inform the Accounts Department exactly what has been received?

Write a short paragraph to show you clearly understand

13 The three types of organisations, commercial, industrial and public service.

14 The difference between internal and external functions of organisations.

15 The difference between customers and suppliers.

Describe data handling systems

After studying this chapter you should be able to describe:

1 the *methods of processing* and *types of data handling systems*

2 the *objectives* of a specified data handling system

3 the *data sources* for a specified data handling system

4 the *methods of data capture* for a specified data handling system

5 the *processes* applied to data in specified data handling systems.

Introduction

There are three stages involved in handling data in a computer system:

1 *Input* – what data the user enters into the system.

2 *Process* – what the computer does with the data.

3 *Output* – what information can be obtained from the system.

In our modern world all organisations, large or small, handle enormous amounts of data. From this data, *information* can be extracted. Let's look at an example. If you are using this book, you are likely to be enrolled on a school or college course. The school/college will need to know your name, sex, address, date of birth, emergency contact number, course on which you are enrolled, any extra classes you are studying, tutor group and more beside.

From this *data*, it is possible to establish *information* such as:

■ how many female/male students are enrolled
■ whether certain courses attract more female/male students
■ how many students are under/over 18
■ in which catchment area the majority of students live, and so on.

Having extracted this information, you might well ask 'Does it matter?' 'Will it make any difference to the school/college?' The answer could well be 'Yes'. As a result of this information, consideration might well be given to issues such as the following:

■ Is the school/college offering equal opportunities?
■ Should courses be structured in a different way?
■ Will the age of students affect the way the course is funded?
■ Do some people find it difficult to get to school/college, and therefore is it worth establishing an out-centre?

Methods of processing

However, before any analysis of the data can be made, it has to be processed (transferred into the computer). We will be looking at two methods, batch and transaction processing.

Batch processing

Batch processing is a method of processing where quantities of data are collected and processed as *one job without direct interaction* between the operator and the system. It is usually used for very large volumes of data which are processed regularly, which are **not required urgently.** Quite typically thousands of input documents may be received in a day, and it is, of course, essential that none is lost or entered twice by mistake, and that all data is transcribed (copied from the source document) correctly. Once a batch is ready for the computer it is not necessary for the operator to be involved. Typical uses of batch processing include producing gas bills (see below for more detail), electricity bills, Heinemann Publishers prints address labels for orders at night, and stock requests for branches of stores, such as Marks and Spencer, can be run at night.

Main characteristics of batch processing:

■ used for large amounts of data
■ used when there is no urgent need to be up to date right *now*
■ used for data which is processed regularly – each week/each month/each quarter
■ **all** the data is available **before** the batch is processed
■ the program is so routine that there is no interaction between the operator and the computer whilst the program is being run
■ often done on large mainframe computers.

Did you know?

Because batch processing does not need to be entered immediately into the computer, it is often run at night when computer time is cheaper.

Figure 3.8 Batch processing is often done at night

The main steps in batch processing are as follows:

- Source documents are checked by the **data control clerk** to ensure they are legible and all necessary information is present.
- Documents are sorted into batches of 50 or 100 which is called a **job** and the operator writes out what has to be done on preprinted sheets.
- Control totals are calculated manually for each batch, e.g.:
  - customer payments could be added and this total (the **control total**) entered on the batch slip. Such a total would be a *meaningful* number;
  - account numbers could be added and this total entered on the batch slip. Such a total would be *meaningless,* but is useful for checking that the data has been entered correctly and is known as a **hash total.**
- A data entry clerk enters the work in **record mode** and saves it on tape or disk.

- A second data entry clerk enters the work a second time in **verify mode**. Any differences are noticed by the computer and the clerk can correct the work if necessary. This process is called **verification** and is an efficient, although expensive, method of checking for errors.
- The work is saved in a transaction file and the job is put into a queue and processed by the computer.
- Output is stored on disk and printed later.
- Printout is returned to operator.

Batch processing is quite a difficult concept – so let's just look at an example. After the gas company has read the meters in a locality, batch processing is an ideal method of producing the new gas bills:

- The meters are read and the new meter reading is written on a card, showing the customer's account number.
- Customer cards with the new meter readings are sorted into a batch.
- The data entry clerk keys in the unique customer account number and the new meter reading, in record mode.
- The total of the meter readings might be added as a check for accuracy – this would be a hash total as the meter reading itself is meaningless.
- A second clerk would enter the data again in verify (check) mode and the computer would compare that the two sets of data match. Any differences would be indicated by the computer, and the error found and amended.
- The details of the meter readings would then be stored in a transaction file which is temporary.
- Later, often at night because it is cheaper, the master file, which is permanent and contains the full details of the account, would be updated with the data in the transaction file.
- Using the account number entered into the transaction file as a reference, the computer would calculate the difference between the old and new readings.
- This figure would be the number of units used, from which the computer would calculate the gas bill.
- The bill is printed and sent out to customers (see Figure 3.9, showing the flow diagram of this process).
- The transaction file would be kept as a back-up, until the next time the meter readings are taken.

The meter reading is the *data* which is then processed by the computer. Two processes will take place – calculating the difference between the new

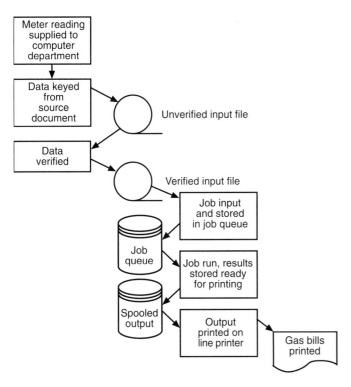

Figure 3.9 Flow diagram showing process from data collection – reading the meter – to producing a gas bill

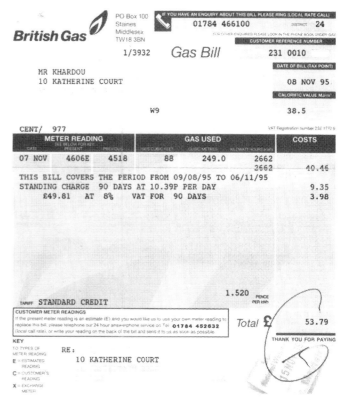

Figure 3.10 A typical gas bill

reading and the old reading and also the cost of the gas used. Finally the bill can be produced – i.e. *information* – how much the customer owes. To summarise:

1 meter reading = data
2 process = subtracting old reading from new one
3 process = calculating the cost of the gas used
4 information = how much the customer owes.

Activity

1 Look back at the list of organisations given for Element 3.1 (see page 82). Think of at least one type of data handling activity they might undertake which could use batch processing and explain your reasons.
2 Would batch processing be a suitable method for transferring college enrolments into the computer? What advantages/disadvantages could arise?
3 List five examples of data handling systems where *batch processing* would be suitable.

Transaction processing

Transaction processing is a method of processing where each transaction is carried out immediately by direct interaction between the operator and the system. It is used when it is important that information held on computer is up to date. For example, your family has decided to book a package holiday to Spain, which includes flight and accommodation. You do not want to arrive at the airport to find too many people have been booked and there are not enough seats on the plane, or that two families have been booked into the same rooms at the hotel.

So when you go to the travel agent to book the holiday, the clerk searches the Computerised Reservation Service, checks for availability, and a booking is made and recorded *immediately*. Obviously, it would be foolish to wait until the end of the day to enter all the bookings into the computer as a batch. If batch processing were used, inevitably there would be frequent clashes in the bookings and on arrival at the airport or hotel, customers would become very irate to find other people booked in the same seats or rooms.

Figure 3.11 Transaction processing prevents overbooking

This type of interactive processing, where the operator enters all the data for one transaction and the computer is updated immediately, is called *transaction processing* and is known as a *real time* system. Real time, because it is *continually* and *immediately* updated. This type of real time system often involves very large databases held on a mainframe computer.

Main characteristics of transaction processing:

- used for small amounts of data
- used when there is an urgent need to be up to date right *now*
- each item of data is keyed in as it 'arrives'
- interaction between the operator and the computer is essential
- operator would sit at a terminal.

Activity

1 Look back at the list of organisations given for Element 3.1 (see page 82). Think of at least one type of data handling activity they might undertake which could use transaction processing and explain your choice.

2 List five other examples of data handling systems where real time processing is important, and

therefore *transaction processing* would be necessary. Apart from obvious commercial uses, think about more unusual uses for computers such as in hospitals, in aeroplanes.

Did you know?

IBM's first general-purpose digital computer, completed in 1944, was capable of making 21,000 calculations a second. Today IBM's most powerful computers can perform millions of instructions per second.

Figure 3.12 Today's IBM computers are extremely powerful

Types of data handling systems

There is a wide variety of data handling systems, and many very sophisticated systems can be bought 'off the shelf' ready prepared for use. It is also possible to have systems made specifically to your own requirements – rather like the difference between buying clothes 'off the peg' – ready to wear, or using a 'bespoke' tailor – made to measure. However there are disadvantages to 'custom-designed' systems – they are more expensive, and there is not as much user documentation or 'help' available.

All sophisticated, commercial data handling systems have common characteristics. Although these complex database packages (see Element 3.3 for more detail on databases) are designed to serve different commercial purposes, their main features will include the following:

1 *Constant* information which mostly remains the same, e.g. employee/customer names, addressees and telephone numbers. Obviously sometimes these details will change, but most of the time they stay the same.

2 *Variable* data which changes frequently – daily, weekly, monthly, e.g. hours worked, overtime, income tax rates, prices, items left in stock, etc.

Bookings

We have already looked briefly at the booking system in a travel agent, and observed how crucial it is for the data to be up to date all the time. A system for a travel agent must be available throughout the country or even worldwide, but a small hotel or leisure centre could also use a computerised booking system. Whether the system is on a large or small scale, it must be capable of recording:

■ who has made the booking
■ for what purpose
■ on what date.

Let's consider in more detail an airline booking system. Such a system often includes:

■ a central computer where data is stored and co-ordinated
■ the ability to accept bookings via different booking methods
■ immediate communication between booking points and the central computer.

An airline data handling system must be able to:

■ store information about flights – times and costs
■ accept bookings and amend flight availability data

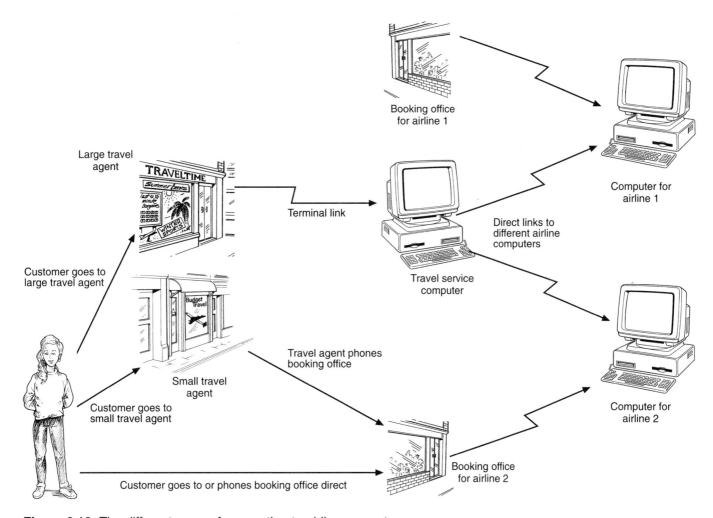

Figure 3.13 The different ways of connecting to airline computers

- refuse bookings once a flight is full
- accept cancellations and amend flight availability data
- prepare and issue tickets.

The system will include:

- a timetable file giving details of flights for about six months ahead
- a bookings file showing the exact availability of seats on any flight
- a passenger file showing who has booked which seats on a particular flight.

An airline ticket can be booked direct by the customer over the telephone, via a small travel agent, again by telephone, or through a large travel agent with direct access into the Computerised Reservation Service.

Payroll

A payroll system is used to calculate employees' wages or salaries. It will calculate:

- the gross pay (i.e. total pay before tax, etc., is deducted)
- deductions for income tax
- national insurance contributions
- pension contributions
- the net pay (i.e. the amount you actually receive)
- and also print out the pay slip.

People are paid either in cash, by cheque or by credit transfer directly into their bank account. The payroll system can:

- print out a list of cheques required
- even print the actual cheques
- print a list of the credit transfer details for the bank
- the most up-to-date payroll systems can even transfer the credit electronically directly to the bank account of the employee.

The payroll system will also:

- produce P60s (certificate of pay, tax deducted and national insurance contributions for the year)
- produce P45s (certificate to show pay, tax deducted and national insurance contributions to date, issued when you leave or change jobs)
- give a complete listing of tax paid to the Inland Revenue at the end of the year.

Ordering, invoicing and stock control

As we have already discovered these three areas are linked together in a modern computerised system

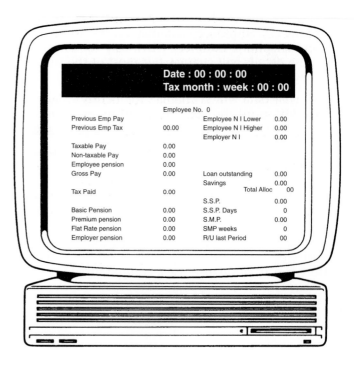

Figure 3.14 Using a payroll package

(see section on flow of information in Element 3.1 and flow diagram, pages 85–7). When an order is received the details are entered into the computer – the electronic data processing system – which:

- checks availability of stock
- produces the delivery/advice note
- charges the customer's account
- automatically alters the stock record to show that these items are no longer available
- produces the invoice (customer's bill).

This system is used typically by manufacturers or wholesalers who supply in bulk to retail outlets in the local high street or shopping centre.

When you buy goods from Sainsbury's or similar stores you do not place an order, you simply walk in and buy. In this situation the electronic data processing:

- records what has been sold
- checks the cost of the item
- totals the bill
- prints a receipt.

Stock control The stock of a business is all the goods it has for sale and stock control is how the stock is managed. It is very important to:

- know as accurately as possible what is in stock
- have enough stock so that you do not have to turn customers away
- not have too much stock.

It is bad for business if you run out of stock a customer wants, but is also bad for profits to have a great deal of stock which is not selling.

Prior to computerisation the **only way** was physically to count the stock, which was very time-consuming. From time to time this is still necessary to check that what is actually in stock matches the computer records, but a computerised data handling system provides a very accurate picture of stock availability all the time. It is also possible to build in an alert mechanism to indicate when stocks are low. The main purposes of a stock control system are to:

- check exactly what is in stock
- track which goods are selling and then to fix minimum and maximum stock levels
- reorder goods when the minimum stock level is reached.

Personal records

Personal records are exactly that – data held about a person. Typical systems include employee records,

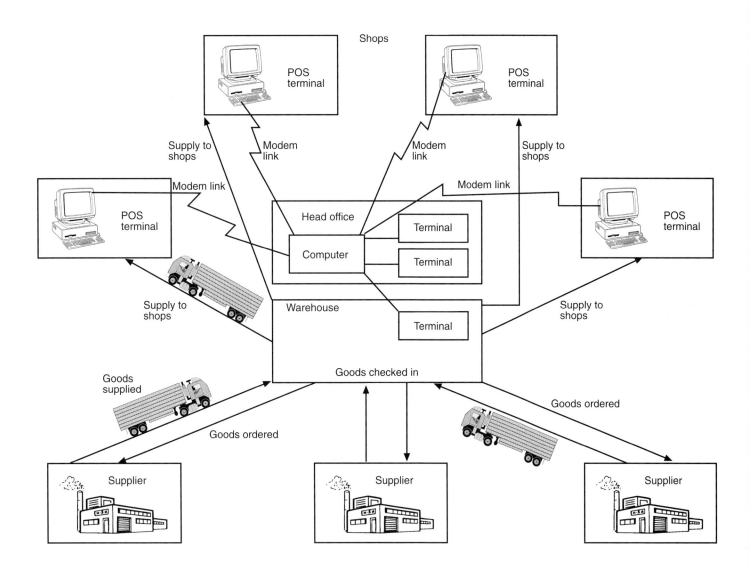

Figure 3.15 Anytown supermarket chain

customer accounts, club membership, school, college, criminal or medical records. You would expect all the usual details – title (e.g. Mr, Mrs, Ms, Miss, Dr, Sir, etc.), first name, surname, address, town/city, post code, telephone number, date of birth – to be included for any of these examples.

Clearly once this basic data is included, the further details required will vary for the different purposes. Let's consider employee records. The other details might include:

- job title
- special skills – such as speaks fluent French, holds HGV (heavy goods vehicle) licence
- department/branch where you work (if the organisation is large)
- employee number ⎱ unique reference
- national insurance number ⎰ numbers
- tax code
- annual salary, weekly wage or hourly rate of pay.

The data handling system for employee records is likely to be in two parts: one database contains the basic details – name, address, etc. – and another linked or related database which deals with the pay. This is known as a relational database, which will be looked at in more detail in Element 3.3.

Activity

Think about a database for medical records, both at the doctor's and also at a hospital. Apart from those already mentioned above, what other details would be required?

Objectives of a data handling activity

A computerised data handling system is usually more accurate, less expensive, quicker and provides more information more quickly to support decision-making than previous manual methods. Generally the objectives of accuracy, cost, speed and supporting decision-making are relevant no matter what the type of activity. However, depending on the activity, certain objectives take a higher priority or are more important than others.

Accuracy

Accuracy is always important, because the information produced by the computer is only as

accurate as the data entered. Apart from visual checking by the operator, it is possible to build accuracy checks into the computer system. Validation and verification are methods of checking accuracy, and will be looked at in more detail in Element 3.4.

Cost

A computer system may seem very expensive, but in comparison with paying enough people to do the same work, it is relatively cheap. You have already discovered that batch processing is cheaper than transaction processing, but for reasons already explained, sometimes consideration of cost is less important than the speed at which the system operates. At other times the speed is less important than the cost.

Speed

People tend to think that computers are cleverer than the human brain. It is not so much that they are cleverer, but there is no doubt that the computer is much faster. Modern computers are capable of handling vast amounts of data extremely fast, much faster than even a team of people could. If you were

Figure 3.16 Sorting through thousands of index cards by hand would be possible – but time-consuming

given two thousand index cards and asked to search through them to find specific information, given enough time you could do it. It would be very boring and quite slow, but it could be done. The power of the computer can handle and sift such data in seconds. Computers can also transfer data from one place to another immediately.

Did you know?

The British Library contains 16 million books and manuscripts, stored on 367 miles of shelves. You can find out virtually anything if you know where to look for it. The power of a computerised index system will help you find what you want quickly.

Activity

List six data handling systems – three where saving money might be more important than speed and three where the speed of the computer operation is more important than cost. Try to think of less obvious systems, e.g. how are computers used in aeroplanes? Which is most important in this situation – speed or cost of the computer?

Support decision-making

Clearly, it was perfectly possible to make decisions in business prior to computerisation, but because a computer handles data – especially large volumes of data – so quickly, it is a very important tool in decision-making in the modern world, and very crucial in today's extremely competitive market. In our everyday lives we make decisions from the moment we wake until we go to sleep. Often the decisions are very simple – 'What shall I wear today?' In a business context making the right decision can mean the difference between making a profit or bankruptcy (going out of business).

Let's look at some ways computers assist the decision-making process in business:

Staff pay People at work do expect to receive a salary increase from time to time, but if the staff are given more money, somehow it has to be paid for. A spreadsheet package can very quickly calculate how much extra will need to be earned, in order to give staff an extra 2%, 3%, 5% or more. Knowing exactly how much each option will cost helps in deciding how much can be offered.

More or fewer staff Our Video Manufacture company would have sales representatives in different areas of the country. Some areas are densely populated and therefore have more shops, whereas other country areas have far fewer stores. The computer can easily establish how much each employee costs for salary, car, telephone, expenses, etc., compared to the volume of sales and the profit earned. This might result in adding a new member of staff in a busy area, or making someone redundant in a quiet area.

New accounts Lists of companies' addresses are available on computer, sorted into area and category. Video Manufacture might use such a list to find suitable businesses with whom they are not yet trading. The representative for that area could then be asked to call on appropriate shops to try to open new accounts.

Which goods A manufacturer may have in stock various components, from which it is possible to make different items. The details of how many and which type of components are available, together with the details of the various items which might be produced, can be entered into a spreadsheet model. This will very quickly determine how many of which items should be produced to make the most profit.

The possibility for decision-making is endless, and it is the power of the computer to provide the required information easily and quickly which supports the complex business world of today.

Sources of data and data capture

Data capture simply means the method of entering data into a computer. The *source* from which the data is obtained will vary depending on the type of information required. Obviously the two go together, so let's consider some different sources and methods of data capture.

Bar-codes/bar-code readers

Look at the back cover of this book and you will find a bar-code. Books, CDs, almost any item of groceries, are all printed with bar-codes these days. A bar-code is a set of printed parallel lines of varying thickness, usually black and white. Each line represents a number, frequently printed above or below the bar. The numbers are codes which typically might be used to indicate:

Figure 3.17 An example of a bar-code

- country of origin
- the company which made the product
- the reference number for the product, and
- the check digit (this is a number calculated through a specific formula as an accuracy check).

The bar-code does not include the actual price, because prices do change. However, the details of the item and price are stored in the computer and prices logged against that particular code. If the prices change, the data in the computer is altered and next time the bar-code is read the new price will be registered.

Data on bar-codes is captured when they are *read* by light pens or scanners at the POS (point of sale) terminal. Data is sent to the computer which immediately returns the item and price to the checkout where they are printed on the receipt and the amount added to the total. In addition the computer records what has been sold, and alters the stock level for each item, which is useful for stock taking and reordering. For each product, the number sold is deducted from the number in stock. From time to time a stock report is printed, and any items which have less in stock than the minimum required will be emphasised. The manager can then reorder the necessary products.

If the store wants to, any item which has less in stock than the minimum required can be ordered automatically. The store's computer will use electronic mail (see Element 4.3, page 151), via a modem and the telephone line, and send an order direct to the supplier's computer. This is particularly useful for supermarkets, where there is such a variety of goods and they are sold very quickly.

Bar-codes aren't just used for identifying tins of beans on supermarket shelves. They are used for many reasons, not just items that are sold. For example, nowadays, when blood is donated, the same bar-code is stuck on the bag of plasma, the platelet bag and the blood sample from one particular individual, to identify data such as the blood group. Bar-codes are also used at the post office when you register a letter.

Figure 3.18 Bar-code scanner being used to check a library ticket

Activity

Consider the advantages and disadvantages of using bar-codes. Why would it be necessary physically to check stock occasionally? List five different occasions you have experienced where bar-codes are used and the method of scanning the code. Compare your answers with the others in your group. What purposes did you discover apart from items for sale?

Documents/keyboard/mouse

Any paper data source is a document. It might be a college enrolment form, from which a student's details are entered into the college database of student records. An application form for a job might be a data source, if you are fortunate enough to get the job. Any kind of completed form – application for a driving licence, a driving test, to open a bank account – can be a data source. In these cases the keyboard will be used for data capture.

Along with the keyboard, the mouse (discussed in detail in Element 1.2) is used as a method of data capture.

Did you know?

The mouse is now an endangered species! Hard to believe – but new systems based on pens, touch screens and voice input could mean the end of this most user-friendly tool.

Figure 3.19 The computer mouse may become an endangered species

Electronic files/magnetic reader

Prior to computerisation all documents had to be stored on paper. Nowadays, of course, documents can be stored electronically on floppy or hard disks, CD-ROM or on magnetic tape (refer back to Element 1.2 for more detail). Two read/write heads use magnetic pulses to receive data from or record data on to the disks, CD or tape. When the heads are reading data, they react to magnetic fields generated by metallic particles on the disk. When data is saved to the disk the heads use electrical impulses to create a magnetic field to write data on to the disk.

This is a very complex area, and it is sufficient to know that a magnetic reader scans magnetic data and transfers the data into the computer. This is one of the most common methods of automated data input. Apart from electronic files, other methods of reading data magnetically include the following:

- *The small magnetic strip* on goods labels used as an alternative to bar-codes, and operating in a very similar fashion. The item code is read from the

magnetic strip by the computer which then establishes the price and deletes the item from the stock record.

- *Magnetic ink character recognition* (MICR), which is generally used on bank cheques. Each bank cheque has a unique number. Each branch has its own unique sort code and each customer has his or her own unique account number. All these numbers are preprinted using magnetic ink. When the cheque is used to pay for something, the shopkeeper pays it into the bank, where the only item left to enter is the amount, which is entered on to the cheque using magnetic ink.

The cheque can now be processed using the magnetic reader, and the money is transferred from the customer's to the shopkeeper's account. The only possibility for error is the clerk entering the amount in the magnetic ink, so it is very accurate and fast.

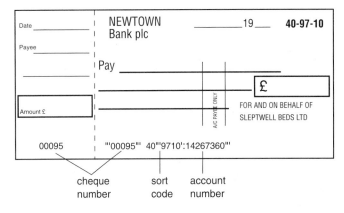

Figure 3.20 A cheque with information in preprinted magnetic ink

 Did you know?

About 2,000 cheques per minute can be processed using this method.

- *Magnetic stripes* – we are all familiar these days with the sight of people standing apparently staring very intently at the wall. In fact, of course, they are taking cash out of their bank account. The black stripe sealed into the back of a plastic card contains details of your bank account, and

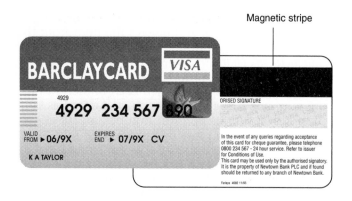

Figure 3.21 A credit card showing the magnetic stripe

you can use it with a PIN (personal identification number) to find out the balance in your account, to order a statement of your account or to withdraw cash.

Similar cards are also used as phone cards, to gain access to buildings with high security or to gain entry to car parks where the use of the card raises the barrier.

At this point it is also worth considering briefly OMR and OCR, although these are *not* read magnetically.

- *OMR – an optical mark reader –* is a scanning device which can recognise marks made in preset positions on a special form. This form of data capture is often used for *marking* multiple-choice tests, and indeed it is used for the unit tests for GNVQ programmes. The marks are short lines made in pencil on cards or documents. Pencil is used so that the mark can be rubbed out and placed in another position if an error is made.

  National Lottery tickets are sold by using a scanning device to read the customer's preferred numbers, marked in preset positions on a form.

- *OCR – optical character recognition –* is read by recognising the *shape* of the characters or numbers. The problem with OCR is the enormous variety of fonts and styles of writing. At present the acceptable fonts are limited, but it is possible to scan pages from a book which the OCR software will convert into text. Some errors do occur – a 7 and a Y might be mistaken – but the majority of the text can be scanned correctly, and errors corrected more quickly than retyping the whole page. OCR is a very useful method of data capture when the font has been designed specifically for this type of software.

 Did you know?

The new European Union passports use OCR for the back page of the passport, which gives the details of the holder.

Figure 3.22 The back of a passport, showing the OCR strip

People

It may seem strange to consider people as a method of data capture, but interviews, such as those conducted for market research, and completion of questionnaires are very important sources of data.

As mentioned above, when you do your unit tests – which is a form of questionnaire – you will answer the questions using a form where you place a line opposite the correct choice. This form will then be *read* by an optical mark reader. The main reason for using this method is that it is quick and cheap to mark the tests. The same is true for recording the results of market research.

Interviews/questionnaires are usually designed so that the answers can easily be transferred into a database. You will have noticed that usually choices are offered, such as:

Quality	Age range
Excellent	under 18
Very good	18–29
Good	30–49
Fairly good	50–59
Poor	60 or over

The reason people are guided into answering within restricted categories is to make it possible to collate the data into a computer and then extract information from it. Frequently we see reports which say something like, 'Most people over 60 do not like loud music!' or 'Those under the age of 18 prefer X pop group.'

Sensors

Sensors, as explained in the section in Element 1.2, can work through contact, heat, light, proximity (being near) or sound. The important point about sensors is that the information received by the sensor will control whether something else happens.

The following are some examples of the way sensors are used:

- These days it is not unusual when you are passing a house at night for outside lights to come on. Your proximity to a sensor, connected to a computer, switches on the lights, and once you walk past and are no longer near the sensor, the lights go out.
- A greenhouse containing sensitive plants, which will die if it is too cold, can be fitted with a heat sensor, and when the temperature drops below a predetermined level, the computer activates a motor to switch on the heaters. This is particularly useful in Britain, which has such an erratic climate.
- Contact sensors are frequently used in burglar alarms. They may be fitted to a door or window and if either is opened the alarm sounds.

Processes applied to data in specified data handling systems

We handle data in order to turn it into *information* we can use. Once the data is stored in the computer then you can use the computer to perform these functions:

- *Calculating* – adding up, subtraction, division, multiplication
- *Searching* – looking through files or records
- *Selecting* – choosing particular item/s
- *Sorting* – putting into the same group or category
- *Validating* – checking that something is suitable or correct.

All these processes were possible before computers and indeed took place in business every day. The difference is the speed at which the computer handles them. Let's look at which process is mainly used for which system:

Process	Examples of how each process is used in a data handling system
Calculating	Cost of a booking made Working out wages/salaries in a payroll system Totalling the cost of goods and the VAT for invoices Adjusting the stock level when an order is placed, or goods are sold
Searching, selecting	To find information or to check what is available when booking or ordering To answer a query on a pay slip or invoice To search through personal records to find details on a particular person, or those in a specific area
Sorting	Putting records into a particular order – alphabetical, highest to lowest, lowest to highest, date order
Validating	Checking that something is valid (suitable) for its purpose or correct, e.g. on a paper form it is very easy to put numbers where there should be text, or a date where the post code should be, but a computerised system can be designed so that text cannot be entered in a field for numbers, and a post code would not be accepted where the date should go – they are not valid (see Element 3.3 for more detail).

Evidence assignment

Scenario

Chris Jones, the manager of 3L (Loose Limbs Leisure), has plans for expanding the current premises and even opening new clubs in other areas. At present aerobics, badminton, squash, swimming and tennis facilities are offered. She is considering opening a multi-gym, and providing other classes such as karate, weight training, sunbeds, indoor tennis, etc.

Chris wants to convince Anytown Council that her ideas are financially viable, and realises that some costs could be reduced by using the existing computer's facilities, but is not exactly sure of the possibilities. She is very pleased with the new computer system, but so far the word processing and spreadsheet software is being used at only a very basic level, e.g. simple letters and recording income and expenditure in the spreadsheet. The database has not even been established.

Now that staff are becoming more confident with the system, Chris has requested more detailed information on other benefits and uses of which the software is capable.

Prepare a report to include the following:

1 An explanation of how various application packages can be useful to process and handle data for the organisation, for bookings, payroll, ordering, invoicing, stock control, personal records.

2 Explain which method of processing – batch or transaction – would be suitable for which activity and why.

3 Explain the objectives of the system – accuracy, cost, speed, support decision-making.

4 Describe data sources or methods of data capture.

5 Describe the processes which could apply to the data handling activity – calculating, searching, selecting, sorting, validating.

Application software	Suitable for which data handling activity	Method of processing	Relevant objectives	Data source/ method of data capture	Processes applicable
Database	Bookings	Transaction – because it must be continually up to date	Accuracy – it is important that bookings are recorded accurately Speed – customers do not like to be kept waiting so the system should be quick and efficient Support decision-making – checks can be made easily on which activities are most popular and most profitable, which may result in decisions to close classes or add extra ones	Membership cards with bar-codes could be used in conjunction with a light pen. This would be a very quick method of taking bookings If the booking is made by telephone, then the number on the bar-code can be entered via the keyboard	Money earned from each activity can be calculated The database can easily be searched to select the activity, date and time, in order for the booking to be recorded The activities can be sorted in order of the most profitable The total number of clients per class can easily be validated against the number of bookings made

6 Explain the problems which may arise when using computers, such as accidental loss of data and how to avoid such pitfalls, such as making back-ups.

Be imaginative, e.g. don't just write lots of words, describing the packages. Instead, prepare a small example of how she could use the word processor, spreadsheet, database and graphics packages. Think about mail shots, advertising leaflets, market research of existing customers and potential new ones. Wherever possible include suitable samples to illustrate your points, e.g. you might use the word processor or desk-top publishing package to produce a leaflet advertising the expansion plans and promoting the new facilities, thus saving the costs of professional printing.

This may seem overwhelming, but start by listing the points to include in your report in a table under the headings as shown on page 102. One example has been given as a guide, and if you make brief notes similar to this, you should find it much easier to write the report and produce suitable examples. You will also find this helpful for revision of this element in preparation for the unit tests.

Note:

Make sure you retain source information for IT core skills Element 2.1.

Refer to the section on IT core skills Element 2.4 on page 182, which you should find helpful for this report.

Revision test

True or false?

1 Transaction processing does not require direct interaction between the operator and the system.

2 Batch processing is often done at night because it is cheaper.

3 A stock control system is a method of tracking as accurately as possible which items are in stock.

Complete the blanks

4 A _____ system is used to calculate employees' wages.

5 An employee number, name, address and date of birth are examples of data kept in _____ records.

6 A _____ contains information about a product, but not the price, which is stored in the computer.

7 The design of a _____ is important, to make the data easy to collate.

Short answer questions

8 Why is it important to know exactly what is in stock?

9 Why is it necessary to identify employees, students, products, invoices, etc., with a unique reference number?

10 Give five ways sensors receive information and the basic principles of how sensors operate.

11 Which method of processing would be suitable for

a a stock control system?
b a payroll system?
c a theatre booking system?

In each case explain your choice.

Write a short paragraph to show you clearly understand

12 How a bar-code reader captures data from the bar-codes.

13 How a magnetic reader captures data, giving three examples of magnetic information.

14 The processes of calculating, searching, selecting, sorting and validating, giving examples of possible uses in a data handling activity.

Use information technology for a data handling activity

Organisations and information technology

After studying this chapter you should be able to:

1 identify *database components*, *data types* and *keys* required for a given data handling activity
2 create a database
3 enter and *edit* data
4 use *facilities* to generate database reports.

This element is largely concerned with the practical activity of designing and using a database, which is the best way to learn and understand the concepts. Therefore we will look at the theoretical background fairly briefly, and then put that knowledge into practice.

What is a database?

Do you have an address book? Well, that's a database.

In simple terms a database is a store of *related* information. In an address book you will have the same types of information for each person:

■ surname
■ first name
■ address
■ telephone number
■ and possibly date of birth.

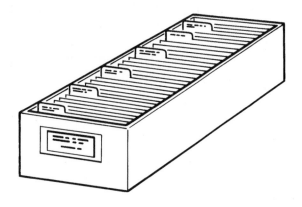

Figure 3.23 A card index box

These days we tend to think of a database as existing only in computers, but databases have always existed. It used to be commonplace in offices to have card index boxes. Each card would be written out with the same kind of details, just like the address book, and most often filed in alphabetical order. This too is a database.

Think about a school or college – what details about the students might have been written on the card? It's been started for you. What else could be useful?

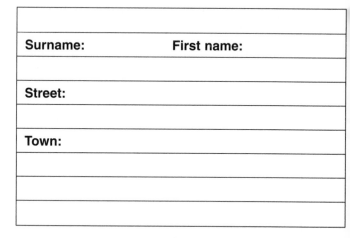

Figure 3.24 An index card for student records

You might think of several other possible fields, such as post code, telephone number, identity number, date of birth, emergency contact number, course, previous exam results, exams entered for, grades achieved, etc.

So why bother with a *computerised database,* if you can simply flick through a set of cards in a small box sitting conveniently on your desk?

Computerised database – advantages	Card index – disadvantages
A vast amount of data can be stored on one disk	You would need many, many boxes to store the same quantity of data
Records are entered once – but can be *searched* in all kinds of ways – e.g. alphabetically, numerically, selectively	If the index cards are stored alphabetically, but you would also like them in, say, order of birth dates, *a second set of cards* would need to be written and stored in date order
Searching is fast – even in a huge database	Searching can be very slow
Data can be lost – but should be able to be retrieved if back-ups are kept	Cards are easily lost, misfiled or mislaid
Can perform calculations, e.g. could ask the database to calculate the VAT on a price and give the cost price, VAT and total price. If the rate of VAT changes, this is easy to update	Would have to be written out manually and difficult to update

Database components

Records

A database consists of a file, containing many records. Each record will include the fields, into which will be entered the appropriate data. Each record will contain the same fields, but sometimes a field is left blank in a particular record, e.g. if someone does not have a telephone, then the phone field will be left blank.

Cover the diagram below and check if you can label the one in Figure 3.26, on the next page.

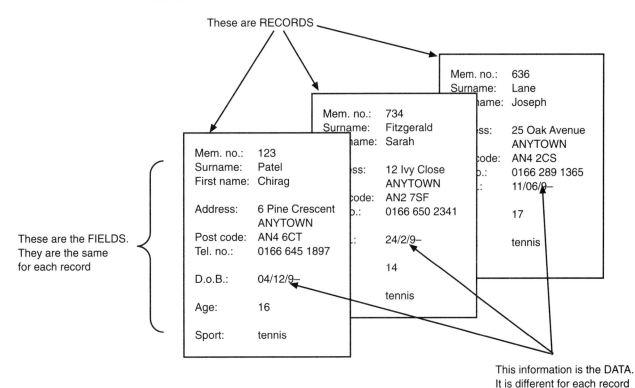

These are RECORDS

Mem. no.:	123
Surname:	Patel
First name:	Chirag
Address:	6 Pine Crescent ANYTOWN
Post code:	AN4 6CT
Tel. no.:	0166 645 1897
D.o.B.:	04/12/9–
Age:	16
Sport:	tennis

Mem. no.:	734
Surname:	Fitzgerald
...ame:	Sarah
...ss:	12 Ivy Close ANYTOWN
...ode:	AN2 7SF
...:	0166 650 2341
...:	24/2/9–
	14
	tennis

Mem. no.:	636
Surname:	Lane
...ame:	Joseph
...ss:	25 Oak Avenue ANYTOWN
...ode:	AN4 2CS
...:	0166 289 1365
...:	11/06/9–
	17
	tennis

These are the FIELDS. They are the same for each record

This information is the DATA. It is different for each record

Figure 3.25 A database is a collection of records

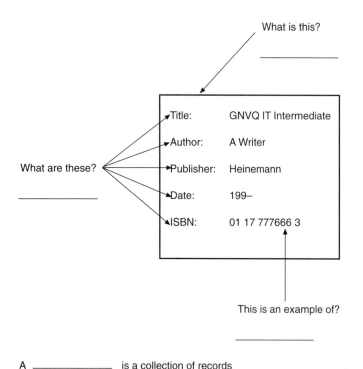

What is this?

_____

Title: GNVQ IT Intermediate

Author: A Writer

Publisher: Heinemann

Date: 199–

ISBN: 01 17 7776663

What are these?

_____

This is an example of?

_____

A _____ is a collection of records

Figure 3.26 Check your understanding

Tables

The layout of a database record can be designed however you wish (see Figure 3.25) – just as forms for different purposes are laid out differently. When you look at the record on screen, you see just one record at a time – just like looking at one card in a card index box. But sometimes this is not convenient – you would like to see a list of the records, under the different field names, or a list of certain selected fields. In a computerised database it is possible to have such a list in *table view*. In this format each *row* is equivalent to one *record*, although it is not necessary to include every field in the table.

Let's consider a database of the members of 3L (Loose Limbs Leisure) mentioned in Unit 1. Supposing the manager of the club wanted to find members aged between 14 and 16, who might be interested in a tennis tournament. She could search the database for the names, age, sport played and telephone numbers of suitable club members, which might result in a table looking something like the one in Figure 3.27. You would expect to see 'tennis' as the only entry under 'Main leisure interest'.

This is much more convenient than looking at each individual record, especially if there is a large number of suitable records. In practice a search in a full commercial database would probably find far more than the four relevant records shown below.

Database structure

Figure 3.28 Comparison of a database structure for a file and a table

Membership no.	Surname	First name	Main leisure interest	Age	Telephone no.	
						} Fields
734	Fitzgerald	Sarah	tennis	14	0166 650 2341	
123	Patel	Chirag	tennis	16	0166 645 1897	
656	Spiller	Corinne	tennis	15	0166 650 2389	} Rows
317	Chiang	Lee	tennis	14	0166 645 1431	

Figure 3.27 Table view of a selection of records. Notice that only the relevant fields have been requested. Compare this with Figure 3.25 – diagram of a database structure

Setting up a database for a computer: field names, length and type

Once you have decided the purpose of your database, you have to decide on the following:

1 The fields you need – i.e. the *names* of the fields, e.g. surname, date of birth. The name of the field indicates which data should be entered into it.

2 The *length* of the fields – i.e. how many characters do you need? With fields such as names and addresses, obviously you need to allow enough space to enter a long name or long street reference, although it is possible to increase the length of the field later if necessary. For numerical data you would not design a field with decimal places for the price of a house! House prices are not quoted as £56,789.58, but a price field for a stationers would be quite different and decimal places would be necessary. So you might fix the length of the field for a house price at 6 digits, which would allow a price up to £999,999. For items in a stationers, you would probably fix the length at 2 spaces to the left and 2 to the right of the decimal point, which would allow prices up to £99.99.

It is good practice to have just enough space for the data you wish to enter, but not to allow more space than necessary, as this extra space can waste the memory capacity of the computer.

3 The *type* of each field. You could just use TEXT for everything, because text will accept both letters and numbers. However, this would **not** make your database very effective when it comes to searching.

Data types

On the next page we look at some typical fields which are useful in a database. (Please note, you may not find all these data types available in the database program you are using.)

Activity

In a sophisticated database, the age field would **not** be entered as a number, but would be calculated from the member's date of birth and today's date permanently stored in the computer. Why would this be a better way of recording the members' ages, rather than simply keying in their age?

Relationships

When creating a database it is often easier to have two or more files which are *related* or connected to each other, rather than having just one huge file. In order to connect the tables or files one field must be the same. Let's look at a database of personnel records to understand this more clearly.

People working in a factory are usually paid by the hour and they clock in when they arrive at work, and clock out when they leave. A database for such staff is likely to have one table or file, giving the unique employee number, the name, address, etc., and another file which includes the employee number, times clocked in and out, from which the hours worked and then the person's wages would be calculated.

The unique employee number is the **key field** which links the two files together. In this way the files are *related* (see Figure 3.29).

When tables or files are linked in this way, it is possible to search them separately or by selecting fields from both, e.g. the personnel officer might want a list of the names of staff in each department. By using the employee number as the field which links the two files, a list giving just first names, surname taken from the personnel file and the department taken from the wages file could be produced easily and quickly.

Type of field	Purpose	Advantages/possible uses
Text/character – sometimes called alphanumeric	Any data (letters, numbers or symbols on the keyboard) can be entered into a text field	■ Names/addresses ■ Where you might include extra detail/description
Numerical Integer: the number of digits can be restricted to a specified length, e.g. 3	A whole number Gives space for a maximum of 3 digits, e.g. 156	■ Restricts data entry to whole numbers ■ Cannot enter 4 or more digits ■ Reduces errors ■ Can be listed in numerical order ■ Can also ask for list of items above/below or equal to a specific number
Decimal	A number with decimal places – you can usually decide on how many to the right and left of the decimal point, e.g. 15.67	■ Suitable for money where prices include pence – £15.67 ■ Measurements – 4.25 km
Calculation	The database can make calculations for you	Given the cost price the database can calculate: ■ VAT ■ Total price automatically
Range check	The field is designed with a lower and/or upper limit	If items are priced in a range of £20–50: ■ Lower limit can be set at 20 ■ Upper limit set at 50 ■ Entries outside that *range* will not be allowed
Date	A typical date format will be prepared – – / – – / – –	Can search for: ■ Birthdays in a given month ■ Those older or younger than a given age ■ Birthdays between particular dates
Time	A typical time format will be prepared – – : – – : – –	Can be used where: ■ Employees are paid by the hour ■ Hours worked can be calculated from time clocked on and off ■ Wages can be calculated on length of time worked
Choice Yes/No	Data entry is limited to yes or no – any other entry will not be allowed	Can search for all the 'Yes' or 'No' entries
You decide, e.g. colours: red, blue, green, yellow	Again, data entry is limited to the selection which is already decided	Can search specifically for 'green' items

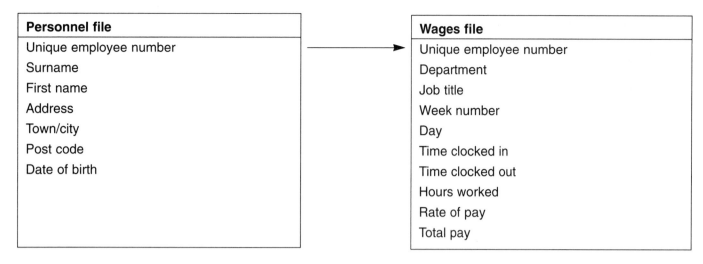

Figure 3.29 The unique employee number is the key field linking two files together

Keys

You know that each record in a database usually has one field which is unique and identifies that record as different from every other record in the file, or in table format identifies each row from every other row. This field is the **primary key**. Look at Figure 3.27 – the primary key in this table would be the *membership number*, as each club member would be given a unique number on joining. It is essential that the primary key is unique, otherwise the computer will not be able to identify the record we want.

The record or table may also have one or more **secondary keys**, which are not unique, but which have been placed in an index. In the example in Figure 3.27, the secondary keys would be *main leisure interest* which could be indexed (grouped together) by category of sport, and *age* which could be indexed in order of date of birth.

 ### Activity

Thinking back to the database for student records mentioned earlier in this chapter, three related files could be created:

Personal details; Academic record; Attendance record

1 Make a list of suitable fields under the three headings.
2 Decide which type of field and how long it would need to be.
3 Decide which field would link the three files together.
4 Identify the primary key and the secondary keys in the three files.

Editing a database

Just as with a word processor, editing a database is usually much easier than with a manual system. From time to time you may need to:

- amend (change or alter) a record, e.g. if someone changes his or her address
- append (add) a new record, e.g. a new employee joins a company
- delete (remove) a record, e.g. an employee leaves the company.

If you need to amend or delete a record, it is very easy to find the correct one in a computerised system: you simple enter suitable data – e.g. employee number – into the correct field, *ask* the computer to search the database and it will very quickly locate the correct record.

When you add a new record to the database, it will automatically be filed in correct order. Any fields which have been indexed (see 'Selection of index key' below) will also automatically be updated.

Facilities to generate database reports

Generating a database report simply means searching the database for particular information required at that time. The report may be presented on screen or printed on paper. Figure 3.27 is an example of a database report. To obtain this information from a manual system where the club members' cards were

109

filed alphabetically, it would have been necessary to:

- look at each individual card
- check the sport played is tennis
- check the date of birth to find players of the correct age
- remove the cards or write down the names and telephone numbers
- refile the cards (every danger that cards will be lost or misfiled)
– a time-consuming process.

A computerised database will use the same criteria, but find the information very quickly, even if the membership list is huge.

As explained earlier in this chapter if the database is created using only text fields, searching for information is limited. Using fields such as date, number, choice provides us with very useful facilities when a report is required. Let's try to understand what these facilities are and how they work.

Relational operators

When you search a database using relational operators, it simply means looking for a number greater than, less than or equal to:

> is the sign for greater than
< is the sign for less than
= is, as you would expect, the sign for equal to.

(If, like me, you confuse the signs for *greater than* and *less than*, try to remember that *Less than* < points to the *Left*.)

The example of the sports club table in Figure 3.27 used relational operators, because one of the criteria for selection was members aged *less than 17 or greater than 13*. Using this criterion only members aged 14, 15 or 16 qualify.

By using relational operators, *greater than, less than* or *equal to*, the selection is limited by the particular relational operator used.

Logical operators

When you search a database using logical operators, the criterion for selection is *and, or, not*. Again the example of the sports club table required members of a specific age *and* those who play tennis. The manager might have wanted members playing tennis *or* badminton. You might be targeting people living outside the main town, in which case you could select *not Anytown*, which would select all those members who do not live in Anytown.

By including *and, or, not* in the search criteria, the selection is limited by the particular logical operator used.

Selection of index key

When you read a novel, you generally start at the first page and carry on until the end (unless you like to cheat!), but, as you well know, with a textbook it is different and the reader often wants to look something up without reading all the previous pages. At the back of this book you will find an alphabetical list of the topics covered in the book, and the page number where that topic can be found – the index. Without an index it would be very difficult to find that topic. Basically the index helps the reader *search* the book for the particular information required.

An index in a database is much the same. A given field in a database can be indexed by categories. For example, the membership file contains a field for the member's sport, so that field can be indexed under the sport played. In the report shown in Figure 3.27, the sport required was tennis, and all the records for members whose main sport is tennis will already be sorted in that category – i.e. indexed.

Sort by selected key field

This simply means producing a report in a particular order, e.g. alphabetical, numerical, order of date. Figure 3.27 might have been requested *in order of age* – which would be the selected key field – in which case the report would have looked like this:

Membership no.	Surname	First name	Main leisure interest	Age	Telephone no.
317	Chiang	Lee	tennis	14	0166 645 1431
734	Fitzgerald	Sarah	tennis	14	0166 650 2341
656	Spiller	Corinne	tennis	15	0166 650 2389
123	Patel	Chirag	tennis	16	0166 645 1897

Sometimes sorting has to be undertaken on two fields. For example, in a telephone directory, the primary field would be the surname, but as you know many people have the same surname. In order to print the directory in alphabetical order, the second name or initials are used as the secondary field. When the database is sorted into alphabetical order, the primary field of surname will be considered first, so that Brown comes before Evans, comes before Smith, etc. Then the second names or initials will be taken into account. In this way Smith Alan will be listed before Smith Andrew.

Primary field (surname)	Secondary field (first name/initial)
↓	↓
Smith	Alan
Smith	Andrew

Activity

Look at the index at the back of this book. Can you find any examples where the list has been sorted using two fields?

As indicated at the beginning of this chapter, the main focus of Element 3.3 is practical – creating a database, entering and editing data, searching the database to produce reports. So let's look at an activity which will use the knowledge learnt in this chapter.

Evidence assignment

Scenario

3L (Loose Limbs Leisure) has not yet established a database of members. As a result Chris Jones, the manager, has been finding it very difficult to keep track of:

- members' details
- membership renewal dates
- targeting particular members with advertising for special events
- bookings, and especially knowing when classes are full
- which instructors worked on which days.

On behalf of Computer Consultants Ltd, you have been asked to plan, design and implement a suitable database to simplify the problems outlined above.

Members' details

Currently the members' details are written in a card index system and include the following information:

Title, surname, first name, address (street, town, county), post code, telephone number, date of birth, date joined, membership renewal date, fee payable, leisure interests.

There are four categories of membership:

1 Adult – full – 7 days per week, £35 per month.
2 Adult – part – weekdays only, £25 per month.
3 Junior – full – 7 days per week, £25 per month.
4 Junior – part – weekdays only, £15 per month (junior members must be under 18).

1A Design a suitable database file which will provide **two related tables**:

- Members
- Main leisure interest.

Look back to the sections on 'Setting up a database for a computer' and 'Data types'. Think carefully about:

- the primary key for each table
- how these two tables can be linked together
- the other fields required – are there any extra fields not included in the manual system which would be beneficial?
- which of those fields would be secondary keys (indexed)
- the length and type of field – consider carefully the best way to design the fields.

1B

Members table

Create the necessary fields for this table, remembering that modern software has powerful facilities, e.g.:

- The members need a unique membership number, which may be created as a field with a *sequenced counter*, so each new member is automatically given the next number in the sequence.
- You might be able to use an *If* function automatically to enter the data for 'Fee paid' depending on the 'Membership category'.

1C

Main leisure interest table

For this table create two fields, one for membership number and one for the facilities offered by the club – aerobics, badminton, karate, squash, swimming, tennis and weight training.

1D Build the relationship between the two tables.

1E If the software you are using is suitable, add an image and enhance the form design as you feel fit – e.g. use suitable fonts, point size, a heading, colour/shading. The form design should **not** occupy more than one screen page.

1F Print a copy of the form design for each of the two tables. You should indicate the field types and the reasons for your choice.

2A

Members

Enter the data on page 113 into your members table. **If possible**, use the facilities described above for the 'Membership number' and 'Fee paid' fields, but otherwise simply key in the data.

2B

Main leisure interest

Enter the data opposite into the table for 'Main leisure interest' indicating against each category whether the member uses that facility.

2C *Proof-read* each record in both the members and main leisure interest tables carefully, to check for errors.

3A A new member has joined *today*. His name is David Gordon and his date of birth is 14/8/69. He wants a full monthly membership, and his main leisure interests are weight training, swimming and squash. Print a report for this record *only*.

3B Ms Wainwright has married Mr Albridge and their new address is 23 Merryview Court, ANYTOWN AN6 7VC and their new telephone number has changed to 0166 317 9001.

3C Mrs Vanderwall has moved to Manchester, so delete her record from the file.

Membership no.	Main leisure interests
1	karate weight training
2	swimming badminton
3	swimming tennis squash
4	swimming tennis aerobics
5	swimming tennis karate
6	swimming tennis
7	weight training squash
8	swimming karate
9	swimming badminton tennis
10	swimming badminton tennis
11	weight training squash
12	weight training squash
13	swimming aerobics step aerobics
14	swimming badminton tennis
15	karate swimming
16	swimming weight training
17	swimming aerobics tennis
18	karate

Members table

Membership no.	Title	Surname	First name	Address	Tel. No.	Date of birth	Membership category	Date joined	Fee
1	Mr	Johnson	Paul	15 Upper Thames St ANYTOWN AN1 4TH	0166 563 5622	01/03/50	Adult – full	10/06/85	
2	Ms	Wainwright	Jean	95 Cathedral Drive ANYTOWN AN4 6TX	0166 563 3144	20/02/71	Adult – part	12/02/95	
3	Mr	Nicholls	James	45 Commercial St ANYTOWN AN1 5TV	0166 674 3198	14/03/50	Adult – full	20/10/92	
4	Mrs	Nicholls	Anne	45 Commercial St ANYTOWN AN1 5TV	0166 674 3198	20/08/52	Adult – full	20/10/92	
5	Mr	Nicholls	John	45 Commercial St ANYTOWN AN1 5TV	0166 674 3198	14/03/80	Junior – full	20/10/92	
6	Miss	Nicholls	Rachel	45 Commercial St ANYTOWN AN1 5TV	0166 674 3198	09/09/81	Junior – full	20/10/92	
7	Mr	Patel	Prashant	24 The Close ANYTOWN AN6 4EH	0166 342 7145	12/11/60	Adult – part	24/03/95	
8	Miss	Wong	Kim	17 Church Drive ANYTOWN AN5 7GH	0166 212 5689	12/03/82	Junior – full	30/04/92	
9	Miss	Jones	Sarah	19 Church Drive ANYTOWN AN5 7GH	0166 212 4453	04/05/82	Junior – part	12/05/92	
10	Mr	Kellman	Leon	39 Pine Ave ANYTOWN AN4 7GD	0166 212 3773	17/07/65	Adult – full	06/08/90	
11	Mr	Phillips	Dwayne	33 Pine Ave ANYTOWN AN4 6GD	0166 212 3221	23/10/65	Adult – part	07/09/89	
12	Mrs	Phillips	Charmaine	33 Pine Ave ANYTOWN AN4 6GD	0166 212 3221	19/12/66	Adult – part	07/09/89	
13	Miss	Phillips	Leona	33 Pine Ave ANYTOWN AN4 6GD	0166 212 3221	01/02/88	Junior – part	07/09/89	
14	Mr	Phillips	Eugene	33 Pine Ave ANYTOWN AN4 6GD	0166 212 3221	30/04/90	Junior – part	07/09/89	
15	Mr	Albridge	Samuel	16 Chamberlain Crescent ANYTOWN AN9 3BV	0166 443 7832	09/08/69	Adult – full	16/11/91	
16	Mr	Hogg	Peter	16 Torrance Square ANYTOWN AN3 6UP	0166 443 9819	19/05/84	Junior – full	08/07/94	
17	Mrs	Mackenzie	Jenny	20 William St ANYTOWN AN2 1GH	0166 674 3388	10/06/73	Adult – part	18/12/90	
18	Mrs	Vanderwall	Louise	24 William St ANYTOWN AN2 2GH	0166 674 4901	14/09/55	Adult – full	21/06/86	

3D Having amended the records accordingly to show these changes, print a report showing only the names and addresses of the members.

4A The sports manager is trying to find a junior player for a forthcoming swimming competition. Produce a report giving only a list of the names and telephone numbers of any members who might be interested.

4B The club wants to start a new karate class for ladies over 30. Produce a report of members who would be eligible showing only their names and addresses.

4C The secretary wishes to remind all members whose subscription is due during next month. Produce a suitable report.

4D Produce a list of all members names in order of their date of birth.

4E Decide on two other searches of your own choice. These should be different from other members of your group. Write down what information you are hoping to obtain from the database, stating which facilities the report uses, and produce two reports to provide this data.

5A Other related tables could be designed for subscriptions, bookings, instructors and wages. In order to develop your understanding of this element, with the help of your tutor try to think what fields could be included in these three tables, and how they would link or relate to the members and main leisure interest tables already designed.

Please note: The Evidence Assignment for Element 3.4 includes some tasks which relate to this database. It would therefore be useful to complete these tasks before handing in this assignment.

Revision test

True or false?

1 The fields in a database file will be different for each record.

2 The primary key will be unique in each record.

3 A table is similar to a file, and a row is similar to a record.

4 It does not matter if you create all the fields as text or character.

5 Choosing different data types provides improved facilities when searching the database.

Complete the blanks

6 To _____ a record means that you change some of the data in it.

7 To _____ a record means that you add a new record to the database.

8 To _____ a record means that you remove a record from the database.

Short answer questions

9 Suggest examples of when you would edit records as described in questions 6, 7 and 8.

10 Give three examples of relational operators and how they might be used.

11 Give three examples of logical operators and how they might be used.

12 *Write a short paragraph to show you clearly understand:*

What you mean by a relationship in a database. What is the advantage of indexing a field?

Examine safety and security issues

After studying this chapter you should be able to:

1 apply *accuracy checks* to a data handling activity
2 apply *security checks* to a data handling system
3 describe *health and safety* issues for information technology users
4 describe the *obligations of users* of information technology.

Accuracy checks

The most sophisticated data handling system in the world, which uses all the modern methods of data capture and is capable of applying all the processes described in Element 3.3, is completely useless if the data entered into the system is not accurate in the first place. A common phrase used in the computer world is 'garbage in, garbage out'.

In a manual system accuracy relies heavily on the operator to proof-read and check visually, whereas a computerised system can build in accuracy checks to *reduce* the risk of errors. The word 'reduce' is used very deliberately, because mistakes can still be made, but the more built-in checks available, the less chance of errors.

Validation

The word valid simply means suitable. Is it valid or suitable for its purposes? If you mix a cake carefully, with all the right ingredients, but try to cook it in the fridge, you will not bake a cake! If you have fantastic equipment for a mobile disco, but try to play CDs on a tape deck, you will not have any music! Silly examples, but the fridge was not suitable

Figure 3.30 Garbage in, garbage out

or valid for the purpose of cooking, and the tape deck was not suitable or valid for playing CDs. So what is the relevance for a computer system? Two very important validation checks are type and range.

Type check

In Element 3.3 we looked at the various data types which could be used in a database. If a field has been designed for numbers, the computer will not accept letters in that field. If a field has been designed to accept a choice of colours – red, blue, green, yellow – it will not accept any other colour in that field. Clearly, it is still possible for the data entry clerk to make errors but some errors will be immediately apparent:

Data to be entered	Data actually entered	Data correct
156	156	✔
156	516	✗ but is accepted because it is of the correct type.
156	1q	Computer immediately signals an error, because 'q' is not a number.
red	red	✔
red	blue	✗ but the choice of blue is accepted because it is included in the list of options - i.e. the correct type.
red	purple	Computer immediately signals an error, because none of the colours listed in the choice above starts with a 'p'.

115

Range check

If a field in a database has been designed as a number field, it is possible to include a further check as well as the type check. The field can be limited within a set *range*, by giving a minimum or maximum figure or both. Computer Consultants Ltd could include a range check for the computers it supplies. The models they normally supply range in price between £500 and £3,000. Therefore the minimum price could be set at 500 and the maximum at 3000.

Data to be entered	Data actually entered	Data correct
£500	500	✔
£500	509	✗ but is accepted because it is within the correct *range*.
£500	400	Computer immediately signals an error, because 400 is below the minimum level – outside the *range*.
£3,000	3000	✔
£3,000	2000	✗ but is accepted because it is within the correct *range*.
£3,000	4000	Computer immediately signals an error, because 4000 is above the maximum level – outside the *range*.

Sometimes only a minimum level or only a maximum level is appropriate for the particular field, rather than both, but in every case some data entry errors will be signalled by the computer – often by a bleep and an error message on screen saying something like 'data not within acceptable range'.

Verification

The word verify means to check, and sometimes this is carried out quite simply by the operator reading the entries and checking them again against the original document. Sometimes a second operator will read the data out loud from the original document to the first operator, who checks on screen that the entries match. This is particularly useful for numerical data, as it is notoriously easy to make keying-in errors with numbers and these cannot be spotted just by proof-reading, whereas spelling or grammatical errors, or words missed out or repeated, will be noticeable.

Verification can also be undertaken by one operator keying in the data once and another operator keying it again (see section on batch processing on page 89). Any differences are indicated by the computer and a check can be made against the original document to establish whether the first or second entry is the correct one. It is an excellent method of ensuring accuracy, but it is time-consuming and expensive, because the information is entered into the computer twice and therefore two people are paid for the same work.

Another useful method of verification is to **spell check** the work. The words are checked against a list in the computer's dictionary. Any words not matching are queried and possible alternatives are suggested. *It is still, however, important for the operator to have a reasonable level of spelling!* The words 'a lot' meaning 'many' are frequently written as 'alot'. The spell check will suggest 'allot' which means 'to give a share', but even though the sense is wrong this alternative is usually accepted.

Most sophisticated word processors also contain **grammar checks,** but in my experience as yet the suggestions are not always easy to understand, even for someone old enough to have been taught English grammar extensively! The average student will probably find the grammar check very confusing – I know I do.

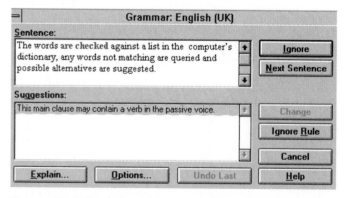

Figure 3.31 Part of a dialogue box from the Grammar Check in Word for Windows

I highlighted the paragraph above about spell checking, and selected the Grammar Check. As you can see the comments in Figure 3.31 are not easy to follow. However, if you use the grammar check for words such as *there* and *their,* you may find it very useful.

In the example in Figure 3.32 I highlighted the sentence 'They ate there dinner early', and the check shows correctly that *there* should be changed to *their*.

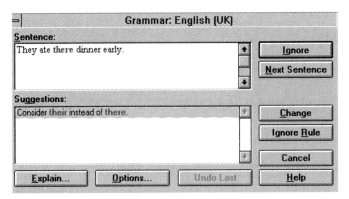

Figure 3.32 Part of a dialogue box from the Grammar Check in Word for Windows

However, when I used the correct version of *their* – 'They ate their dinner early' – and used the Grammar Check, the result was as shown in Figure 3.33.

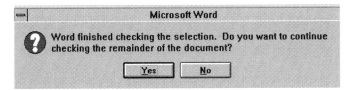

Figure 3.33 Part of a dialogue box for the Grammar Check in Word for Windows

As you can see, no error was detected. With both spelling and grammar checks, if an error is suggested, it is very probable, but not definite, that you have made a mistake. You need to look at the suggestions given and try to decide the correct version.

Correctness

This means checking data to ensure that it is meaningful. It is perfectly possible to use all the validation and verification techniques available in a modern computer, but still produce meaningless

information. (Garbage out!) The example of the words 'a lot' being replaced by 'allot' is one such mistake, although in this case the intended sense is still obvious. However, sometimes the wrong spelling may lead to confusion or even complete misunderstanding of what the writer meant.

Once we have entered data into the computer, *none of us is keen to have to read it all again, especially if it is a long report. But there is no other way to ensure that the data makes sense.* Often our thoughts and ideas run faster than our fingers can type, so words are omitted or repeated, or the sense is muddled and can be improved with some minor changes. With numerical data, the number entered might be in the acceptable range, but inappropriate. For example, a database of children's records in a primary school might include fields for the year group, and the date of birth from which the child's age is calculated. The age field has a range check from 4 to 11. One record lists a child in the reception class, but aged 8. The reception class is for 4–5 year-olds, therefore one of the entries must be wrong. Both fields contained *valid* data – reception is a suitable choice for the year group, and *8* is within the range for ages, but nevertheless the data is not correct. This is where the power of the computer is so useful – editing can be undertaken easily and swiftly, without starting all over again.

Activity

Refer back to the Video Manufacture plc sales order and invoice discussed in Element 3.1. What validation checks could be made for the following?

- *Sales order* – order no. and goods reference number
- *Invoice* – unit price. (Will it be possible to have a specific check for Anytown's customer order number, A129634, shown on the invoice?)

In what ways could the purchase order, sales order, delivery note and invoice be verified? Write down your answers, then check the answers at the end of the book to see whether you were right (see page 206).

It would be possible to ensure verification if the work were entered twice but, in practice, in a busy commercial or industrial situation, getting orders out quickly is likely to take priority. This would be a time-consuming method of checking, so it is better for any errors to be rectified later. Of course, the data entry clerk should check carefully that the data has been entered correctly.

As far as goods reference numbers are concerned, a list of all the codes used by the company could be stored in the computer and, if the code entered does not match one in the list, then an error would be indicated. Of course, it would still be possible to enter one of the listed codes, but not the correct one.

To prevent errors on the unit price, the goods reference number would automatically generate the relevant price. The total cost and VAT would also be calculated automatically from the number of items and the unit price. If the code for the correct item has been entered, then these fields will be correct.

Security checks

Security checks are designed to protect the data in the files, to ensure that the data is not lost, corrupted or misused. In many ways protecting the data is more important than protecting the hardware, because it is easier, if expensive, to replace the actual hardware; it is very difficult, sometimes even impossible, to replace the data.

Loss of data can be caused accidentally or deliberately by:

- fire
- hardware failure such as scratches on a disk which damages all or part of the data
- unintentionally writing over the data or deleting a file
- unintentionally updating with incorrect data
- theft
- fraudulent changes made by employees or others for malicious reasons.

Security checks are also designed to prevent unauthorised access which may result in:

- competitors gaining important information
- deliberate corruption of data
- loss of confidential/private information about individuals or organisations.

So how can data be protected to prevent situations such as this arising?

Regular saving

Have you had the experience of entering a great deal of information into the computer, only to lose it because of a power failure, a breakdown in the system or simply deleting the work accidentally?

Figure 3.34 Saving work regularly prevents frustration and anger!

Haven't we all at some time? Frustrating, isn't it? The only answer is to save work regularly.

Did you know?

Modern sophisticated software has an automatic save feature, which will save documents at set intervals, e.g. every 10 minutes, in a special location and format, until you save them into the normal file format. In the event of a power failure or some other problem occurring before you save your work, when you reopen the program a list of automatically saved documents will be displayed so that you can recover them.

Back-up copies

Probably the most important security check is to have a back-up copy of the data. We have all done it – saved some very important work, but the disk has been lost or corrupted and we have not made a copy. Often this is no more than very irritating and time-consuming to rectify but, in business, loss of crucial data could be just as serious as losing all the stock through theft or fire. It could even result in bankruptcy.

Data stored on the hard disk of the computer can be backed up on:

- floppy disks, which are generally used for small computers – PCs or portables
- a tape streamer which is a magnetic tape and generally used as an off-line backing store for large computers.

If there is no hard drive (less common as costs of computers come down) then the data can be stored on two separate floppy disks.

The advantage of storing back-up copies on disk is that files can be accessed directly and quickly, whereas a magnetic tape has to be read starting from the beginning until you reach the file you want – just like a tape for music.

The advantage of backing up on tape is that tapes are light and compact, easy to store for long periods, and far cheaper than disks.

Tape is therefore an ideal medium for storing large volumes of data in a business context, especially when the use of the tape is anticipated *only* if the original disks are lost or damaged, and therefore the speed and ease of access is not a prime consideration, whereas cost and ease of storage are more important.

Confidentiality

Non-disclosure

To some extent, protection of data will always be dependent on the trustworthiness of the employees, and therefore companies need to be as careful as possible about whom they employ. Inevitably some people will break that trust and use information gained illegally. It is also important to inform employees about laws relating to confidentiality, so that they do not unintentionally disclose information which should be confidential.

Organisations have an obligation of confidentiality both for their own self-interest and also to protect the public whose data is held on their files. The data can be protected physically by making access to the data by unauthorised personnel as difficult as possible.

To protect very important data against fire or theft, back-up copies are often stored in a fire-proof safe or even in a building on another site.

The ability to identify the system user is another important aspect of security, both to ensure that only authorised personnel gain access to the data and also

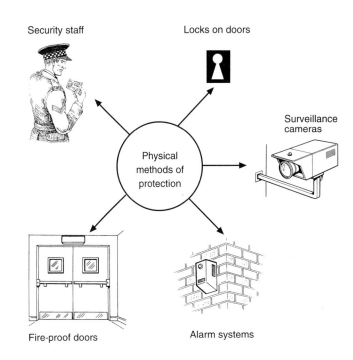

Figure 3.35 Various methods of protecting the data (and hardware) physically

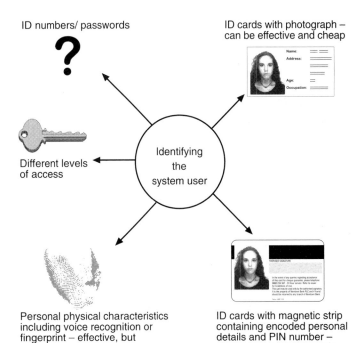

Figure 3.36 Various methods of identifying the system user

to identify any unauthorised access, whether from within or outside the organisation.

Passwords

If you use a network system in your school or college, you will almost certainly use a unique ID number to gain access to the system, followed by a password which you personally choose. When selecting a password, it is crucial to choose a word which:

- is easy to remember – but not your boy/girlfriend's name – in a few weeks you might have had several new ones (!) and you forget which is the right one
- is not obvious – e.g. your own name.

This password should be kept confidential and in a business context should also be changed frequently, to make it more difficult for the password to be discovered. You will notice that when you enter the password, the characters are not displayed on screen, but appear in a coded form, frequently as a series of asterisks (******). This is known as *encryption* and is designed to prevent someone casually observing your password as it is shown on the screen.

In addition to passwords for access to the system, modern software programs also allow the use of passwords when saving files. Figure 3.37 is a screen dump showing part of the options dialogue box from the 'Save As' facility in Word for Windows.

A password entered in the Protection Password box prevents anyone opening the file unless he or she knows the password. A password entered in the Write Preservation Password box allows access to *read* the file, but prevents anyone saving changes to the file, unless he or she knows the password. Passwords entered into these boxes will again appear as a series of asterisks. An X in the Read-Only Recommended box indicates that it is advisable to read but not to amend the file. If the user wishes to write *to* the file,

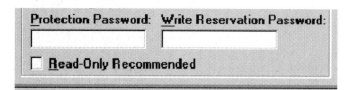

Figure 3.37 Part of a dialogue box which enables passwords to limit access to the file from Word for Windows

then it should be saved under a new name, so that the original version is retained.

Giving staff different privileges or security levels which allow access only to some files or some fields within a file is a common method of protecting data and maintaining confidentiality. The most senior staff would have:

- greater privileges
- a high security level
- access to all or most of the data

whereas more junior staff would have:

- fewer privileges
- low security
- access only to less important data.

As indicated earlier some staff can read the file, but not write to the file (i.e. make changes).

Did you know?

Another method used to check security is to program the system to track exactly which user has logged on, to which files and for how long. This is known as an **audit trail** and its purpose is to check whether someone has accessed information to which he or she is not authorised.

Activity

Ask the members of your group:

1 Do they make back-ups of their files?
2 If so, how?
3 Do they use any passwords?

Then ask friends or family who use computers at work:

1 What systems are in place where they work for backing up files?
2 What storage medium is used for back-up files?
3 Do they use any passwords?
4 Does their organisation use audit trails?

Next time you meet, compare the results with the other group members. Finally, check out the software programs you are using to find out whether the files can be protected by passwords.

Copyright

In the same way that the author of a book or composer of a piece of music is protected by law from someone copying the work and selling it as his or her own, the Copyright, Designs and Patents Act 1988 protects original work created using a computer, such as:

- documents produced using a word processor
- accounts reports using a spreadsheet
- drawings using a CAD (computer-aided design) program .
- music written using a program designed to assist composition
- and, of course, all the software packages.

The author of the work is usually the person who creates the work, unless it is created in the course of his or her employment, when the employer may be the author. The author is the only one with the right to:

- copy or adapt the work
- sell or rent copies to the public
- broadcast the work – including as part of a cable programme service.

In practice this means that you must not:

- give or sell copies of software
- copy data/documents/programs saved on a computer and pretend the work is your own, even if you do not sell it.

If the author believes that someone has infringed the copyright, then he or she may sue and if the case is proven, then damages may be awarded. Copyright lasts for 70 years after the author has died (or if two or more people have been involved together as authors, until 70 years after the last author dies).

One way to protect valuable computer programs from piracy, especially during the developmental stage, is to distribute copies of the work in object code. (Object code is a machine code version of the program, which is more difficult to utilise.) The company name or names of the programmers can also be written into the code, in the event that a 'software pirate' denies copying. In addition copies of the software at different stages of development can be deposited with someone independent, such as the bank manager, the date being noted. This may prove valuable later if there is a debate concerning the author of the work, or who first wrote it.

Health and safety

Stress

As the use of computers has become more widespread, concerns have been voiced from time to time about the health and safety of the operators and stress suffered by them through the course of their work. The main worries relate to:

- backache
- eyestrain
- headaches and migraine
- RSI – repetitive strain injury
- radiation, especially if using VDUs when pregnant.

These problems can generally be avoided if sensible precautions are taken.

Backache

This can usually be prevented by suitable seating, good posture and taking a break from time to time. Chairs should:

- be capable of swivelling
- have a movable base, i.e. castors
- have an adjustable back rest to give support where needed.

In addition an operator should not be expected to sit working at a VDU for hours without a break, and indeed should take responsibility for changing his or her posture – perhaps taking a walk in the lunchbreak to exercise and relieve the muscles.

Figure 3.38 Suitable seating is important for people working at VDUs

Did you know?

To ensure that employers provide suitable conditions for computer operators, the EU introduced legislation which has to be put into practice for new workstations installed after 31 December 1992 and existing workstations have to be upgraded, if necessary, by 31 December 1996. A video entitled 'VDUs in the Workplace' and available from Team Projects, Technical Presentations, Eagle Court, High Street, Rochester ME1 1JT, clearly explains the European directives in respect of working with VDUs. If you can gain access to a copy, it is well worth watching.

Eye strain/headaches/migraine

Problems with eye strain or headaches are likely to occur *only* if the VDU is fuzzy, flickers or is in a poorly lit position. The EU directives require that:

- the screen should not flicker, nor reflect light
- the angle, brightness and contrast of the screen must be adjustable
- desks and keyboards should have a matt finish to prevent reflection of light and to avoid glare
- lighting should ensure correct contrast between the screen and the general background
- VDU operators must have the right to a free eye test before commencing VDU work and regularly afterwards.

Repetitive strain injury (RSI)

RSI is caused by making the same or awkward movements continuously. This problem affects any operators constantly hitting computer keys for long periods. The tendon sheaths in the hand, wrist or arm become inflamed, causing pain, numbness and swelling, which, if untreated, can result in permanent disability. Ironically it is believed that the *light* touch required by the modern keyboard, compared to the much heavier keys of old-fashioned typewriters, may aggravate the problem.

To prevent or reduce the risk of RSI, keyboards should:

- be separate from the VDU
- be adjustable to lie flat or slope at an angle of approximately 10 degrees
- have concave keys
  - to reduce the risk of the fingers slipping off them

  - to reduce shock on the fingertips, fingers, wrist and arms.

Radiation

There have been concerns that there is a risk of radiation from working with VDUs, and it has been suggested that pregnant women have suffered miscarriages as a result of radiation from VDUs. Special shields can be attached to the VDU to protect users from radiation, but the evidence indicates the risk from radiation is less than from natural sources.

Other hazards

Hazards such as electrical faults, fire or obstruction are no more or less relevant when working with computers than in any other area of employment. The Health and Safety at Work Act 1974 (HASAWA) and the Control of Substances Hazardous to Health Act 1989 (COSHH) require all employers to ensure that their place of work is a safe environment. This includes provision of:

- safe entrances and exits including fire escapes
- safe equipment – electrical equipment must be checked regularly
- safe storage for hazardous substances and warning signs indicating their location
- a statement in writing on the organisation's health and safety policy
- training for staff – their rights, obligations, fire drills
- accident investigation procedures.

Employees also have a duty to undertake safe working practices. For example, they should:

- report/deal with (as appropriate) any hazards, such as trailing wires, obstructions – especially to fire exits
- not lift heavy equipment
- know the fire drill
- take suitable breaks as mentioned earlier
- know and use correct posture at the keyboard.

Obligations of users

Much of the security of data relies on the integrity and trustworthiness of those who use the system. Organisations have always been at risk from dishonest staff, but the main difference since the advent of computers is that it is so much easier to obtain the information – you do not even need to be in the room or even the building! The organisation has an obligation to ensure security of data as far as possible, but the users, both in terms of their personal and their business use of computers, must also take responsibility in respect of the following.

Confidentiality of data

If you are in a position of trust, you must not pass on information, no matter how innocently. In fact you could be prosecuted under the Data Protection Act (see below).

Think about the receptionist at a local doctor's surgery. He or she will almost certainly know some of the patients personally, and will also, inevitably, be aware of the confidential medical history of those patients. Imagine this scenario. The receptionist is aware of a bad history of heart problems in members of your close family, but you are in perfect health. He or she intends no harm, but gossips about it. Your insurance company gains illegal access to this information and refuses life insurance or increases your premiums. If you discovered what information the insurance company had obtained and how it was obtained, you could sue for compensation under the Data Protection Act.

"YOU'LL NEVER BELIEVE THIS, BUT JOHN'S BROTHER'S HAD A HEART ATTACK NOW."

Copyright

The law relating to copyright also includes theft of software or work produced on a computer (refer back to page 120). If you are found to be copying data or software illegally, you may be prosecuted. It is **essential** to realise that **you** have to be aware of the law. It is not just the responsibility of employers. Ignorance of the law is not an acceptable excuse and you can still be prosecuted even though you did not realise you were doing anything wrong.

When you buy software programs you are given a licence and your 'ownership' of that copy is registered with the software company. You will be given details of the 'Grant of Licence'. Typically (although this may vary) the licence permits you to:

- install the software on a single computer
- make one copy of the disks as a back-up only
- load the software on to the hard disk keeping the original disks for back up only.

You are not allowed to copy the software on to a network unless you purchase a network licence, which is more expensive than a single-user licence.

Responsible attitudes to uncensored or private materials

Inevitably there has to be trust in and reliance on the users of information technology, especially in a business environment. Most people are in fact quite honest, have no intention of defrauding their employer or disclosing confidential information. It is, however, essential to take security issues seriously, so that you do not *unintentionally* give access to uncensored or private materials to someone else. Also if you *accidentally* discover uncensored or private materials, you must not take advantage of the opportunity, and it may be appropriate to report that a breach of security has occurred.

One of the major concerns of parents today is that children will be exposed to pornography or be contacted by paedophiles through the Internet. (The Internet is a worldwide network of databases linked together. Users can read information from the Internet and also write to the Internet.) A report in *The Daily Telegraph,* 8 August 1995, describes programs, now available, which are designed to prevent access to hazardous areas of the World Wide Web. Also, in America an association called Safe Surf acts rather like a board of censors and provides ratings for web sites. Child-friendly sites are encouraged to include a code in their address so that parents know they have been approved.

Another concern is the availability of pornographic material on disks, but in reality this is simply a new version of old problems – pornography in art, literature, films and videos. It is not possible to prevent misuse of computers, any more than abuse of freedom in any other area of life. It is up to each individual to take responsibility for his or her own use of facilities.

Theft

Theft of computer equipment – monitors, keyboards, printers, etc. – is less of a problem than theft of the memory chips, which are tiny but very valuable components. They are easily removable and clip in or out of the computer. If equipment is stolen, often keyboards and monitors are ignored, as they are relatively cheap and easy to obtain, but the CPU (central processing unit) or 'brains' of the computer is taken. Factories making the memory chips are frequent targets for criminals. The chips can be more valuable than gold to a criminal – their smallness and lightness make them so easy to transport, often across the world.

Theft of software has already been discussed under the sections relating to copyright.

Virus checking

A computer virus is a harmful program, developed by someone either for general mischief or to attack a particular organisation. The virus copies itself without the user intending it to, or even being aware of it happening until problems occur. Sometimes, in attempt to defy virus detection, the program will mutate (change) slightly each time it is copied. Problems caused by viruses can include clearing screens, deleting data and even making the whole system unusable.

Viruses can affect both floppy and hard disks and are usually transferred from one computer to another via floppy disks. If disks are used only on one system then the risk of 'catching' a virus is much less. The more often disks are used in different computers, the greater the risk of 'catching' a virus. In fact some organisations do not allow floppy disks to be taken from work to home or vice versa, for this very reason. If the disk is to be loaded into a computer just to show or demonstrate

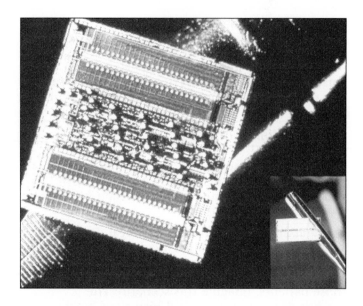

Figure 3.39 A computer memory chip, showing its size relative to the eye of a needle

the contents, then write-protecting the disk will prevent any viruses on that computer being transferred on to the disk. It is a good idea to write-protect disks containing the software programs before putting into the disk drive, to ensure that they are not accidentally infected. You may need to reload the program at a future date and it would be very annoying to find the disks damaged.

Computer viruses have become an ever more serious problem, but anti-virus software, such as 'Dr Solomon's Anti-Virus Toolkit', is available, which can detect and remove any known viruses. You may find anti-virus software installed on your school or college network, which automatically checks every disk as it is accessed, and prevents loading of files from an 'infected' disk. It is annoying to find one of your disks has a virus, but if you do find out, at least you can stop using it or have it 'disinfected', thereby preventing the virus from being passed on.

Did you know?

Computer 'viruses' are far more of a threat to security of data than industrial espionage, dishonest employees, fire, theft or simple errors.

Data Protection Act 1984

The Data Protection Act relates specifically to **personal data held on computers.** It was introduced because of concerns that more and more data was being held on computers about each of us, with the potential for misuse. For example, companies have been known to sell lists of names and addresses to other companies, with the result that large quantities of unwelcome promotional literature arrive in the post (junk mail).

Personal information has always been held on paper, but now that it is stored electronically, it is so much easier for information to be passed from one computer to another, possibly with disastrous consequences. Some people were anxious that sensitive personal details were held on computer, without their knowledge, and could be more easily obtained than from a manual system. Part of this anxiety stems from lack of understanding of computers – people often do feel threatened by things they do not understand. Other people felt that it is all a fuss about nothing, that if you are not doing anything illegal there is no need to worry, and in fact the more information is available on computers, the easier it is to catch criminals.

The 'worriers' eventually won the day, and the Data Protection Act 1984 was passed to protect the rights of individuals against misuse of personal data held on computer.

The main points of the Act are as follows:

1 Any organisation holding personal data in a computer system must register with the Data Protection Registrar, stating clearly what details are to be included and for what purpose.

2 The data must be obtained fairly and legally and held **only** for the purpose stated.

3 Only necessary data should be included – in other words, extra, irrelevant data is not allowed – and it must be accurate, up to date and kept only as long as it is needed.

4 The data must not be given to anyone who is not entitled to it.

5 The data must be protected against loss or disclosure to unauthorised users.

6 The data subjects – the people to whom the data refers – are entitled to see what information is held on them, with certain exceptions.

7 If data held is inaccurate the subject has the right for it to be corrected, and in the event he or she has suffered personal damage through incorrect or lost data, there is a right to compensation.

(A student pack containing further information can be obtained from the Office of the Data Protection Registrar, Wycliff House, Water Lane, Wilmslow, Cheshire SK9 5AF.)

Right of individual to disclosure

As indicated in points 6 and 7 above, individuals have the right to know what information is held on computer about them and to have any errors corrected. Exemptions from the Act include personal data kept for purposes of national security, medical and social service records, some police files and details kept on a home computer, such as an address list of your friends, or a list of their birthdays.

Did you know?

A gentleman in America suddenly discovered he was listed as dead in one computer, because cheques were returned marked 'deceased' across his signature. He spoke to his bank who reassured him that the error would be

"YOU'RE DEAD-LIE DOWN!"

rectified, but his troubles had just begun. The rumours of his death spread through the computer systems much faster than he could hope to correct the information! As a result his social security was stopped, his Medicare was stopped and he felt helpless against the power of the computer. It took over a year to rectify all the errors. You might think this is an isolated incident, but thousands of lives are disrupted each year by faulty data in computer systems.

Evidence assignment

1 Using the database designed for Element 3.3, select suitable fields to which you can apply the validation checks of range and type. If necessary amend the fields to include these checks. Demonstrate to your tutor what happens when you enter data of both the correct and incorrect range and type. Explain why incorrect data is not accepted by the computer.

2 Before handing in this database assignment verify the accuracy of the work by checking carefully against the original text.

3 Save your work at regular intervals in the right directory, using a suitable file name, print and make a back-up copy. Protect your file with a password, demonstrating both the back-up and the password to your tutor. If the software you are using does not have password protection facilities, then write a paragraph explaining the procedure.

4 This task provides evidence for Communication Core Skills Element 2.1 – take part in discussions. You must prepare for this discussion by researching the following questions:

- Why do you think giving away copies of software breaks the copyright law?
- Why do you think it is not acceptable to pretend work generated on a computer is yours, even if you do not sell it?
- Do you feel the cost of purchasing software, which is often very expensive, has any effect on illegal copying of programs?
- Do you feel the copyright laws are too strict, too easy, should be changed in any way?

Look for relevant information in computer textbooks, newspaper articles or magazines, making notes which **should be handed in** to your lecturer after the discussion.

Working in pairs:

- explain what information you have obtained

- explain whether you agree or disagree with the present copyright laws and why
- be prepared to answer questions
- note any points raised by your partner which are different from your own, and **hand in** these notes as well as your original notes.

Scenario

The manager of 3L (Loose Limbs Leisure) has realised that computerising the system has implications for staff, apart from knowing how to use it. She has asked Computer Consultants Ltd for advice. In the past such requests were handled simply by giving out a free leaflet with the most basic details, but the company has realised that it could provide a much better service to its clients and also charge for the information. You and a small team have been asked to prepare a presentation for 3L which, if successful, will be used in future.

The presentation must cover the health and safety issues for information technology users and also the obligations of those users (see the range for Element 3.4). You and your colleague are anxious to impress your boss with this project, and take a great deal of trouble with handouts and overhead transparencies.

Revision test

True or false?

1 Numerical data would be a suitable type to enter in a character field.

2 A range check could be used for the months of the year.

3 It does not matter if you tell someone your password.

4 Data about stock held on a computer is covered by the Data Protection Act.

5 Only employers have an obligation to ensure confidentiality, copyright or data protection.

Complete the blanks

6 _____ means checking, but this does not guarantee _____ .

7 When using a VDU the risk from _____ is no more than from natural causes.

8 It is important to make _____ copies of your files, in case the data is lost or corrupted.

Short answer questions

State whether the following actions infringe (break) the copyright law and explain your reason:

9 Your friend has purchased a new software package and sells you a copy of it at a reduced price.

10 Your friend has purchased a new software package and gives you a copy of it.

11 Your friend has purchased a new software package and makes a back-up copy for his own use, in case the original disks are ever damaged or lost.

Write a short paragraph

For each of the following situations, decide whether the law on data protection has been or would be broken, and explain your answer:

12 Anytown College keeps records of students' names, addresses, dates of birth, emergency contact numbers and previous qualifications on computer.

13 Some students have to pay for their courses, and it has been suggested that the individual's credit rating could also be added to the file.

14 The course tutor needs to contact a student urgently and is given the student's home telephone number by the administration office.

15 A student is very attracted to another student and wants to send a Valentine card. One of the staff in the administration office is a romantic at heart, sees no harm in it and passes on the address.

127

Describe electronic communication systems

The need and desire to communicate is a basic requirement of humankind, from the hieroglyphics frequently found by archaeologists to modern people with a mobile phone. The instinctive desire to improve communications has been a driving force resulting in easier, better, quicker ways of communicating across the world – even the universe. The advancements have never been more rapid than in this century. This section is concerned with the development of electronic communications and the way information technology is used to transfer, receive and store information. It will also consider computer networks and the facilities available through using such networks.

After studying this chapter you should be able to describe:

1 *electronic communication systems* (and give examples)
2 *protocols* (the rules for using electronic communication)
3 *modes* (different methods) *of communication.*

Electronic communication systems

Broadcast systems

The combination of telecommunication and computer technology has produced an 'information explosion', one result of which has been the enormous expansion of different types of broadcast systems, in addition to the radio and television entertainment programmes with which we have long been familiar.

Mobile telephones and *cell broadcast networks* use **cellular radio**, a technique developed in recent years to enable the use of mobile telephones. It would be impossible to provide each phone with an individual radio frequency, so the idea of cellular radio has evolved. The country is divided into geographical areas called cells, varying in size depending on the number of mobile-phone users in the area. In cities cells are small, whereas in the country cells are much larger. Cells use a set of frequencies which will be different from the cell next to it, but can be the same set as another cell as long as it is further away. This may be difficult to understand, so Figure 4.1 illustrates the concept.

Cell A using frequencies 1–100	Cell B using frequencies 101–200	Cell C using frequencies 201–300	Cell D using frequencies 101–200

Figure 4.1 Radio cells and frequency distribution. It should be noted that the numbers **do not represent the actual frequencies;** they are simply a reference for the purpose of clarification

Each phone within a cell uses a different frequency to maintain privacy, and the system keeps track of which cell a phone is in, so that calls are routed to the right cell. Just as with the normal phone system, the cellular phone system can transmit voice or data.

Videotext describes any information system transmitted to a user's screen via a computer. The main *public* systems are *Teletext* and *Ceefax,* which provide a public service based on a central computer database, accessed via a television set fitted with a Teletext adapter, using the remote control. The database contains thousands of *pages* or frames of information regularly updated by the information provider.

Most, if not all, of us will be familiar with this facility which enables us to check the latest weather reports, sports results, news headlines and much more. The pages are broadcast continuously, whether they are selected or not, until the user wishes to access or look up the required information, by pressing the Teletext button and entering the appropriate page number into the remote control.

The main drawback of Teletext is that it is not inter-active, but a *one-way communication system* from the provider to the user.

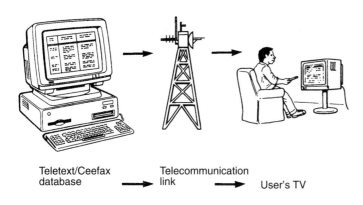

Teletext/Ceefax database → Telecommunication link → User's TV

Activity

Investigate the Teletext systems provided by the BBC and ITV:

1 Which broadcasting service uses which system?
2 List the topics covered by each.
3 Are there any differences?

Viewdata is also an information system, again based on pages or frames of information from a central database and its appearance on screen is very similar to Teletext and Ceefax. A *menu* listing information such as details about flights or ferries is shown on screen, giving a page number, which you enter from the keyboard. The relevant page is then shown on screen. The main difference is that viewdata is a *two-way communication service* – data can both be received and transmitted.

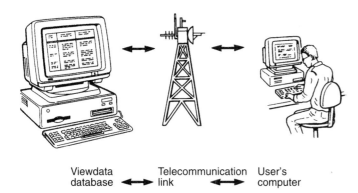

Viewdata database ↔ Telecommunication link ↔ User's computer

Typically, a viewdata system will be available for a specific group of businesses with similar interests/requirements, providing access to many mainframe computer systems. A typical viewdata system, with which many of us may be familiar as a customer, is used by travel agents. It has two main functions:

1 To *provide information* on holidays, hotels, flights, car hire, cruises – anything connected with travel.
2 It is an online, real-time (see Element 3.2, page 92) reservations system. If the customer decides to make a reservation the travel agent can record the details *directly* into the computer system, which is *immediately updated.*

Two major providers within the travel industry are Fastrak and Istel. Tour operators such as Thomsons, or airline companies such as British Airways, are information *providers* who pay to have their pages included in the database. Some providers will choose to go with both Fastrak and Istel, whereas others will be unique to one. The user – i.e. the travel agency – needs a telephone line, pays only for the cost of the calls and will almost certainly have a dedicated viewdata terminal or, alternatively, a computer, a modem and the necessary software. (A modem is necessary because computers store and use digital data – i.e. on/off – whereas much of the telephone network still uses analogue data – i.e. continuous. See Element 4.2, page 142, for more detail on modems.) If you wanted to book a flight, the travel agent would be able to view on screen a *timetable* of flights, and then

Viewdata system	Provider	User	Customer
For example, Fastrak or Istel ⇓ establishes a viewdata database ⇓ sells this service to organisations such as Thomson, British Airways	For example, Thomson, British Airways ⇓ pays to have pages of information on their holidays, flights, etc., included in the Fastrak or Istel viewdata database ⇓ Each provider has its own password to allow users to access the system	For example, Anytown Travel Agency ⇓ decides to computerise the business ⇓ has to contact providers who issue the password ⇓ accesses the system paying only for the cost of the calls ⇓ is able to obtain information from the viewdata database ⇓ can also put information into the viewdata database – i.e. make reservations	Customer makes inquiry with travel agent (can be in person or by telephone) ⇓ Travel agent checks viewdata system on flight/holiday/hotel availability ⇓ Customer decides to book a flight/ holiday/hotel ⇓ Travel agent enters details directly into the computer ⇓ Viewdata system is immediately updated

Figure 4.2 Providers, users and customers of viewdata systems

check, also on screen, whether the flight you choose has seats available, and how much it costs.

To understand this more clearly, see Figure 4.2, which looks at it from the point of view of the viewdata system, the provider, the user and the customer.

UK systems include the following:

- *Campus 2000* – a service for education, providing electronic mail, access to databases and telesoftware (computer programs transmitted via viewdata or Teletext).
- *New Prestel* – which is mainly an information retrieval system, with over a thousand providers, including banks, travel agents, transport companies, universities, trade unions, insurance companies, the government and many more. You can obtain information on stocks and shares, worldwide weather, availability of airline/theatre seats, road reports, press articles, extracts from major international publications. If you want to decide whether a potential new customer is a good credit risk, financial databases will give you details on the profit and loss accounts of the business. The list is endless.

Radio and TV

Conventional radio signals are limited by the number of frequencies available. Digital satellite broadcasting is the future for radio transmission and opens up the possibility of hundreds of different radio stations. This could mean, for example, that a radio station might be devoted exclusively to a type of music enjoyed by only a small minority and, whereas in the past each radio station was trying to

attract as many listeners as possible, nowadays broadcasters do look for what is known as 'niche' or specialised markets.

You may have noticed that miles of suburban roads are being dug up to lay cables, for cable TV. Cable companies are linking homes over a wide area to the services they provide. Subscribers pay a monthly line rental for the use of the cable, which allows the user to receive satellite and terrestrial TV broadcasts, and/or standard telephone services.

Plans for further expansion of cable facilities include the ability to watch films of your choice at a time of your choice. At present viewers can watch films as they are broadcast, or record them for later viewing, but experiments are now being carried out to develop *video on demand*. The aim of this service is to allow subscribers access to a vast library of films which they can then watch immediately. The advantages of this facility are that you will not be limited to the choice offered by the TV station, and it provides the facilities of a video rental shop, without the need to go there to select your film. Perhaps more importantly, you won't have to take it back! Inevitably there will be a charge, and time will tell whether the benefits are worth the cost.

Did you know?

Two experimental television projects are currently taking place in East Anglia, which could change the face of broadcasting. These trials are the latest stage in the development of interactive television or video on demand. The aim is to develop a television network which allows viewers to watch what they want when they want. Instead of the television schedule as we now know it, viewers would have a huge library of programmes from which to select, which could be started and stopped whenever they want. The programmes would be held in a central computer (like a digital juke box) and selected for watching as and when the viewers wanted.

The race to develop such a system is taking place worldwide, with around 70 pilot projects underway in the USA, Europe and the Far East – the BBC alone is involved in ten trials. There are two potential methods of sending the pictures into homes – one uses ordinary telephone lines (you can still make or receive a telephone call while the system is in use) and the other uses fibre-optic cable.

Citizens Band Radio use radio channels to allow two-way, short-distance business and personal communication. CB continues to be used by the drivers of trucks, by factory personnel for internal communication, but since the early 1980s has been less popular on a personal level, undoubtedly because of the facilities provided by electronic communications. Marine and aircraft control and the police use set frequencies which are unique to each operation.

Networks

As people became more and more civilised, they needed to find different ways to communicate, and especially ways to communicate quickly over a distance. In times of danger, bonfires were lit to warn of the progress of invaders. Semaphore (using flags) could provide instructions from one ship to another in a battle, and Morse code (using long and short signals to represent the letters of the alphabet) could be transmitted by telegraph, or simply by sound or light and the message decoded. These could all be described as early *network* communication systems. Nowadays network communication is available electronically and we have already discussed some very familiar uses:

- cash-point machines – also known as automatic teller machines (ATMs)
- electronic point-of-sale terminals (EPOS)
- Cable TV is a form of network.

Networks allow the sharing of resources and information by users and come in two broad categories – local area networks (LANs) and wide area networks (WANs). As its name suggests, a LAN system is located in a small area – usually within one building – whereas a WAN connects users over a much larger geographical area – even between continents. (LANs and WANs will be discussed in more detail in Element 4.3.)

Telephone

Telephone communication was originally designed for speech, but it is now also possible to send digital data via the telephone system. This ability to send words, files, pictures along telephone lines has led to the increase in electronic communication networks, which provide facilities such as viewdata. The ability to transmit digital data has resulted in one of the latest advances, the videophone which, although rare at present, will no doubt become commonplace. Videophones enable you to see as well as hear the person on the other end of a telephone. Don't worry,

you can choose whether to let the other caller see you or not! To activate the video link, you just press one button and if the person at the other end wishes to accept the link, a full colour image appears on a small screen attached to the telephone unit. If you wish to *show* the other person a still picture, the quality is even better.

Did you know?

Alexander Bell spoke the first distinct words over a telephone line in Boston, Mass, on 10 March 1876. Bell taught deaf children to speak, and his detailed knowledge of the way speech is produced had given him the idea that electrical signals might be used to transmit speech over telegraph cables. He brought his invention to England in 1877 and impressed Queen Victoria with a demonstration. However, it was 1956 before the first transatlantic telephone cable was laid connecting America and Britain.

Facsimile

Facsimile – known as fax – is used to send the contents of a document, including text and/or pictures, via a telephone line. The image is converted into electronic form so that it can be transmitted via the telephone line, and an exact copy of the document is printed by the receiving fax machine.

PC fax machines do not even need the document to be fed into the machine as hard copy. The fax software creates your header sheet for you and you just type in your message. The computer communicates directly with the receiving fax machine. Similarly a fax received by a computer will be stored *electronically* and printed as hard copy only if desired.

Did you know?

In 1995 Mercury Communications and PA Sport established a Cricket FaxBack service, whereby users can dial a number on their fax keypad and obtain information including details of England's tour to South Africa, World Cup results, visiting teams from India and Pakistan, the domestic season in England, the next season's fixtures list, plus the real-time match scores on paper, as they were actually happening around the world.

Protocols

Electronic communication only works if the receiving machine understands the signals coming from the sending machine. They both have to use the same 'language' or follow the same set of rules – the protocols.

To illustrate the point, when home video recording was first introduced, three systems came on to the market: VHS, Betamax and Philips. All were capable of recording programmes and playing them back, but tapes for one system could not be used in machines designed for the others. They were using different protocols. The public found it inconvenient not to be able to play any tapes on their machine. In the end because VHS was licensed to more VCR manufacturers, there were more and more machines able to play VHS tapes, and eventually the Betamax and Philips 2000 systems were no longer popular. There are numerous manufacturers of domestic video recorders, but nowadays they all use the VHS system (protocol). Similarly there are numerous manufacturers of computer equipment, but as yet a total standardisation has not been achieved for the computer industry and different companies use different protocols.

In data communication and networks, there are many protocols or rules to ensure that when messages are transmitted electronically, they arrive at their destination, any errors being detected and corrected. To enable correct, accurate communication, settings or parameters need to be agreed by both the sending and receiving station. The transmitting station sends a signal to say, in effect, 'I want to send a message – are you ready to receive?' If all is well, the receiving station replies, 'Yes, go ahead', and this exchange of signals is sometimes referred to as *handshaking*. Any equipment which uses the same communication protocol can be connected together, but devices with different systems can sometimes communicate via a 'protocol conversion computer'.

Let's consider some of the criteria or parameters **which have to be agreed** in order to transmit the data.

Baud rate

The speed at which data is transmitted is known as the *baud rate*, where 1 baud = 1 bit per second (bps). This method usually transmits ten bits for each character. The sending and receiving computer must both be set to the same baud rate, otherwise the data will not be received correctly, or possibly nothing will be received at all.

Speed at which data is transmitted

Baud rate (bps)	Character rate (cps)
50	5
100	10

 Activity

Complete the following table giving the respective character rate per second for the baud rate shown:

Transfer rate (bps)	Character rate (cps)
300	
600	
2,400	
9,600	

Clearly, the higher the baud rate, the faster the data can be transmitted. The lowest baud rate used for data communications is 300, but normal telephone lines can transmit at baud rates up to 19,200. (The terms baud or bps used to describe transmission speeds are, for most purposes, the same.)

Flow control

When you take notes in class, if the lecturer speaks faster than you can write, then you lose track of what is being said and the notes become jumbled. You can, of course, politely ask him or her to pause for you to catch up. Data transmission is much the same, and it is essential for the receiver to be able to say in effect 'please wait a minute'. A typical example of this is transferring data from a personal computer to the printer. The PC can transmit data much faster than the printer can handle. Data is stored in the receiver's memory, known as the buffer, but there is a limit to the buffer's capacity. Flow control prevents the receiver being swamped by the amount of data arriving.

Let's see how this works:

Sender → data → receiver

Receiver (cannot handle more data)
→ sends message 'receiver not ready'

Receiver (processes the data) → sends message 'now ready' to receive more data

Sender → data → receiver

There are several methods of sending flow control characters within the protocol, and whichever method is used, these must be agreed between the sender and receiver.

Data bits

Computers hold all information in the form of binary numbers, and the smallest unit of information is the binary digit (bit) which is either a 0 or a 1. A group of *8 bits* is called a *byte,* and all the characters on the keyboard are represented in the computer by bytes. It is very similar to a code such as Morse code, and each computer uses a standard set of 0s and 1s to represent letters and numbers in order to be able to communicate. Most personal computers use *ASCII* – American Standard Code for Information Interchange. The original ASCII code used 7 bits, which provided 128 codes – more than enough to represent all the upper or lower-case letters on the English keyboard, as well as numbers, symbols and control codes (Figure 4.3). The eighth bit was added to the left and used as a parity bit (see **Parity** below).

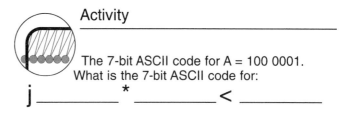

Activity

The 7-bit ASCII code for A = 100 0001. What is the 7-bit ASCII code for:

j _____ * _____ < _____

Parity

It is very easy for data to be changed or corrupted during transmission by interference or crosstalk, but accuracy should be one of the main benefits of a computer system, so it is essential that any discrepancies between the data sent and the data received are detected. One method of error checking is to add a *parity bit*. Both ends of the communication link agree that there must be either an *even* number of 1 bits in each byte of data or an *odd* number.

If even parity is chosen the 7-bit ASCII code is examined and if there is already an even number of 1 bits, then the eighth bit or parity bit is set to 0. If the character has an odd number of 1 bits, then the eighth or parity bit is set to 1 to make an even number of 1 bits. If odd parity is chosen, the eighth or parity bit will be set to an odd number of 1 bits. Even parity is most typical. The extra bit – either a 0 or 1 – is usually added to the left of the string. For example:

Character	ASCII code	Character	ASCII code	Character	ASCII code	Character	ASCII code
Null	000 0000	SOH	000 00001	STX	000 0010	ETX	000 0011
EOT	000 0100	ENQ	000 00101	ACK	000 0110	BEL	000 0111
BS	000 1000	HT	000 01001	LF	000 1010	VT	000 1011
FF	000 1100	CR	000 01101	SO	000 1110	SI	000 1111
DLE	001 0000	DC1	000 10001	DC2	001 0010	DC3	001 0011
DC4	001 0100	NAK	001 0101	SYN	001 0110	ETB	001 0111
CAN	001 1000	EM	001 1001	SUB	001 1010	ESC	001 1011
FS	001 1100	GS	001 1101	RS	001 1110	US	001 1111
SPACE	010 0000	!	010 0001	"	010 0010	#	010 0011
$	010 0100	%	010 0101	&	010 0110	'	010 0111
(	010 1000	)	010 1001	*	010 1010	+	010 1011
,	010 1100	_	010 1101	.	010 1110	/	010 1111
0	011 0000	1	011 0001	2	011 0010	3	011 0011
4	011 0100	5	011 0101	6	011 0110	7	011 0111
8	011 1000	9	011 1001	:	011 1010	;	011 1011
<	011 1100	=	011 1101	>	011 1110	?	011 1111
@	100 0000	A	100 0001	B	100 0010	C	100 0011
D	100 0100	E	100 0101	F	100 0110	G	100 0111
H	100 1000	I	100 1001	J	100 1010	K	100 1011
L	100 1100	M	100 1101	N	100 1110	O	100 1111
P	101 0000	Q	101 0001	R	101 0010	S	101 0011
T	101 0100	U	101 0101	V	101 0110	W	101 0111
X	101 1000	Y	101 1001	Z	101 1010	[	101 1011
\	101 1100	]	101 1101	I	101 1110	_	101 1111
-	110 0000	a	110 0001	b	110 0010	c	110 0011
d	110 0100	e	110 0101	f	110 0110	g	110 0111
h	110 1000	i	110 1001	j	110 1010	k	110 1011
I	110 1100	m	110 1101	n	110 1110	o	110 1111
p	111 0000	q	111 0001	r	111 0010	s	111 0011
t	111 0100	u	111 0101	v	111 0110	w	111 0111
x	111 1000	y	111 1001	z	111 1010	{	111 1011
I	111 1100	}	111 1101	~	111 1110	DEL	111 1111

Figure 4.3 ASCII table showing 7-bit code

Character	7-bit code	Even parity	Odd parity
a	110 0001	1110 0001	0110 0001
	⇓	⇓	⇓
	There are 3 '1 bits', i.e. an *odd* number	To make the parity *even* a '1 bit' is added to the left of the string	To keep the parity *odd*, a '0 bit' is added to the string
q	111 0001	0111 0001	1111 0001
	⇓	⇓	⇓
	There are 4 '1 bits', i.e. an *even* number	To keep the parity *even*, a '0 bit' is added to the left of the string	To make the parity *odd*, a '1 bit' is added to the left of the string

With even parity the receiving computer checks that the number of 1 bits is even, to detect any errors. If an odd number is detected then the data is rejected and a request for retransmission is made – known as error correction. This method does have limitations, in that if more than one bit is corrupted during transmission, then the parity may still be correct, but the data is wrong. Therefore most protocols use more complex methods of detecting and correcting errors.

Let's look at how the parity can be right, but still an error is made:

Sender		Receiver
1001 1001	$\rightarrow$ Parity is *even*, but there is a 1-bit corruption	1001 1000
Sender		Receiver recognises the parity is odd, so an error is detected and request made for data to be transmitted again
1100 0011	$\rightarrow$ 2-bit corruption	0100 0001
Sender		Receiver recognises that the parity is even, so no error is detected

Activity

1   Add an extra bit to the following bit strings to show both even and odd parity:

Character	7-bit ASCII code	Even parity	Odd parity
h	110 1000		
%	010 0101		
U	101 0101		
z	111 1010		

2   Check whether the following parity and the data received are correct:

Even parity

Character	Data sent	Data received	Parity correct?	Data correct?
G	0100 0111	0100 0111		
!	0010 0001	0000 0001		
w	0111 0111	0110 0101		
t	0111 0100	0110 0100		

Odd parity

Character	Data sent	Data received	Parity correct?	Data correct?
\	1101 1100	0110 1101		
<	1011 1100	1011 1100		
L	0100 1100	1100 1100		
5	1011 0101	1011 0101		

Stop bit

We have already looked at the flow control, by which the receiver informs the transmitter that it is ready to accept data or needs a pause. Similarly, the transmitter needs to inform the receiver when each character or byte of data begins and ends. If there were no start and stop bits, the data would become a meaningless stream of 0s and 1s. A start bit indicates the beginning of a byte, followed by the 8 bits of the character, and a stop bit indicates that the character is complete. These start and stop bits indicate the boundaries of a character, and it is important that both the transmitter and receiver recognise what are start and stop bits.

Start Bit	1 byte or character	Stop bit
☐	0011 1010	■

Terminal emulation

A mainframe computer is very large, may occupy a whole floor or even a whole building, is capable of storing and processing a vast amount of data, can cost millions of pounds, and is used by large organisations, such as governments, the armed forces, banks, and very big industrial corporations. It can support possibly hundreds of 'dumb' terminals – i.e. special terminals which look very similar to today's PCs, but they have no processing power of their own. The terminals are designed to operate with a particular mainframe, but cannot be used with a different type of mainframe, rather like the tapes manufactured for VCR, Betmax and Philips video recorders. Each terminal has its own features, which set the character and control codes used in transmission and reception, and these are built into the *hardware*.

As personal computers have become so widely used, it has been necessary and desirable to make today's PCs *emulate* (mimic or copy) the terminal standards, to enable them to communicate with mainframes. This is possible through special *software* programs, which provide a selection of types of mainframe computers. Just as a PC can link with different types of printers, it can link with different mainframes by selecting the right choice which has been coded into the software.

Modes of communication

If you wish to listen to music you have a variety of options available to you – you can go to a live concert, or listen to a recording on TV, play a tape, a record or a CD; indeed, you can even play back music on your computer. Similarly, there are different methods or *modes* of electronic communication, depending on the type of cable and its facilities.

Simplex

When communication is transmitted in one direction only, it is known as simplex. A good example of this is television – the TV station transmits information to the TV set, but no

information flows in the other direction. Another example is a sensor which feeds information to a computer, but does not need a response. For example, a sensor in a greenhouse transmits the temperature to the computer. If the temperature drops below a certain level, then the computer activates the heating system.

The sensor *sends* information to the computer, but the sensor itself receives no information *from* the computer.

Half-duplex

Sometimes information can flow in either direction, but **not** at the same time, which is known as half-duplex. An example of this mode of communication is a two-way radio such as Citizens' Band (CB), where you must switch between transmit and receive. No doubt you have seen this in films when someone says 'Roger', meaning message received, or 'Over', meaning, in effect, the communication link is being given *over* to the other person. Half-duplex transmission is often used between a central computer and terminals.

Full duplex

When information can flow in both directions simultaneously (e.g. a telephone conversation) it is known as full duplex. This is typically used for interactive computer applications. Examples include the 'tutorial' disk often provided with modern software, which shows users how to use the program and informs him or her if he or she has gone wrong.

Activity

The best way to understand an interactive computer application is to check whether the 'tutorial' option for one of the programs you use is available and try it out for yourself. Alternatively, your centre may have a keyboarding program which teaches you to touch type – if so, experiment with that.

To illustrate the three modes of communication, think about traffic systems:

Simplex is rather like a one-way street

Half-duplex is rather like a street with road works and temporary traffic lights – you can travel in both directions, but not at the same time

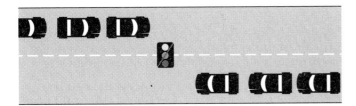

Duplex is similar to a normal two-way road

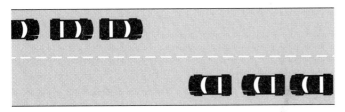

Parallel transmission

We discovered earlier that, using ASCII code, each character consists of 8 bits (0s or 1s). When this data is *transported* around the computer, it is moved in groups of 8, 16, 32 or 64 bits. All the bits are moved together along separate parallel wires or lines, these wires being known as a *bus*, and therefore transmission is very fast. Ideally they should all travel along in line and arrive together at their destination.

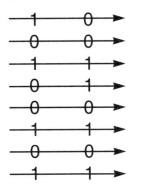

The group of wires together are known as a **bus**

In this example, the parity is set to even and if you look at the ASCII table, the first data string is *5* and the second *%* – so *5%* should be received

Figure 4.4 The data bits in parallel transmission all arriving together

The problem is that each wire will be slightly different, so that the bits may not arrive at exactly the same time, leading to errors.

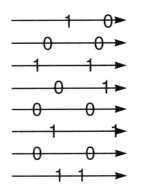

The data bits have become very jumbled, and there is a risk that the message received is not *5%*, but something entirely different

Figure 4.5 The same data bits arriving at different times. The risk is that errors will occur

It is important that the bits making up one byte of data do arrive together, so parallel transmission is only suitable for short distances such as inside the computer, where speed is an advantage. It can also be used outside the computer to disks and printers, but beyond a few metres becomes unreliable, and is also too expensive over long distances, because of the cost of large numbers of parallel wires.

To help you remember and understand the concept of parallel transmission, think about the Red Arrows giving an aerobatics display. The planes are trying to keep exactly in line with each other, but the further they travel the more difficult it is to stay synchronised.

Serial transmission

Serial transmission is slower than parallel, but is more accurate, reliable and less expensive over long distances. Each bit of the byte is sent down the wire in turn and reassembled at the other end (see Figure 4.6).

A special-purpose chip converts the parallel transmission inside the computer to serial transmission for the communication line.

> transmitter $0 \rightarrow 1 \rightarrow 1 \rightarrow 0 \rightarrow 0 \rightarrow 0 \rightarrow 0 \rightarrow 0 \rightarrow$ receiver

Figure 4.6 Serial transmission

Evidence assignment

Create a directory for Unit 4 and save all your work for this unit in the appropriate directory.

Please note: Be extra careful to save this assignment, as you will need to come back to it when you complete the evidence assignment for Element 4.3.

Computer Consultants Ltd have developed a name for giving excellent, personal service, and as a result the business is going from strength to strength. The managing director has decided that a series of fact sheets, which can be kept separate or be sections of a small booklet explaining the benefits to business of electronic communication and the jargon used, would be really useful. This could be left with clients after initial discussions or sent to prospective new clients.

1 First, create a file in which you word process the basic information about each of the topics. To obtain the information required you may:

■ use notes taken in class *
■ research from textbooks/magazines in the library
■ use data down-loaded from CD-ROM facilities available in your school or college, e.g. encyclopaedias on CD or newspapers stored on CD.

* NB: To be credited with Communication Core 2.2 it is essential that one piece of written material should be **hand written**. The notes taken in class or obtained from other research for this assignment can be used to cover this aspect of the range. It will be necessary for the notes to be written up neatly and legibly, and handed in with the assignment.

Your *first fact sheet* will describe electronic communication systems, and you must include information about all the following:

Method of communication	Suggested benefits
Mobile telephones	Sales representatives who travel around
CB and shortwave radio	Staff in remote situations (soldiers on active service, forestry workers)
Teletext and viewdata	Differences and benefits
Telephone/facsimile	What are the advantages/disadvantages of each method?

People also find some of the terminology used very difficult to understand, so your *second* and *third fact sheets* must include explanations of the following:

Protocols Baud rate, flow control, data bits, start and stop bits, terminal emulation	Protocols have to be agreed to communicate in a wide area network. You will learn more about WANs in Element 4.3, when you can complete this fact sheet
Modes of communication Simplex, half-duplex, full duplex, serial and parallel	These also link with wide and local area networks – WANs and LANs – so you may also wish to complete this fact sheet after studying Element 4.3

By **saving** and **printing** these two *uncompleted* fact sheets, and then returning to them for Element 4.3, you will provide evidence for IT Core 2.2, editing information.

2 Having selected appropriate information for your notes, you are now ready to design the fact sheets. Open a new file which must be produced in *landscape layout* and either in *two* or *three columns*, so that they can be easily folded, as shown on the next page.

You must also decide on the font style you wish to use for the fact sheets – make sure you choose a **different font from the default style in your system.**

You must import the text from your notes, but be imaginative in your design – remember people find diagrams and pictures much easier to understand than too many words. Perhaps you could select from ClipArt or scan suitable pictures to include in the fact sheet/ booklet. Once you have added pictures/ diagrams you will probably find you can reduce the amount of text needed to explain the topic.

Landscape layout showing 2 columns.

Fact Sheet

Landscape layout showing 3 columns.

Fact Sheet

Fact Sheet

NB: To be credited with the relevant IT core it is essential to:

- have two separate files (IT Core 2.3.1)
- create the fact sheets for task 2 in a different font and page layout, being careful to use appropriate headings and subheadings (IT Core 2.2.4)
- make sure you resolve any differences to obtain a consistent format (IT Core 2.2.6; 2.3.4).

3 Having presented the information in different ways, select which method best meets the requirements of the task and explain the reasons for your choice. Refer to the section for IT Core 2.3 on page 181 which you should find helpful when completing this task (IT Core 2.3.1).

Revision test

True or false?

1 Every mobile telephone has its own radio frequency.

2 Flow control prevents data being received too quickly to be processed.

3 Teletext is an interactive communication system.

4 Data sent at a baud rate of 600 will be received more quickly than data sent at 300 bps.

5 A videophone enables you to see as well as hear the other person.

Complete the blanks

6 A _____ is a method of communicating over a distance, and allows the sharing of resources and information by users.

7 A _____ machine is able to send text or pictures via a telephone line.

8 The smallest unit of information in a computer is a 0 or 1 and is known as a _____ , and a group of 8 _____ is known as a _____ .

9 Even _____ means that the number of 1s in a byte is even.

10 When a modern PC is made to behave in the same way as a terminal for a mainframe computer, the process is known as terminal _____ .

Short answer questions

11 Describe the facilities and benefits provided by a viewdata system used in a typical modern travel agent.

12 What is the purpose of a stop bit?

13 Explain the difference between simplex, half-duplex and full duplex.

14 Explain the difference between serial and parallel transmission and the advantages and disadvantages.

Use an electronic communication system

This element requires you to put into practice much of what you learnt about electronic communication systems for Element 4.1, at the end of which you should be able to:

1 prepare *information* to be transferred

2 describe how to *set up* an *electronic system* to enable information transfer

3 use an *electronic system* to transfer information

4 use an *electronic system* to receive and store information

5 apply *accuracy* and *security checks*.

Preparing information to be transferred

Information which is to be transferred electronically can be as a paper document or an electronic file transferred direct from the computer. For example, a fax machine may use a paper document or a file direct from PCFax, as described in Element 4.1.

It is essential that a paper document has clearly printed text or sharp pictures or diagrams for the fax machine to recognise and copy them. It is also important that the paper is in good condition in order to feed it through the fax machine. If the paper is very thin or the edges are torn, then it may get damaged as it feeds through the fax, or the machine may not accept the document at all. It is much the same as with a photocopying machine. If the original document is of poor quality, the photocopy will not be satisfactory, and if the paper is unsuitable, it will not go through the automatic feeder. If the image is poor or the fax machine does not accept the document, then you might have to obtain another copy in better condition, or if necessary retype it before sending.

When sending electronic files, it is important to ensure that you have selected the right file, by checking the file name. It is always important to spell check before sending, especially if it is a new file not previously checked.

Setting up an electronic system to enable information transer

We have already discovered in Element 4.1 that a number of issues have to be decided in order to transfer information electronically. These include the *mode of communication* and the *protocols*.

How much you will be able to do as a practical exercise for this performance criterion will depend largely on the facilities available at your centre and the costs involved. Alternatively, work experience may provide practical opportunities. However, you should at least be able to provide a description of the necessary requirements for a given situation.

Facsimile, as already indicated in Element 4.1, can either be used by feeding a paper document through the fax machine, or by transferring files directly from a fax program such as WinFax.

The process of sending a paper fax is as follows:

- make sure the fax machine is switched on
- feed the document into the fax machine – it can be face down or up depending on the machine

Figure 4.7 A phone and fax are often combined in one machine

- check the fax number for the receiving machine and then dial the number
- the document is scanned
- if the transmission is successful, a message is printed – e.g. 'Transmitted OK'.

Fax machines may be single or multifeed. With single feed, if you have several pages to send, you will have to wait for the first page to pass through the machine, and then lay the second page in place. With a multifeed fax, all the pages can be laid on top of each other and the fax will take them in one at a time – rather like the way a laser printer holds a store of paper, but takes one sheet at a time to print.

Programs such as WinFax allow you to store files and a fax *directory*. Instead of having to stand by a fax machine you can also choose to send the fax immediately or set a time when the computer will send the fax, which can take advantage of cheap-rate telephone calls.

The process for using PCFax programs is as follows:

- open or create the file you wish to send – it does not matter what type of file it is – word processing, spreadsheet, database, etc.
- select from the print setup, the fax printer – in this example WinFax on FAXMODEM
- set this as the default printer
- close the dialogue box and click on **OK**.

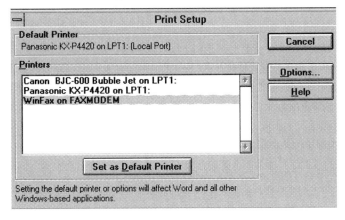

You will then see another dialogue box similar to the one opposite:

- type in the fax number
- if necessary indicate to whom it should be sent – if the fax already has a fax header sheet and all the details mentioned in Element 4.1, you will only need to enter the fax number
- click on **Send**.

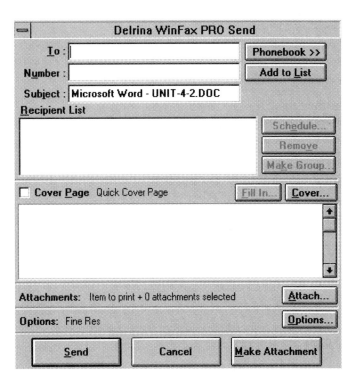

You will probably then find a box indicating that the number is being dialled. If the connection is made another message appears: 'handshaking'. This indicates that the transmitter is checking whether the receiver is ready, and the receiver says in effect, 'Yes, go ahead'. If all is well the fax is sent and when it is finished, a message indicating it is complete will be shown on screen.

Transferring, receiving and storing information

Communications software

If you are going to transfer information electronically, you do need the right software. Examples include Norton PCAnywhere and Procomm, but if you have Microsoft Windows, it already includes a program called Terminal, which is quite suitable for this purpose.

Terminal includes facilities such as:

- setting a telephone number which Terminal *dials*
- deciding the number of seconds to wait before a connect signal from the remote computer is received
- whether to redial if the connection fails
- specifying that the system bell rings when a successful connection has been made
- setting protocols, such as the baud rate or whether the parity should be odd, even or none
- setting a terminal emulation – i.e. selecting the type of mainframe to connect to.

(Check back to the last chapter if you don't understand any of these terms.)

Whichever communications software you are using, it will be necessary to configure it to match the requirements of the rest of your system. The configuration screen for Terminal looks like the one in Figure 4.8.

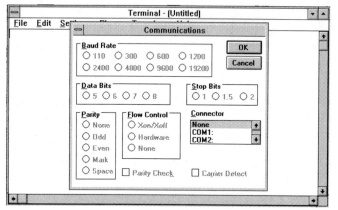

Figure 4.8 The configuration screen for Terminal

Modem

A modem, or modulator/demodulator, to give it its full title, is a translation device for electronic signals. The public telephone system was originally designed to carry sounds or analogue signals, but with the help of a modem, data or digital transmissions can also be made. (In this context the word *data* is used

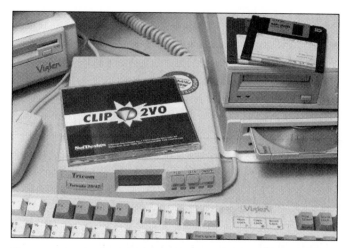

Figure 4.9 Personal computer peripherals on an office desk. At centre is a modem with a CD lying on it

for any information created on your PC, from word processing, to spreadsheet, to graphics.)

The digital or on/off signals transmitted by your computer are translated by the modem into continuous signals, which can be sent down the telephone line. Another receiving modem converts the telephone signal back into digital form, which can be understood by the receiving computer. The modem translates analogue (continuous) to digital (on/off) signals. If you find it difficult to understand, think of a light switch. A conventional switch is either on or off, just like the bits in computer transmission which are either 0s or 1s. However, if you use a dimmer switch the light level can be gradually increased or decreased in a continuous movement – analogue.

There is a wide range of modems available, but some modems are faster than others, and it is important to remember that one operating at less than 9,600 bps will be very slow to transfer data, resulting in large telephone bills.

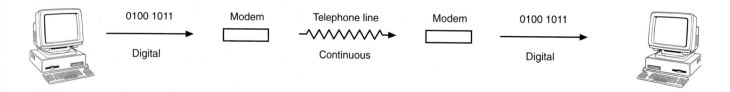

Technology is moving so quickly that even since this section of the book was first planned, new developments have been announced – PC-based videotelephony. Multi-Tech Computers of Ascot have developed a BT-approved modem, which combines videophone, answering machine, fax and data terminal all in one, with one dramatic added feature – those at either end of the telephone will be able to discuss and work on a document *simultaneously*. Until now modems could handle these areas one at a time, but now whilst the telephone conversation continues, documents or faxes can be exchanged from PCs at either end, and the two PCs can even display a *whiteboard* which can be used by either party for the display of slides or for writing on.

Figure 4.10 Using a PC videophone

Accuracy checks

Echo

The echo feature is a useful check on the accuracy of the data. The receiver copies back or *echoes* the data to the transmitting computer, which compares what it sent to what is received back. Sometimes the comparison is automatic and sometimes manual. In the latter case, data entry via the keyboard is transmitted direct to the receiving computer and then echoed back on to the screen. The operator makes a visual check on screen to confirm the data is correct.

Terminal provides a local echo facility. When on, the keystrokes are echoed back to the screen of the transmitting computer; when off, the keystrokes appear only on the screen of the remote computer.

Parity checks

Parity has been described in Element 4.1 and, as indicated above, Terminal provides the facility to set parity to even, odd or none. It is important to ensure that the parity of both transmitting and receiving computers is matching.

Security checks

Encryption

Encryption is simply transposing a message in plain text into a coded text. We are all probably familiar with children's puzzle books where a = 1, b = 2, c = 3 and so on. What do you suppose the following word is?

5 14 3 18 25 16 20 9 15 14

Yes, that's rather basic, but illustrates the concept. In practice encryption in a computer is much more complex, and involves scrambling the data at one end of the line, transmitting the scrambled data, and unscrambling it at the receiver's end. It is a very effective security check.

Lloyds Bank has teamed up with the British computer company Psion to pilot an electronic banking service called the Electronic Cheque Book. The service aims to attract both personal and business customers. With a Psion hand-held computer and a modem to connect to the telephone line, it will be possible to send electronic cheques to any bank in Britain. To maintain security, a special disk is required to access the system, and a password is needed to log on and to carry out any transactions.

User identity, passwords and privileges

These have all been discussed in some detail in Element 3.4. It is common practice when accessing a network to enter your unique user identity followed by a password, which you have chosen. In a commercial setting it is good practice to change the password frequently. It is also possible to include a password for specific files, which may allow other users to read the file, but not to change it, or alternatively prevent them from even loading the file, unless they have the password. You will notice that passwords usually appear as a series of asterisks. The data has been encrypted, to prevent someone casually observing your password.

Another common practice when establishing a network is to allow different privileges to different users. For example, in the college where I work, there is a 'p:\' drive on the network. Staff often save files on the p:\ drive, to make them available for students, e.g. the elements and performance criteria or the assignments for a particular unit might be saved on p:\ drive. Students can then load the file from the p:\ drive, but if they make any changes they must save it either on a floppy disk or on their own section of the network – the f:\ drive. This prevents students either accidentally or deliberately interfering with the original file – in other words, they do not have the same privileges as the staff.

Did you know?

The first automated homes are being tested by Scottish Hydro-Electric at Perth. Users will eventually be able to dial their home telephone and switch on the oven, draw the curtains or turn up the heating. The service also connects the telephone to a burglar alarm and smoke detector which, if activated, would send a signal to a prearranged telephone number. The electricity company will also be able to read the customer's meter remotely.

Evidence assignment

Ideally, to meet the performance criteria in this element, you will need suitable communications software, a personal computer with a spare communications port (COM port), a modem, a cable to connect the modem to the COM port and a suitable telephone socket. Connecting the hardware is a simple matter of plugging the cable into the COM port and the modem, connecting the modem to the telephone line and plugging the PC and modem into the power socket.

Chris Jones, the manager of 3L (Loose Limbs Leisure), really has been bitten by the computer bug, and has now asked you to install a fax machine and PCFax software. You have arrived to install the equipment

and want to check if it is working correctly, by sending a fax back to your office. You can work in pairs, one sending the fax and the other receiving it; then swap over. Your tutor will have to provide a fax number you can use to receive the message.

1 Use the word processor to:

- design a fax header sheet for the leisure centre
- create and save a suitable short message to send to a colleague at Computer Consultants Ltd, 108 King Street, Anytown AT2 3RJ.

2 ■ start up and set up the computer to send a fax
  ■ check that the fax machine is ready to receive messages
  ■ send the message created for task 1.

To hand in:

- copy of your word processed fax header sheet and message
- copy of this message received by fax machine.

3 Word process a suitable reply to indicate the message was received, using a fax header sheet for Computer Consultants Ltd:

- set up the computer to receive a fax
- set up the fax machine to send a fax
- send the reply to the computer
- close down the system.

To hand in:

- copy of your word processed fax header sheet and reply
- printout of this message received by PCFax software.

4 Chris Jones was very interested in what you were doing, and asked you to make notes on the procedure for future reference. Make sure you include full details, especially the accuracy and security checks which were required.

5A If you have Terminal available in Microsoft Windows, working in pairs, you can demonstrate electronic communication, even without the facility of a modem and a telephone line. Indeed, this can be very helpful to aid understanding of the protocols.

You will need a special cable, called a 'modem eliminator' to connect two computers via the COM ports – if your computers have two COM ports, this procedure will be simpler, but if not plug the cable into the COM port usually used for the mouse. (In this event you will have to use the keyboard commands to select menus, etc., rather than the mouse pointer.)

5B Having connected the computers, switch on and open Terminal – you may have an icon available, but if the Program Manager does not include the icon for Terminal, try searching the directories in File Manager for terminal.exe and load the program by double-clicking on this name.

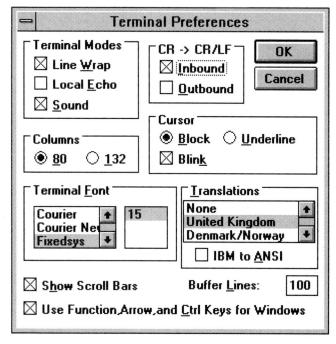

5C Take turns to be the one typing the message, and **make notes** of what happens in each of these stages, to use as evidence for your portfolio.

Type a simple message: 'This is an experiment to learn about protocols.'

On which computer does the message appear?

5D From the **Settings** menu on the *transmitting computer*, select **Terminal Preferences** and click on **Local Echo** – as shown in Figure 4.11 – and **OK**.

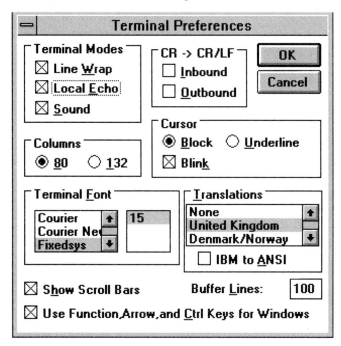

Figure 4.11 Terminal Preferences screen on transmitting computer

Type the message again, and this time you will find the text *echoed back* to the transmitting computer screen, where you can check for and correct any errors.

After the word 'protocols', add these words: 'such as baud rate'.

You will notice the additional words appear on the receiving screen, but you can edit the text only on the transmitting computer. Try deleting the words on the receiver – can you make any changes?

5E 'This is an experiment using Terminal to see what happens when a message is typed which needs two or three lines. Did you find a problem when this message was received? If so, describe the problem.'

Make a note of any difficulty.

5F From the **Settings** menu on the *receiving computer*, select **Terminal Preferences** and click on the box **Inbound**, as shown shown in Figure 4.12.

Type the message again and notice the difference.

Figure 4.12 Terminal Preferences screen on receiving computer

5G This time on *both* computers, from the **Settings** menu, select **Communications**, as shown in Figure 4.13.

You should find that the protocols – baud rate, data bits, parity, etc. – are the same.

Experiment with different baud rates – either slower or faster, but you must *both choose the same one.*

Click on the **Transfers** menu and select **Send Text File** – choose any text file already saved in your directory to send.

Notice how quickly the file is transferred when you choose a high baud rate. When you are sending data to a remote computer, the baud rate you choose will

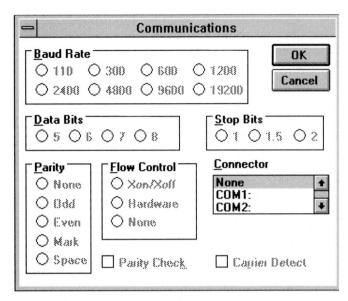

Figure 4.13 Communications screen

depend on the capability of the modem. Old modems worked at about 1,200 or 2,400 bps, but modems are now available which operate at speeds up to 28,800 bps. Anything over 14,400 will give an excellent performance.

5H This time, use a different baud rate on each machine, and type this message:

'Different baud rates have been chosen. Does this cause a problem?'

5I Experiment with the parity settings. Also from the **Settings** menu select **Communications**, but this time choose different parities for each computer, and note what happens when you type this message:

'This is an experiment to see what happens if the parity settings do not agree.'

If you are able to experiment with Terminal or another similar program, you will, it is hoped, find it much easier to understand computer protocols. If you are able to use Terminal via a modem, you can *dial* a phone number to which you wish to send a message.

6 Hand in the notes you made at each of these stages, explaining what happened.

Revision test

True or false?

1 A fax machine allows you to send data and pictures via a telephone line.

2 A parity bit tells the receiving computer when the data string has ended.

3 A modem converts analogue signals to digital form for transmission via the telephone line.

4 With a PCFax it is possible to transmit data directly without having a hard copy.

5 Encryption is a form of accuracy check.

Complete the blanks

6 _____ _____ is essential to transmit information electronically.

7 In order to communicate electronically, it is necessary to ensure that the _____ agree.

8 The use of _____ is one method of checking security.

9 When transmitting data electronically, if you use the _____ facility, the data will be sent to the receiving computer, and sent back to the transmitting computer, where it can be read and checked for accuracy.

Short answer questions

10 Why is it necessary to ensure that the protocols agree when using electronic communication?

11 Encryption prevents outsiders from reading the data. Explain what this means.

Element 4.3

Examine computer networks

After studying this chapter you should be able to:

1 describe *types of networks* and *services* available on networks
2 explain the *benefits* of networks
3 describe *components* of networks
4 produce diagrams of *network topologies*
5 describe *security requirements* for computer networks.

Types of networks

The two main types of networks, LANs and WANs, were introduced briefly in Element 4.1 (see page 131). Let's look at them in more detail.

Local area networks

A LAN is located in a building or where there may be several buildings on one site such as a school or college. A LAN can be set up anywhere it is practicable to link the system with *direct cabling*. The purpose of a LAN is to link physically a number of PCs to each other in order to share resources. The LAN can be as small as two PCs or may connect a large number of computers housed in several buildings, constrained only by the physical problems of laying direct cables. There are a number of ways in which the LAN can be linked logically, but each different network configuration (layout) is known as a *topology*.

The advantages of a LAN compared to having several stand-alone PCs include:

■ sharing the resources of disk drives, printers or a powerful computer
■ sharing software
■ accessing files stored on the network from any PC, without having to pass disks from one user to another
■ communicating with other PCs on the network – especially useful if they are not all in the same room.

The basic function of the network is to allow the user to send and receive messages:

■ from one PC to another, e.g. e-mail sent to other users on the network
■ between a PC and the file server, e.g. a request to run a program – Word
■ between a PC and the print server, e.g. a request to print a file.

Sometimes a LAN includes a mini or mainframe computer with a number of 'dumb' terminals connected to it, but commonly the PCs are connected to one powerful computer known as a *file server*. The file server is not used by any one person, but contains a large hard drive to store data which can be accessed very quickly by all the other PCs in the network. The network will probably also include a *print server* (sometimes the file server and print server will be the same), which is a PC connected to a printer or printers, and allows everyone using the network to print their work. If you are familiar with using a network, you will know that the print server in effect controls the requests for printing. As each print request is received, it is placed in a print queue and once the previous request has been completed, it commences the next one.

This is quite a difficult and complex topic, so let's look at a simple diagram to represent this activity. In Figure 4.14, the arrows represent the flow of information between the network components.

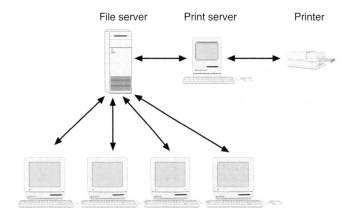

Figure 4.14 Flow of information in a local area network

Activity

It is highly probable that the computers you use at school or college are linked together in a LAN. Find out:

- whether the PCs you use are connected in a LAN
- if so, how many computers are linked
- whether they are linked to a mainframe, minicomputer or powerful PC
- whether the school or college uses any other LAN or WAN, possibly the administrative office.

Now list as many organisations as you can which will almost certainly use a LAN or WAN.

Wide area networks

A WAN is spread over a very large geographical area, even worldwide, and communication is made not by a physical cable between the computers, but by ordinary telephone lines supplied by companies such as British Telecom or Mercury, or via microwave or satellite link. The original telephone link – the Public Switched Telephone Network (PSTN) – operated at fairly low speeds, but more recently high-speed networks have been built. Public Data Networks (PDNs) are specifically for *data* transmission, whereas the Integrated Services Digital Network (ISDN) carries voice, data, images and video through a single *digital* line. With the PDN and ISDN systems, it is no longer necessary to convert the signal into analogue form for transmission.

There are two types of WANs – public wide-area networks and private wide-area networks. Public WANs are available to most of the public, usually through telephone and cable TV networks, whereas private WANs use privately owned or rented lines.

Cable television, mentioned in Element 4.1, is one examples of a public WAN. Another example, which you have probably heard of, is the Internet or *information superhighway*. The Internet is an international web of interconnected commercial, educational and government networks, which started in North America when a number of universities linked their computer systems together to exchange information. The Internet now enables the subscriber to receive information from or send information to anywhere in the world. There are around 30,000 networks connected to the Internet and an estimated 25 million users, the majority of whom live in Europe or North America. Any digital data, including sound, can be transmitted via the Internet. Indeed it is possible to obtain the details of elements, performance criteria, etc., for this course from the Internet and Heinemann puts out some GNVQ-type assignments on the Internet.

Many large organisations today will use a private WAN, established specifically for their own benefit. Let's look at how Video Manufacture plc could use the benefits of a wide-area network.

Electronic communications and Video Manufacture plc

Video Manufacture plc has a head office based in Bridgetown, factories in Wales and Scotland, and a nationwide sales force of 15 representatives and three regional managers. Each day the representatives were required to phone in to head office at least twice, but often it was impossible to find a public telephone box, and even when they did, on winter days it was cold and draughty making the calls. Therefore, the news that the sales force would be issued with mobile phones was greeted with great enthusiasm. The benefits and convenience were immediately obvious – representatives, managers and head office could all contact each other whenever it was necessary.

However, when the announcement was made that the sales force would be given portable computers, the reactions were very mixed. Many of the staff had never used a computer and were somewhat sceptical of the idea, so criticised it with comments like 'new-fangled things', 'not necessary', 'managed fine without them up to now', 'but I can't type'. However the sales director was adamant as he could foresee the advantages to be gained, and was convinced that once the *doubters* had been trained in their use, they would realise how the system would improve their efficiency and help them manage their accounts more effectively.

So how can a WAN assist sales representatives and regional managers?

A portable computer can *communicate electronically* with the head-office computer, by using a modem and the telephone line. Each user is given an individual password, which allows access only to those areas of the company's files relevant to that user. The portable is then very versatile and can be used by connection to the mains electricity supply, a battery or a car adapter connection to plug into the cigarette lighter.

The advantages are as follows:

■ Every evening the latest turnover figures can be downloaded from the head-office computer to update the data on the portable and saved.
■ Each month the representative has a sales target to meet, and if successful he or she will receive a bonus. Obtaining accurate daily sales figures makes it much easier to track progress.
■ The regional manager is responsible for the overall target of the region and can track progress of each representative on his or her team and the total sales for the region.
■ The representative no longer needs to maintain or rely on cumbersome files and computer printouts containing all the information relating to particular accounts. Representatives need to consider

   – historical data, e.g. how much was purchased this year against last year, month by month
   – sales by product
   – sales by value
   – whether payments are up to date or in arrears
   – back order status, e.g. last month 50 units were ordered, but only 25 were delivered, so the representative can check whether the outstanding quantity is still required.

Such information will be easily available and *up to date* on the portable.

■ When visiting a customer, the representative can check the current stock situation immediately – particularly useful if an urgent order is required.
■ At night the representative can upload the day's orders directly into the head-office computer, ready for the sales clerks to process the next day. An urgent order could even be made there and then at the customer's shop.

How can a WAN assist head office?

■ During the day any memos, price changes, special promotions, indeed any information that would normally be posted to the representative can be sent as a PCFax. Similarly the representatives and managers can communicate with head office or each other.
■ The faxes would be stored until the representative/manager logs on at night, when he or she would download and save the information.
■ On visiting a customer the representative could display on screen details of special promotions or price reductions.
■ With programs such as PowerPoint it is possible to create an eye-catching and interesting presentation display. The marketing department could create such a display to be downloaded into the representatives' portables, which they could then demonstrate to their customers.

Figure 4.15 Portable computers can be used to present product information to potential customers

Head office can also use the facilities of the WAN to communicate with the factories:

- each day's orders can be transmitted directly to a PC in the factory
- the factory can transmit details of each day's deliveries to head office
- the WAN can also be used for electronic mail and faxing between the various locations and also to send faxes directly to customers.

Activity

Many of you will be familiar with mail-order shopping. No doubt you, or another member of the family, has ordered something from a catalogue.

If you place the order by *telephone,* think about the process and how this might involve a WAN. First, write down the steps which you take to place the order and then decide if and where the mail-order company might be using a WAN.

Did you know?

By 1996 thousands of British people may be able to do their shopping from their armchair, by pointing a remote control at their television. Interactive television shopping will make this possible.

All you need is a set-top box similar to that used for cable television and a customised remote control. If you have a computer, an added bonus included in the cost of rental is an incorporated modem which allows access to the Internet. The only snag is that so far the choice of products is limited as few retailers have opened a store in the online shopping centre.

Activity

- Look in newspapers and magazines for articles about the Internet.
- Discuss what you have learnt with the rest of the group.
- Does anyone in the group already have access to the Internet?
- What use might you make of the Internet?
- List three specific examples of organisations which use private WANs.

Types of service available on networks and their benefits

The main services available on networks are:

- bulletin boards
- conferencing
- electronic mail
- file transfer
- interacting with databases.

The main benefits are sharing the hardware and software resources and sharing the data.

Did you know?

A service launched in November 1995 promises to offer worldwide telephone calls for little more than the price of a local UK call – by using the Internet. Free World Dialup, a consortium of Internet companies and individuals, allows anyone with a sound-card, microphone and a modem to initiate a call to telephone users anywhere in the world. Previous Internet telephone services have been possible only between two computer users. The big difference with this new system is that you start the call from a computer, but it can be routed to a normal phone.

Bulletin board services (BBS)

Bulletin boards are rather like electronic notice boards and allow you to look up messages left by others, or to read information, some of which is like reading a newspaper on screen instead of on paper. A typical provider might be a manufacturer, especially hardware and software companies which provide information about their products and in return you might report back any comments or problems. Sometimes software is available to 'download', but this can lead to virus *infection* of your system. Some bulletin boards are free, but usually you must pay a subscription. A notice board is a very useful way of giving information – no doubt there are several in your school or college – but relies on someone physically being able to stand in front of it, whereas a bulletin board can be accessed wherever you are, provided you have the necessary hardware and software.

Conferencing

For many years BT has had the facility to link a number of people together (rather than just the usual

Figure 4.16 A video-conference in progress

two-way link) so that all of them can hold a conversation. Following from this video-conferencing centres were established, where both audio and visual links are possible, although this is expensive. Computer conferencing allows a number of computers to be linked together so that the subscribers can *discuss* a particular subject. This facility is especially useful to researchers who wish to share ideas worldwide, providing a rapid exchange of ideas, almost as good as communicating face to face.

Electronic mail

E-mail is like an electronic letter, sent via the computer instead of the postal service. It is a very sophisticated method of electronic transfer, where messages and documents can be *sent* from one computer to another using a modem and a telephone line. Mail prepared on a word processor or a document scanned into the computer can be transferred either immediately if it is urgent, or can be stored along with the e-mail address of the receiving computer, and the computer automatically transfers the mail at night. Remember, computer time is cheaper at night. It's very much like taking all the mail to the post box at the end of the day, except that transfer is immediate. Just like the letters which come through our letter boxes, electronic mail waits until the recipient *opens* his or her electronic mailbox. Sometimes electronic mail is sent to an intermediate computer which is always available – a bit like the sorting office at the post office – where it is held until the receiving computer is ready to accept it.

More and more organisations are including an e-mail address, as well as the usual postal address and

telephone number, on their letter heading. Guinness advertisements now carry an e-mail address; the BBC Radio 4's *Today* programme has an e-mail address. Sending the electronic mail at night can be very useful to companies which service/repair household appliances – washing machines, tumble dryers, freezers, etc. The e-mail is sent at a set time at night to the service engineer's computer and in the morning he or she can check exactly which calls need to be made.

File transfer

File transfer might simply mean sending a file to the printer, or using a network to transfer data electronically between computers remote from each other. Special software allows fast transfer of files and checks for and corrects any errors occurring during the transfer. Sometimes the transfer is made automatically without the user even being aware it has happened. You must:

- know where you wish to send the data, e.g. which printer, a fax number, an e-mail address
- make sure the two devices are connected
- name the file to be transferred
- transfer the file
- close the connection – especially if you are using a telephone link, or it will become quite expensive.

If you were able to use Terminal as described in Element 4.2, you may already have used the file transfer facility (see the evidence assignment for 4.2, task 5G).

Interacting with databases

Databases and the facilities available to banks and sales organisations have been covered extensively in Unit 3. Central databases provide a large store of information, and can be accessed or updated from a wide geographical area. These shared resources are stored centrally, but are available locally, and are continually updated. We considered in some detail the benefits of a centralised database when booking a holiday or making a flight reservation (see page 91).

Different departments of an organisation can also benefit from accessing a range of services on a large system. A central database of company information will allow simultaneous access to different users. At any one time the marketing department might be using the customer file for names and addresses for a mail shot on a new promotion, whereas the accounts department is checking which customers are behind with payment, whilst the administration department might be adding a new account to the file. If the database was stored on disk passed from PC to PC, each user would have to wait until the other had finished with the disk.

Central services

The security of a network and user-support services can be provided by a central specialist or group of specialists. Security is of particular importance and is more difficult to control if an organisation is using a large number of individual PCs, when each individual user has to take responsibility for the security and confidentiality of his or her particular computer.

The network manager will take responsibility for loading the software on to the network and for providing users with appropriate access rights in respect of sensitive data, which helps to ensure that neither the copyright nor data protection laws are infringed. Individual users or departments can also set read/write privileges on files as necessary for added security. The network manager will also ensure that files are backed up regularly, unnecessary files are deleted and that the network runs smoothly. When problems do occur he or she can help resolve them for the user, whereas when organisations had only stand-alone PCs, the user had little or no support.

Figure 4.17 Teamwork builds on the strengths of the various team members

It was also commonplace for different PCs to have different software programs – e.g. one person used Word, another WordStar and yet another WordPerfect. On a network it would be more likely that everyone uses the same type of word processing, spreadsheet, database program, etc., with the result that staff are able to share their knowledge of the programs.

Teamwork

As indicated above a shared network allows many people access to the data at the same time and also enables a number of people to work together on a project, keeping in close touch with other members of the team and their progress. Some team members will be good at different aspects of the job, and teamwork can take advantage of and build on the various strengths of the team members, each helping the other and sharing and resolving problems.

Shared resources

A stand-alone system requires a powerful PC to run modern software efficiently, and also its own printer. A network requires a powerful file server, but this is not necessary for each of the individual terminals, which can therefore be far less expensive. In addition a large number of terminals can share just one or two printers. It is also convenient to store data and software on one machine (the file server) and for all users to access the data and the printers through the file server. Data is an essential resource to all organisations, and it is much easier to transfer data via a network than passing diskettes between users. It is also very difficult to ensure that each stand-alone PC holds updated files, whereas shared data in a network – as in the travel agency – enables every user to have access to the latest information.

Network components

As has already become evident, a network is simply linking together a series of PCs to share facilities of software and printing. Communication across the network can be achieved by microwave or satellite link, necessary to send signals over long distances for a WAN, or by some type of cable, which would be typical in a LAN.

Cabling

The type of cable used to connect a network has a major impact on the speed and accuracy with which it operates, and the ease of installation – a very thick cable being difficult to embed in or along walls. The three main types are as follows:

- Twisted pair, similar to telephone wire, is cheap but suffers from electronic interference and the transmission rate of data is slow, approximately 64,000 bps, e.g. phone calls, low-quality images.
- Coaxial is of high quality, well insulated and data is transmitted much faster and more accurately than twisted pair. It can carry between 10 million and 1,000 million bps, e.g. several channels of high-definition TV.
- Fibre optic is the latest development, very fine but capable of carrying 2,400 million bps, e.g. hundreds of conventional TV channels, 30 high-definition TV channels, all the world's telephone calls at once (almost!).

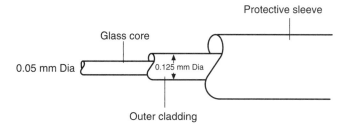

Figure 4.18 Optical fibre

File servers

As already explained the file server is a powerful PC or larger computer (mainframe or minicomputer) which stores the software required by the workstations, including the network operating system, which *supervises* or *controls* the operation of the network. Files are *downloaded* from the file server to the workstation and *uploaded* from the workstation to the file server.

Print servers

Sometimes the file server also controls the printing on the network, but often there is a separate PC controlling one or more printers. Requests from workstations for printing are sent from the file server to the print server and placed in a print queue. Different types of printers are often available – dot matrix for draft quality, laser for high quality or colour for special effect – in which case the print server will also direct the print request to the appropriate printer.

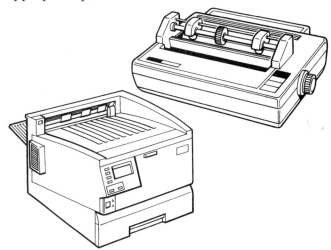

Figure 4.19 Dot-matrix printers may be used for draft quality, and laser printers for high quality printing

Workstations

A workstation is a single-user PC connected to the network. Generally workstations do not have their own hard disk, but use the facilities of the file server.

Network cards

To access the network, each PC must be fitted with a network card. This is similar to a printed circuit board, which slots into the CPU (central processing unit), and contains all the necessary electronics and connections to allow the PC to link into the network.

Network software

The average computer user is familiar with application software – word processing, spreadsheet, database, graphics, desk-top publishing programs – but computers also require an operating system which:

- controls the loading and running of programs
- controls the use of peripherals such as disk drives and printers
- makes the hardware easier to use and helps the operator decide what to do by displaying simple messages on screen, e.g. printer out of paper
- allows formatting of disks, files to be renamed, copied, backed up, etc.
- maintains a directory of files stored on disk
- makes sure no problems arise but tries to overcome them if they do.

MS-DOS is a very familiar disk-operating system which was designed for stand-alone PCs. Similarly a network requires its own software to operate the system. Novell's Netware is one method which is a separate networking operating system in charge of the operating systems of the individual PCs. In addition to the above facilities, network software can:

- produce a log of the programs as they are run, recording who has used the computer, for how long and what they did
- charge the appropriate account if the user is paying
- organise the use of hardware and software facilities, ensuring that everyone has a fair share, but giving precedence to those users with a *high* priority over those with *low* priority
- maintain security.

Network topologies

The network topology is the way in which the *nodes* – a node may be a computer or another device such as a printer – in a network are arranged. The way in which the network is arranged affects the way in which it operates. Let's look at the four topologies required for this course.

Bus network

In a bus network all the nodes (devices) share a single cable (see Figure 4.20). The messages are transmitted in either direction from one point along a single *bus* from any PC to any other. Problems arise when more than one user wishes to send a message at the same time. To overcome this the station checks first whether the bus is busy. If it is, then the station has to wait.

A bus network is cheap and easy to install. Extra workstations can be added without disrupting the network, and it is also fairly easy to locate faults in the cable. However, if there is a problem with the cable the whole network fails, and if too many work-stations are attached to the network, performance is slow.

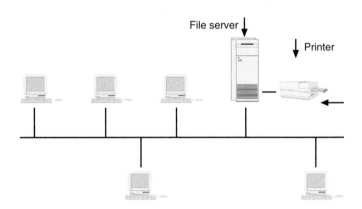

Figure 4.20 Diagram of a bus network

Ring network

A ring network is a similar to a bus network with *ends* joined up (see Figure 4.21), and may or may not depend on a central file server. All the computers within the network can communicate with each other, but messages are transmitted in only one

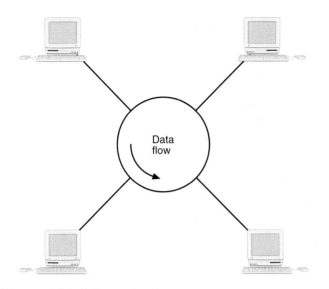

Figure 4.21 A ring network

direction, which provides fast, simple transmission. A *message token* (a unique reference) addressed specifically to the destination computer is sent around the ring. Each node checks the token address, with the addressed node accepting the message. The drawback of a ring network, just as with the bus network, is that if there is a fault at any point in the system, the whole network breaks down.

Star network

The main difference in a star network compared to a bus or ring topology is that each node is connected individually to the file server (see Figure 4.22). The server handles signals in turn as they are received from the workstations.

A star topology has a good, reliable performance even when the network is busy, and there are no *collisions* of data, because each station is served by its own cable. A breakdown in one cable does not affect the other stations, and it is simple to add workstations without interfering with the network. However, as cable can be a significant cost of a network, a star topology may be expensive to install.

Mesh network

Each node in a mesh network is connected to a number of other nodes (see Figure 4.23), and if the mesh is fully connected, each node is connected to every other node in the system. This topology is suitable only for a very small network, as data usually has to pass through one or more nodes before reaching its destination.

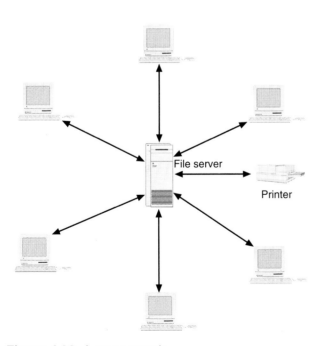

Figure 4.22 A star network

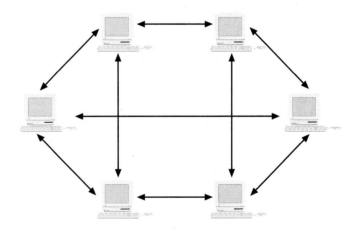

Figure 4.23 A mesh network

155

Activity

1 Does the ring network shown in Figure 4.21 include a file server?
2 Is the mesh network illustrated in Figure 4.23 fully connected?
3 If you use a LAN at your school or college, find out which topology has been used to configure it.
4 Draw diagrams of the four network topologies, and explain briefly how each works and its advantages and disadvantages.

Security requirements

The data held on an organisation's computer is one of its most valuable assets, and the more widespread the use of networks becomes, the greater the risk of interference from unauthorised users. We frequently read about cases of computer hackers (someone who obtains illegal access to computer data) or viruses which corrupt apparently secure systems. There are a number of ways in which computer security can be maintained.

User identity, passwords and access rights

Entering a user identity number and password is a common method of accessing a network, and can also be used to limit the user's access to certain information. Sometimes files are made *read* only, which means that the user can look at the file, but cannot make any changes to it, unless it is saved under another name, thereby keeping the original file intact. To obtain *write access* it is necessary to know the password. If the file has been saved using a password for both read and write access, then the file cannot be opened unless you know the passwords. These issues have already been covered in detail in Element 3.4 (see page 120).

Legal requirements

The law relating to data protection, copyright and health and safety has also been discussed in Element 3.4 (see pages 120–123). In 1990 another Act came into force, the Computer Misuse Act, in order to deal with the problems of hacking and viruses. The Act made it illegal to:

- access data without authorisation
- access data without authorisation with the intention of using the data for criminal purposes
- modify data without authorisation.

The latter includes introducing a virus into a system or creating a new virus, even if it is not known which systems the virus will *infect*.

Topic	Some suggestions are given to help get you started
Local area networks	Advantage of sharing resources/data by linking PCs in a business – check the range for Performance Criteria 2
Network topologies	Diagrams of three types
Network components	You might be able to include the components (or some) with the diagrams of topologies
Wide area networks	Benefits of communicating with sales force/customers and obtaining information from commercial databases. The whole topic of WANs could be covered as a series of sheets – starting with what a WAN is, then continuing with the protocols and mode of communication covered in Element 4.1
Types of services	These could be linked to WANs
Security requirements	Explain the range – try to include suitable screen dumps, such as the one illustrating passwords shown in Element 3.4 on page 120. (You can usually print what is shown on screen by pressing the **PrtSc** key. This copies the screen dump into the clipboard, which can then be pasted into the required place in your fact sheet. You are probably familiar with resizing images by clicking with the mouse and dragging the double arrows. Screen dumps can also be *cropped* – i.e. the unrequired sections removed – by holding the shift key whilst dragging the *handles* with the mouse. The double arrow will change shape to look rather like this:

Figure 4.24 Topics for your evidence assignment

Evidence assignment

1 Complete the series of fact sheets you have started for Element 4.1 and/or design further ones to cover the topics in Figure 4.24.

Make sure you save your work at regular intervals in the right directory, using a suitable file name, print and make a back-up copy.

2 This task provides evidence for Communication Core 2.1 – Take part in discussions. It should be noted that, in order to cover the range, on this occasion some members of the audience should include people who do not know you.

With the help of your tutor, organise a debate on the issue:

'Thousands of children worldwide are being corrupted by obtaining pornographic material via the Internet.'

Invite some guests to attend, and agree who will propose the motion (in a debate the topic to be discussed is called the *motion*) and who will second it. In order to participate you will need to research information on the problems of access to pornographic material via the Internet. Look for relevant information in computer textbooks, newspaper articles or magazines, making notes, which **should be handed in** to your lecturer after the discussion. Newspaper articles will probably be the most useful source for your research for this task. If you have a CD-ROM for *The Times* newspapers in your library, it will be easy to search for a suitable article,

When undertaking your research, consider the following points:

- What evidence is there that pornographic material is available on the Internet?
- What methods are available to limit access to such material?
- Do you feel this is a genuine problem or something hyped up by the press?

Having completed your research you should prepare for the debate by:

- summarising the information you have researched into concise points
- deciding whether you agree or disagree with the motion
- listing your reasons for your decision
- studying the section on Communication Core 2.1 starting on page 179.

During the debate you should:

- make your points clearly, taking notice of the advice given in the section for Communication Core 2.1
- listen to other people's points, taking notice of the advice given in the section for Communication Core 2.1
- if you disagree, challenge their statements quoting suitable evidence.

At the end of the debate, take a vote on whether the group agrees or disagrees with the motion.

Did you know?

There is so much concern about pornographic material being available to children via the Internet that software has been designed to censor and filter out obscene material. Parents can select 'trigger' words such as 'sex', and if the child types in or receives an electronic message including the specified words, the system automatically closes down. There are, however, teething problems – a demonstration was thwarted when the word 'Middlesex' caused a shutdown.

Revision test

True or false?

1 It is possible to transmit data between cities using a LAN.

2 A WAN allows a user to access information from a database located in a different city or even another country.

3 A bulletin board is rather like a notice board, but it is available on a computer.

4 Electronic mail can be sent only if the person receiving it is logged on to his or her computer.

5 More data can be sent more quickly using fibre-optic cable.

Complete the blanks

6 LAN stands for _____ _____ _____ , whereas WAN stands for _____ _____ _____ .

7 The computers or workstations in a LAN are physically connected using a _____ .

8 The computers or workstations in a WAN are connected via the ——————— ——————— , ——————— or ——————— link.

9 Name four different network topologies: ——————— , ——————— , ——————— and ——————— .

10 The advantage of a ——————— network is that if the cable to one workstation breaks, the other workstations are not affected.

Short answer questions

11 Explain the difference between a LAN and a WAN.

12 In order to maintain security of the network, access rights or privileges are sometimes allocated. What does this mean?

13 Sometimes files are write-protected. What do you understand by this term?

Element 4.4

Use a computer network

As with Element 4.2, this element is largely practical and, if you are using a network, the evidence for it should be provided naturally through the course of producing assignments.

After studying this section you should be able to:

1 access a computer network and observe *security procedures*

2 create your own subdirectory structure on a network

3 *manage your own files* on a network

4 access network applications

5 create, edit, save and print data files using a network.

Accessing a computer network and observing security procedures

It is very probable that your school or college uses a LAN of PCs and RM Nimbus or Novell Netware are among the most popular. If you are using a network, you will have been given a user identity and you will have chosen your own password. When you log in to the system, you will have access to certain programs and also to disk space to save your own work. If you keep your password secret, other students will not be able to interfere with or copy your files. Ideally passwords should be changed at regular intervals.

We have also looked at security procedures in some detail in Element 3.4 and Element 4.2.

Did you know?

An American microchip manufacturer has recently launched a new product that seems like something only previously heard of in old spy films – a ring that stores your identity, opens doors and gains access to computers. These digital decoder rings have hidden computer memories for storing photographs and passwords. Inside each ring is a touch button with a 64 k memory – equivalent to approximately three pages of type. Using a special probe, the contents can be transferred to a computer in four seconds.

Creating your own subdirectory structure on a network

When you file documents in a filing cabinet, it is important to have structure and organisation to the filing. If all the papers are thrown in the drawers in no particular order, then it is very difficult to find a specific document when you want it. Sometimes filing is done alphabetically, numerically or geographically and, if each cradle in the filing cabinet is labelled sensibly, this will make it easy to find what you want.

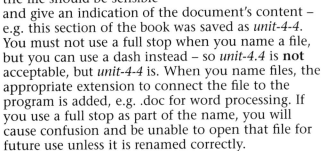

If you are using Windows software, you will notice that the icon for the file manager is a filing cabinet, and organising electronic files on a computer is much the same as organising paper files in a filing cabinet.

In the first place the name of the file should be sensible and give an indication of the document's content – e.g. this section of the book was saved as *unit-4-4*. You must not use a full stop when you name a file, but you can use a dash instead – so *unit-4.4* is **not** acceptable, but *unit-4-4* is. When you name files, the appropriate extension to connect the file to the program is added, e.g. .doc for word processing. If you use a full stop as part of the name, you will cause confusion and be unable to open that file for future use unless it is renamed correctly.

The next important step to *good housekeeping,* as it is described, is to create directories. A directory can be compared to one of the drawers of the filing cabinet. Appropriate directories for this course might be the names of the mandatory units. Once the directories are created, then all the work relating to the particular unit should be saved in the directory for that unit. Later on when you have perhaps 20 or 30 files relating to the course, it is much easier to find work if it is organised in this way.

Figure 4.25 is an example of a File Manager screen with directory tree for units 1, 2, 3 and 4, and list of files saved in the unit 4 directory.

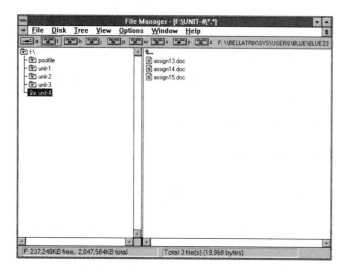

Figure 4.25 A File Manager screen with directory tree

Managing your own files on a network

The importance of having *back-up* copies of your work cannot be stressed enough. Apart from saving your work on the network, it is essential to *copy* the files on to disk. In a business environment back-up copies would be maintained in another building to avoid loss by theft or fire. From time to time it is also important to *delete* any unwanted files. However, do be certain that the contents are no longer required!

If work has been saved in the wrong directory, then it is a simple matter to *move* the file to the correct place.

File protection

As shown in Element 3.4, when saving files you can protect their security with passwords (see page 120). Most LANs also enable users to set up rights to their files and subdirectories, but establishing or changing access rights is usually the job of the network manager.

Accessing network applications

If you are using a network, then you will inevitably access at least two network applications, as required in the evidence indicators for this unit, and you will also automatically create, edit, save and print files using a network.

Evidence assignment

Much of the evidence for this element will be through direct observation, which can be recorded on a log sheet, as in the example shown on page 161.

1 From the **File Manager** show the list of files *both* on the hard drive and the floppy drive, by selecting **Window** and **Tile**.

2 Print a screen dump showing the directories for both the network and your disk *before* housekeeping activities – it should look something like the one in Figure 4.26.

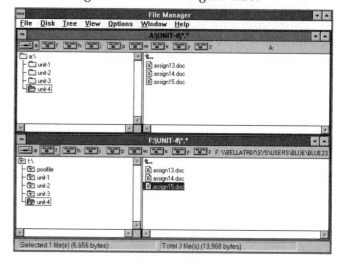

Figure 4.26 File Manager screen showing directories for both network and disk

You will notice that, although a directory for unit 4 has been created on the floppy disk in a:\ drive, no files are listed, so back-ups of assignments 13, 14 and 15 have not yet been made.

3 If you have not already done so, create a directory for each of the mandatory units, called unit-1, unit-2, unit-3, unit-4. It should look something like Figure 4.27.

Figure 4.27 Directories for each unit

4 Delete any files which are no longer required, but **be careful not** to delete any files related to assignments.

5 Reorganise the remaining files by moving them into the appropriate directory.

6 Copy the directories and files on to a disk as a back-up.

7 Print a screen dump showing the directories for both the network and the disk *after* undertaking housekeeping activities, show your tutor or lecturer your directories on screen and ask him or her to sign the log below.

8 Select one file and use a protection password (refer back to Element 3.4, page 120) and again demonstrate the password to your lecturer and ask him or her to sign the log.

9 Investigate the network and establish which areas have different levels of access privilege. For example:

■ What user areas have been established on the network?

■ Do staff accounts have facilities unavailable to students?

■ Are certain files *read only* to students?

■ Is it possible to *copy* these files to your own account?

■ If so, is it then possible to *write to* the files?

10 Write a short commentary on network protection procedures established in your school or college to ensure that copyright of software and confidentiality of users are maintained.

Revision test

True or false?

1 The problem with networks is that you cannot stop everyone having access to your files.

2 It is permissible to copy software for back-up purposes only.

3 If you make a file 'read only', this stops other people looking at your file.

4 It is legal to copy software as long as you do not charge someone for a copy.

5 Directories and sub-directories help to organise files.

Complete the blanks

6 You should _____ _____ files on a regular basis to guard against data loss.

7 If you _____ _____ files, you cannot open them unless you know the password.

8 Every time a user needs to access the network system, it is necessary to _____ .

9 Some network users are not allowed access to certain files containing personal data. This is to comply with the _____ _____ _____ .

Evidence log sheet for _____

Activity	Signed	Date
Log in procedures observing security procedures		
Unwanted files deleted		
Back-up created		
Subdirectories created		
File protection password		
Two network applications accessed: 1 _____ 2 _____		
Name of data files created, edited, saved and printed using the network applications above: 1 _____ 2 _____		

Communication

The ability to communicate clearly, easily and fluently, both orally and in writing, is crucial to every part of life, which is why this core skill is so important. You may be brilliant with numbers and an absolute genius with the computer, but you still need to be able to speak to colleagues/customers/friends and to write messages/letters in a manner suitable to the working world or to your personal life, and be aware of the difference. At the end of this course you should be quite a competent computer operator, but if you attend a job interview muttering, mumbling, answering just 'yes' or 'no' whilst looking at your feet, you are very unlikely to have the opportunity to show this prospective employer how capable you are!

At the end of this section you will find a tracking sheet for Communication Core Level 2, to help you identify which evidence assignments provide opportunities to collect evidence towards particular performance criteria. It is worth repeating that even if one assignment enables you to *tick all the performance criteria* of an element, you will need the other pieces of evidence to cover *all the range*.

Element 2.1 Take part in discussions

For this element you are expected to:

1 make contributions which are relevant to the *subject* and *purpose*
2 make contributions in a way that is suited to the *audience* and *situation*
3 confirm that you have understood the contributions of others
4 make contributions which take forward (or help to make progress in) the discussion.

A discussion can be as simple as two students working on an assignment together, or a lecturer checking a student's portfolio and agreeing the strengths and weaknesses, or as formal as a staff meeting or a debate in the Houses of Parliament – although sometimes the latter can seem more like a shouting match than a discussion!

At this point you may be thinking something like this: 'I came on this course to learn about computers. I know how to talk – why should I bother with all this? What a waste of time!'

But wait a minute – have you ever had to telephone an employer to ask for a work experience placement? Many students faced with such situations suddenly realise a *business* telephone call is very different from chatting to a friend, and they don't find it easy. Have you ever listened to an explanation where the person goes on and on and is very confusing, whereas someone else explains clearly and concisely? To whom do you prefer to listen and which kind of person do you want to be? You must have dealt with sales assistants who are helpful, friendly, smiling and those who are grumpy, miserable and seem annoyed to be interrupted by a customer wanting to pay! In which manner do you like to be served?

If you are shy or quiet and don't like speaking publicly, don't panic; aggressive, loud people are not good communicators, because they rarely *listen* to others, and listening is just as important as speaking. Like all skills, it takes practice to communicate orally in the best manner for a particular situation. We learn to speak in the family setting, so talking to family and friends (the informal situation) comes fairly naturally. When speaking in a formal situation (work, dealing with the bank, making a complaint in a shop) it is often very useful to prepare, or think through what you are going to say beforehand.

Activity

1 On this occasion do not prepare beforehand, work in pairs with someone you do not know particularly well in the group, and tell him or her about:

- your family – whether you have any brothers/sisters/aunts/uncles
- why you chose this course
- what you hope to do at the end of it
- any hobbies or interests you have.

The listener must not make written notes, but should check at intervals that he or she has correctly understood the speaker. Join up with another pair and the two listeners then take turns to introduce the speakers. The person being introduced should listen and check the facts are correct, and **at the end** (do not interrupt) correct any errors and also add any important points that he or she forgot to mention originally.

2 Choose a topic which interests you, a sport or hobby, a favourite personality, television programme, your best holiday. This time think about the topic and make some notes before you speak, planning the key points you wish to make and the order you wish to present them. **Do not** refer to your notes whilst describing your chosen topic to your partner. The listener should be thinking of questions to ask once you have finished speaking.

Afterwards, evaluate together honestly how accurate you were, whether you missed anything important you would have liked to include and whether the information was given clearly (unambiguously).

Accuracy and clarity

When communicating it is important:

- to be accurate
- to make sure enough detail is given – 'Come round next week', but when next week? – but not so much that the facts become blurred

- not to be ambiguous or confusing – your boss says 'Make sure those new stands are delivered to Blakes' as he rushes out to a meeting, but there are four branches!

The advantages of oral communication are that it is direct and immediate feedback is received – no waiting for a reply. The disadvantage is that mistakes may be more difficult to correct. You may not notice that you made a mistake – said the 4th when you meant the 5th, whereas when you write you can check the content, correcting any errors, before sending it, and no one else will know you made a mistake.

Body language and tone of voice

One of the advantages of oral communication is that you can see the person's body language, often called non-verbal communication, and hear the tone of his or her voice. Also you can see the reactions of the listener, and immediately correct any wrong impressions you have conveyed, both of which are impossible with written communication.

Body language generally consists of the following:

1 *The expression on your face* – something cheeky or even rude can be quite acceptable if it is said with a smile.

Figure C.1 The same words expressed in a different way can carry contrasting messages

2 *Eye contact* – you don't have to stare constantly, but someone who never looks you in the eye can give the impression of being insincere, untruthful or just shy and nervous.

3 *Personal space* – similarly the person who comes close to you may be friendly and relaxed, but the person who stays back may also be shy rather than unfriendly. Leaning forward when listening tends to show real interest, but is also an indication that you know the person well.

4 *Gestures* – if your mother/father puts an arm round your shoulder and gently says 'You shouldn't have done.....', he or she is much more likely to gain a positive response than if he or she shouts and wags a finger at you.

Study the two pictures in Figure C.1. Is there a difference even though the question is the same?

We all know that the same words said in a different tone of voice and with different mannerisms can convey a quite different message. 'Why did you do that?' said in a friendly, pleasant way can show genuine interest, wanting to find out, but shouted in an angry voice, whilst shaking a fist, indicates annoyance that this act has been committed, and is more likely to result in an aggressive or defensive response.

When taking part in discussion, the tone of voice and body language you use are very important. The person who makes his or her point calmly, clearly with a firm but relaxed manner is much more convincing than someone shouting angrily, whilst thumping the table with his or her fist. The former suggests the person is confident of his or her point, whereas the latter suggests a lack of confidence. It is important to be assertive, but not aggressive.

Activity

1 Two members of the class can *volunteer* to role play the following in an assertive manner, and another two in an aggressive manner:

Customer:	I bought this hair drier last year, but it doesn't blow out any hot air any more.
Shop assistant:	You said last year. How long have you had it?
Customer:	The guarantee ran out two weeks ago, but I bought it in good time for my daughter's birthday and so it wasn't used for four weeks.

Shop assistant:	I will have to check with the manager whether we can replace it under the guarantee.
Customer:	I think he should exchange it as the guarantee has only just expired.

2 In small groups of two or three, consider what types of body language might indicate the following emotions:

- confidence
- happiness
- encouragement
- amusement
- anxiety
- discouragement
- sadness
- annoyance.

Listening

Listening is just as important as speaking in oral communication. The speaker may be brilliant, but if no one is listening, there is no communication. Be aware that it is much easier to listen to something we want to hear and to ignore something we don't want to hear:

Easy listening!	*Not so easy listening!*
Your maths class is cancelled today – everyone rushes home	An extra maths revision class has been arranged for 4.00 pm – hardly anyone manages to turn up!
You have won £100,000. Just take this cheque to the bank. You rush off to the bank at the first opportunity	You owe me £40 – stop at the cashpoint on the way home. You completely forget to get the money!

So often, we listen, but don't really hear! Have you had this experience? You give a message to one of your friends and ask him or her to pass it on to someone else. Later, the message is repeated back to you, but bears little resemblance to what you originally said.

Rosaria:	Jason, be sure to tell Joe and Natalie that the time of the film is not 8.00 pm, it's 7.30.
Jason:	Joe, we're not going to the film at 7.00 – it's 8.00. Tell Natalie when you see her.
Joe:	Natalie, I gather the film's off tonight.
Natalie:	*(sees Rosaria later)* I'm really disappointed to know the film's been cancelled.
Rosaria:	What gave you that idea? I told Joe the film starts at 7.30 not 8.00!

Did you know?

One of the most important skills for a sales person to develop is the art of listening. By listening carefully to what your customer is saying, you can respond effectively and are much more likely to make the sale.

If you are speaking publicly, giving a presentation or taking part in a discussion, there are some simple points to remember which will immediately improve your performance.

Golden rules for giving a presentation

1 Think about the way to speak:

- *Talk slowly* – people tend to speak faster and faster when nervous. If your voice sounds *slightly slow* to you, this will be just right for the listener.
- *Speak clearly* – if you are speaking more slowly than usual, you will be less likely to mutter, mumble or keep saying 'er' and 'um' all the time.
- *Speak up* – it is not necessary to shout, but if the audience cannot hear you, there is no point in speaking at all.

2 Remember your body language is important too:

- Don't gesture wildly or stand poker straight – you will appear nervous.
- Do use relaxed gestures or move around a little.
- Do smile now and then. You will *appear* confident even if you don't feel it.

3 Introduce yourself, your team and the topic.

4 Do prepare, but don't *read* your notes. Use cards or overhead transparencies with main points and expand on them as you speak.

5 Look at the audience – not just at one fixed spot above their heads or down at the floor.

6 Do explain jargon, abbreviations and acronyms (an acronym is a word made by using initials instead of the full title, e.g. Nato for North Atlantic Treaty Organisation). The listener will forget even familiar abbreviations and acronyms if too many are used, and your jargon may be someone else's gobbledegook.

7 Do make your points as concisely as possible. People remember only about 70% of what they hear so don't be too 'wordy'.

8 Do enhance your points with images – either on overhead transparencies or verbal images (vivid descriptions) which help the listener remember.

9 If it is a team effort, introduce the next presenter properly, don't just stop and sit down.

10 Do make sure there is a definite conclusion.

Do your best to follow all the above points, and you will probably be surprised to find that you not only sound confident, you actually feel confident.

Golden rules for taking part in discussions

Rules 1 and 2 for giving presentations are just as applicable in discussions. If you know beforehand that a discussion is planned then you can be prepared.

1 If at all possible make sure:

- the environment is conducive (helpful) to discussions and free from distractions, e.g. an important meeting is much more likely to progress well if there are no interruptions from telephone calls
- the timing is right. Often this is beyond your control, but if you are very tired and the discussion can be postponed, then do so.

2 Think about the important, relevant points you want to make, so that you don't wander off the point, or go on and on about some fairly trivial issue.

3 Do remember to give others a turn to make their points.

4 Learn to concentrate on the speaker, listening politely and carefully to others.

5 Try not to:

- interrupt
- finish sentences for the speaker
- fiddle with papers, paper clips, gaze into space, draw doodles or generally show lack of interest – even if you are bored to death!
- daydream about the film you saw last night or your plans for the weekend. You may be asked a question and won't know what has just been said!

6 Be responsive. Have you ever had a conversation with someone who just answered yes or no? Eventually the conversation becomes an awkward silence. A response such as 'Yes, I do agree that the use of computers has made many people redundant, but many new jobs have been created in the computer industry' moves the discussion along. Someone else can either agree or disagree and expand on why.

7 Do take opportunities to confirm points made, e.g. 'Can I just check? We have agreed to meet at _____'.

Important!

The assignments for the mandatory units provide opportunities to take part in discussions, but do remember – you must join in, you cannot be a silent observer!

Element 2.2 Produce written material

For this element you are expected to:

1 include information which is accurate and relevant to the *subject*

2 check that the text is legible and the meaning is clear, correcting it if necessary

3 follow appropriate standard *conventions*

4 present information in a *format* that suits the *audience* and purpose

5 use structure and style to emphasise meaning.

Business letters

Just as with oral communication, written communication in a business context is more formal than writing to a friend. There are standard conventions for letters used for external correspondence between the organisation and customers or other businesses, and memoranda (usually called memos) used for internal correspondence between staff within the organisation. Fewer secretaries are employed and many people at work are responsible for their own correspondence. Therefore, check that you know how to lay out a business letter.

Modern business letters usually follow what is called a fully blocked style as in Figure C.2.

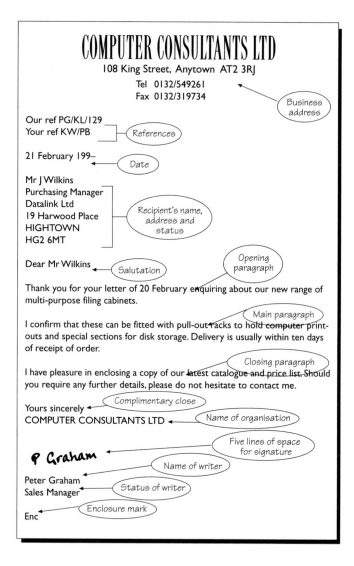

Figure C.2 A typical layout for a business letter

Read the following points and check them against the example letter:

1 There is no punctuation (commas or full stops) in the date, reference, address, after Dear _____ or in the closing section of the letter. In this style, punctuation is used only during the main body of the letter.

2 You will notice that clear lines are left at certain stages of the letter – mostly just one, although five is usual between Yours sincerely/faithfully and the name, to allow room for the signature. Clearly, common sense should prevail and if the letter is very short, you may wish to spread it out slightly – but do not use extra lines in the recipient's address.

3 The name of the postal town/city (not the county) should be in capitals.

4 The post code should be on a new line, but if this is not possible because the letter won't quite fit on the page, allow six spaces between the name of the town/city/county and the post code.

5 The *complimentary close* must match the *opening salutation*:

if you open with	you must close with
Dear Sir/Madam	Yours faithfully
Dear Mr/Mrs/Miss/Ms followed by the name	Yours sincerely

Do not use first names, unless you know the person well and normally use his or her first name in conversation.

Use a capital 'Y' and a small 'f' or 's'.

6 The opening paragraph should briefly introduce the topic. This may be a letter received, or it could be in response to an advertisement for a job. Suitable opening sentences often begin like this:

Thank you for your letter of (date) …
Further to our recent telephone conversation …
I wish to bring to your attention a problem I am having with …
With reference to your advertisement for the post of IT Co-ordinator in the 'Anytown Herald' …

7 The next paragraph(s) will expand more fully on the reason for writing.

8 The final paragraph should conclude the letter, and will often say something like:

I look forward to hearing from you.
Please contact me if you require any further information.
In the light of the above I would be pleased to discuss the possibilities further with you at interview.

9 If any items are enclosed with the letter, then the word 'Enc' should be typed at the very end, allowing one clear line space. This is to remind both you and the recipient that there should be enclosures.

Writing a curriculum vitae (CV)

When you have finished this programme of study, you may be planning to look for a job or you may hope to continue with the advanced course and eventually apply for university. Whatever your plans, sooner or later you will need to prepare a CV. It might just be for work experience or a Saturday or evening job, but it is worth taking trouble to prepare your CV. When you write to a prospective employer, you must remember that he or she will receive many such letters, and your letter and CV is the first impression he or she will gain of you. It may be that you are absolutely right for the job, but unless that letter and CV gains you an interview, you will never have the chance to convince the employer.

Golden rules for writing a CV

1 Prepare your CV on a word processor – it will be easy to update whenever necessary.

2 Always send an original copy, not a photocopy.

3 Presentation is very important. The CV should not be too long – one or two pages should be enough, but don't use a tiny font in order to squash it in one page.(Employers tend to be older and may not bother to read it at all if they find it difficult to see the print!)

4 Include the following:

Personal details
- name, title
- address
- telephone number
- date of birth

Educational details
- schools/colleges attended (not primary schools) and dates
- GCSE results
- any other certificates gained, e.g. typing, word processing exams
- current programme of study, i.e. GNVQ Intermediate IT and results known to date
- any extra courses you are studying at the same time, e.g. GCSE English or maths
- positions of responsibility held
- work experience details

Employment details
- if working, current job, including part-time Saturday or evening work, and a brief description of duties
- any previous jobs. Include any responsibility you held and a brief description of duties

Any other important/useful information
Remember you do not have a long history of employment at present, so you need to *sell*

yourself. What makes you stand out from other applicants? You might include:

- details of any hobbies/interests or sports. Do say if you are/have been part of a team
- details of any organisations to which you belong. Do say if you act/have acted in a position of responsibility, e.g. treasurer/secretary/Sunday-school teacher
- anything else which might be useful – non-smoker/car driver.

Referees
It is useful to include two names, but do ask permission first. Suitable referees are:

- someone who has known you for a long time – can be on a personal level, but not a relative
- a teacher or tutor
- the leader of any organisation to which you belong
- your past employer (if it is not too long ago)
- your current employer – but if you don't want him or her to know you are applying for another job, it is acceptable to say he or she can be contacted only if you are offered the new post.

Activity

1 Look at the two ways of presenting the same CV shown on pages 169 and 170, and then discuss with your tutor the advantages and disadvantages of the two presentations.

2 Look in the local paper to find a job advertisement which might be suitable for you. Using the guidelines above, compose a letter indicating that you are enclosing your CV. It is not enough to simply write 'Please find enclosed a copy of my CV'. Think carefully about what is said in the advertisement and try to target your letter specifically to this position.

Note: This letter, and other similar pieces of work, may be included in the portfolio as further evidence for Communication core skills.

Memos

Read the following points and check them against the example memo in Figure C.3.

1 The heading 'Memorandum' is normally in the centre, although it can be blocked to the left.

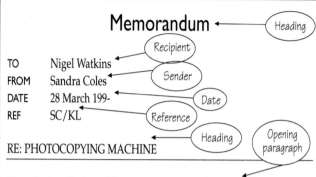

Figure C.3 A typical memo

2 The recipient and sender's names, date and heading all line up on the same column.

3 The main body of the memo will be typed under the line, but it is not essential to have a line across the page – it simply makes a better presentation.

4 The content of the memo is usually short and less formal than a letter.

5 The sender's initials can be included at the bottom of the memo.

Curriculum Vitae

Name: Mr Chris MacAndrews

Address: 24 Pleasant Grove
                      ANYTOWN
                      AN8 4TH

Telephone: 0132 775 2890

Date of birth: 4 September 1979

Education: St James High School   – September 1990 – July 1995
                      Anytown College   – September 1995 to date

GCSE passes: English   (D)
                      Maths   (E)
                      Computer Studies   (C)
                      Science   (E)
                      Geography   (E)
                      History   (F)

                      RSA: Word-processing – Stage 1

                      I am currently studying the GNVQ Intermediate in Information Technology. I have passed all the unit tests, and my grades to date indicate that I will achieve a distinction for my final award.

Work experience: I had a very enjoyable and interesting work experience placement at Anytown Insurance Co. for three weeks in 1995. My duties included filing, inputting data into the computer and answering the telephone.

Employment details: I worked regularly for two years at Anytown Newsagents delivering the papers. Since September 1995 I have been employed by Anytown Supermarket. At first I stacked shelves two evenings a week, but for the past six months I have also worked on the check-out on Friday evenings and Saturdays.

Hobbies: I played for the school first XI football team for two years, and now I play for the College team. I also enjoy swimming, cricket and playing the guitar.

Referees: Mr John Jenkins   Mrs Jane Smith
                      Programme Manager   General Manager
                      Anytown College   Anytown Supermarket
                      The Crescent   25 High Street
                      ANYTOWN   ANYTOWN
                      AN9 2LY   AN6 4SW

Curriculum Vitae

CHRISTOPHER MacANDREWS
24 Pleasant Grove
ANYTOWN
AN8 4TH
0132 775 2890

QUALIFICATIONS

St James High School – September 1990 – July 1995

GCSE (1995):	English	(D)	Computer Studies	(C)
	Maths	(E)	Geography	(E)
	Science	(E)	History	(F)

Anytown College – September 1995 – to date

RSA (1996):   Word-processing – Stage 1

I am currently studying the GNVQ Intermediate in Information Technology.
I have passed all the unit tests, and my grades to date indicate that I will achieve a distinction for my final award.

E M P L O Y M E N T

Work experience – Anytown Insurance Co.   **Summer 1995**
I had a very enjoyable and interesting work experience placement at Anytown Insurance Co. for three weeks in 1995. My duties included filing, inputting data into the computer and answering the telephone.

Anytown Newsagents   **1993 – 1995**
I worked regularly for two years at Anytown Newsagents delivering the papers.

Anytown Supermarket   **September 1995 to date**
Since September 1995 I have been employed by Anytown Supermarket. At first I stacked shelves two evenings a week, but for the past six months I have also worked on the check-out on Friday evenings and Saturdays.

PERSONAL DETAILS

Single	D of B: 4 September 1979
Good health	Non-smoker
Currently learning to drive	

INTERESTS and ACHIEVEMENTS

I played for the school first XI football team for two years.
I now play for the College team.
Keen interest in swimming, cricket and playing the guitar.

REFEREES

Mr John Jenkins	Mrs Jane Smith
Programme Manager	General Manager
Anytown College	Anytown Supermarket
The Crescent	25 High Street
ANYTOWN	ANYTOWN
AN9 2LY	AN6 4SW

Activity

Refer to the evidence assignment for Element 4.2 on page 144, and write a memo confirming that the fax machine and PCFax software have been successfully installed. Use your own name as the sender of the memo, and use your tutor's name as the recipient.

Forms

Completing forms should be very simple. The required information is clearly indicated and a space is given to enter it in. What could be easier? But if you are anything like me, you hate filling in forms. I have never met anyone who likes this task: some don't mind, and most people seem to feel the same as me. Why is this? Probably because we don't concentrate enough, rush it and, as a result, put the wrong details in the wrong places, which is very hard to correct neatly, unless you start again with a new form! It is a good idea to fill it in first lightly in pencil, so that you can be sure the right information is entered into the boxes, then go over it again in ink. No doubt you completed endless forms when you joined this course, and you do have to complete some documents for the evidence assignment for Element 3.1.

Activity

1 Obtain application forms for a passport and driving licence. Practise filling these in.

2 Obtain a holiday brochure. Select one holiday for you and your best friend and fill in the holiday form.

3 You may have already passed your driving test, and if not you probably aim to learn to drive in the future. On today's busy roads, it is probable that at some time you will be involved in an accident, even if it is not your fault. Using the following information, practise filling in forms by completing the accident report form in Figure C.4.

- Policy no.: MX403781.
- Policyholder: use your own name and address.
- Type of licence: use full if you have one, or provisional if not.
- Details of insured vehicle: Fiesta, red, registration number K741 PDW, value £8,500.

The accident occurred last Tuesday evening at about 9.00 pm. It was dark and raining lightly. You were waiting to turn right into a quiet side road, Chamberlain Crescent, Anytown, where you had arranged to collect your friend (choose the name of one of your friends). An oncoming car, driven by Mr Blaycock, of 14 Village Way, Anytown AN6 3PH, 0132 776 3122, turned left into the side road, and right into a narrow lane. After he turned into the side road, there was no more traffic coming towards you, so you turned right into the same side road. Suddenly you realised to your horror that he was reversing out of the lane. He hit your car right between the doors, damaging the front door and the back panel. There were only minor scratches to his car, which is a grey BMW, registration M638 ANT. No one was injured, but there is about £450 of damage to your car. Fortunately, your friend was waiting on the pavement and witnessed that Mr Blaycock had not checked whether anything was coming.

This activity is also useful practice for Communication Element 2.4 – read and respond to written materials – and could be used as evidence.

Spelling, punctuation and grammar

The importance of accuracy has been stressed over and over again throughout the book, and it is not possible for your work to be accurate if the spelling and grammar are incorrect. Refer back to Element 3.4 (the sections on verification and correctness on pages 116–117), to remind yourself of the points already made.

Whether you are good at spelling or not, **always** use the spell checker. Apart from finding misspelt words, it will also find errors where you knew the spelling but made a typing error. Using the grammar check for the whole document may not be helpful, but if in doubt use it for selected text, especially with words such as 'their' and 'there'.

Punctuation is an area which some students frequently find difficult – when to use full stops, commas, question marks, semi-colons or colons, dashes, hyphens and apostrophes – but it is an essential aid to making your text easy to understand and read.

Full stops

Full stops (.) come at the end of a sentence and the word beginning the next sentence starts with a capital letter. When using the word processor, leave one or two spaces after a full stop. It doesn't matter which, but be consistent.

PRIVATE CAR ACCIDENT NOTIFICATION FORM

Policy No.

Details of Policyholder

Name:

Address:

Post code:

Tel. No.:

Driving Licence:

Full ☐   Provisional: ☐

Details of Insured Vehicle

Make: Colour: Reg. No.:   Value

Other vehicle involved:

Name of driver:

Address:

Post code:

Tel. No.:

Make:

Colour:

Reg. No.:

Accident

Date: Time: Weather:

Street/Town where accident occurred:

Who was at fault?   Self ☐   Other party ☐

Plan of Accident:

Draw a sketch stating approximate measurements, showing positions of vehicles and the direction in which they were travelling:

State fully what happened:

Figure C.4 An accident report form

Commas

Commas (,) are more difficult but are used at a point where the sense gives a natural pause to break up sections of a long sentence. If you are not sure whether a comma is in the right place read the sentence without pausing unless you have a comma to find out whether you are out of breath and whether you are pausing too often or in odd places. Use one space after a comma.

Try reading the above sentences about commas. The commas have been deliberately omitted. Did you find you weren't quite sure of the sense and were wanting to take a breath?

This time I have included commas, some in the right place but others in the wrong place:

Commas are more difficult, but are used at a point where the sense gives a natural pause to break, up sections of a long sentence. If you are not sure whether a comma is, in the right place read the sentence without pausing unless you have a comma, to find out whether you are out of breath and whether you are pausing too often or in an odd place. Use one space after a comma.

Decide which commas are correct and which need moving somewhere else. Check it with the version below.

Commas are more difficult, but are used at a point where the sense gives a natural pause, to break up sections of a long sentence. If you are not sure whether a comma is in the right place, read the sentence without pausing unless you have a comma, to find out whether you are out of breath and whether you are pausing too often or in an odd place. Use one space after a comma.

Question marks

Question marks (?) are much easier and come at the end of a sentence which asks a question. Use two spaces after a question mark.

Which colour do you prefer? I like the blue one.

Semi-colons and colons

Semi-colons (;) are also difficult, but indicate a more definite pause or break in the sentence than a comma, but less definite than a full stop. Leave one space after a semi-colon. Use semi-colons when the sections of the sentence are closely linked, e.g.:

Many students at this college study full time; fewer study part time.

or when separating items in a list, e.g.:

Please inform the following of their roles in the school fete: Margaret Smith is in charge of the cake stall, because she owns the local bakery; Hitesh Patel will run the skittle alley because he runs the youth club which owns the equipment; Yen Tran will organise the craft stall, because she teaches arts and crafts.

Colons (:) are often used to introduce a quotation or list, when the colon may be followed by a dash:

Examples:–
Please inform the following of their roles in the school fete: Margaret Smith is ...
As Shakespeare said: 'The quality of mercy is not strained ...'

Use one or two spaces after a colon.

Dashes

Dashes (–) are used to *separate* points and should have one space each side of the dash, e.g.:

Punctuation is an area which students frequently find difficult – when to use full stops, ...

Hyphens

Hyphens (-), which look identical to a dash on a word processor, are used to *join* words together, frequently to describe something; there should be no space each side of the hyphen, e.g.:

The clothes were old-fashioned.

In this example the writer does not want to describe the clothes as old or fashioned, but **old-fashioned**.

Apostrophes

The apostrophe (') is probably the most difficult punctuation mark of all. In English we often say words like 'don't', and the apostrophe is used to indicate that a letter or letters in a word are omitted, e.g.:

don't for *do not*; *won't* for *would not*; *shan't* for *shall not*; *isn't* for *is not*; *can't* for *cannot*; *it's* for *it is*

It is also used to indicate something which *belongs to* someone or something, e.g.:

The girl's coat was blue. The boy's hat was black.

If you can turn the sentence round and use the words *belonging to*, and still make sense, you need an apostrophe, e.g.:

The coat belonging to the girl was blue. The hat belonging to the boy was black.

It is more difficult when using the apostrophe with a plural ending in *s*, e.g.:

All the students' coats were brown, because the school uniform is brown.

The coats belonging to the students were brown, …

All the students wore brown coats.

This time there is no apostrophe because to turn the sentence round – all the brown coats belonging to the students wore – makes no sense.

Try it with these sentences and decide which one doesn't need an extra apostrophe and why.

The cats milk is hot, so he shouldn't drink it until it cools down.
Anytown High School's players were delighted because the grammar school's team hadn't beaten them for the first time.
The cars engines had overheated in the traffic jam, because the drivers hadn't switched off the engines.

Activity

The following paragraph is taken from the section on 'Industrial organisations' in Element 3.1 on page 81. All punctuation and full stops have been removed. Rewrite the paragraph with suitable punctuation and full stops. Would the use of bold, italics or underline improve the writing at any point? Then compare your version against the original text.

steel one of the worlds most important metals is processed from iron and carbon ford motor co manufactures cars in some parts of the uk coal is still mined from underground but in africa something more exciting is found diamonds british petroleum bp extracts oil out of the north sea and refines it for use as petrol or oil for cars these are all examples of industrial organisations we do see garages which are specifically ford agents or petrol stations selling just bp products but these would be the retail or commercial side of the business rather than the industrial side

Structure and style

If this book had been written as one long piece of text, with no paragraphs, headings, subheadings, pictures or diagrams, it would be very difficult to follow. All the information would be contained in the text, but no doubt you would have given up after only a few pages. However, it is no use starting new paragraphs because you haven't had one lately, or making a heading/subheading unless the following text relates to that heading/subheading. The use of bold, italics, underline or different font styles can give emphasis to parts of the text, and the inclusion of images provides added interest and helps the reader understand and remember important points. (Use of images will be dealt with in the next element.)

In order to give structure and style to your writing follow these guidelines:

- Paragraphs should not be too long and should deal with a particular topic or section. For example, the first paragraph under the heading 'Structure and style' above deals with the introduction to this topic. This second paragraph continues on the same theme, but moves on to give examples of how to create structure and style.
- Use a consistent style for your main headings and subheadings; you might choose all capitals and bold for main headings – **MAIN HEADING** – and first initial capitals and bold for subheadings – **Subheadings**. Look at the chapters of this book and identify which are main headings and subheadings and the style used for each.
- Highlighting certain words or phrases in bold, italics or underline emphasises important points, e.g. 'It is **essential** to …' By using bold for the word '**essential**', the reader's attention is drawn to the fact that a very important point will follow.

  Italics have been used in this section to differentiate between examples and explanation.

- Instead of using a long, continuous paragraph, the use of numbered, lettered or bullet points can make the writing clearer. This section uses bullet points for these guidelines. Look for other examples in this book and evaluate whether the use of points makes the topic easier to read, understand and remember.
- Use specialist vocabulary carefully, making sure that you give explanations where necessary, e.g. 'She was using a real-time booking system'. Unless you understand the meaning of 'real-time', this sentence makes no sense.

Activity

The following is an extract from Element 4.2 on page 141, which has been changed into one continuous paragraph and the use of bold, italics or numbered or bullet points removed. Rewrite the text with suitable paragraphs, add bold, italics or change any section as you feel appropriate to numbered or bullet points. Then check your version against the original text.

Transferring, receiving and storing information. Communications software. If you are going to transfer information electronically, you do need the right software. Examples include Norton PCAnywhere and Procomm, but if you have Microsoft Windows, it already includes a program called Terminal, which is quite suitable for this purpose. Terminal includes facilities such as setting a telephone number which Terminal dials; deciding the number of seconds to wait before a connect signal from the remote computer is received; whether to redial if the connection fails; specifying that the system bell rings when a successful connection has been made; setting protocols, such as the baud rate or whether the parity should be odd, even or none; setting a terminal emulation, i.e. selecting the type of mainframe to connect to. (Check back to the last chapter if you don't understand any of these terms.) Whichever communications software you are using, it will be necessary to configure it to match the requirements of the rest of your system.

What else is included in the original which improves the presentation?

Important!

The assignments provide plenty of opportunities to produce written material, but do remember that:

- whilst you may achieve the performance criteria for the mandatory unit, unless you remember to check your spelling, style, etc., you will not achieve this core skill element
- one piece of work must be hand-written *legibly* – the evidence assignment for Element 4.1 (page 138) specifically addresses this point.

Element 2.3 Use images

For this element you are expected to:

1 select *images* which clearly illustrate the *points* being made

2 use *images* which are suited to the *audience, situation* and purpose
3 use *images* at appropriate times and places.

Images are used:

- to catch attention
- to keep the audience interested
- when a visual aid makes the point more easily or clearly.

What do we understand by the word *images*? In this context an image can be as follows:

- *A symbol* to illustrate an object or an instruction – a floppy disk, no U-turns.

No U-turns

- *An actual picture* to illustrate an object – such as the laser printer in Figure C.5.

Figure C.5 A laser printer

- A *cartoon-type drawing* to illustrate someone or something – the family in Figure C.6.

Figure C.6 The family

- *A diagram* – such as an organisation chart or floor plan.
- *A flow chart* such as the one in Figure 3.9 on page 91.
- *A table* – there are many examples in this book such as Figure IT.2 on page 181.
- *A graph* – numerical data in a table is often converted into a graph to present the information in a different way, as with the graph in Figure IT.3 on page 181, produced from the table in Figure IT.2.
- *Photographs* – with modern scanners a relevant photograph could be included in an assignment.

These are all different ways of using images to illustrate points in the text. The image must be relevant to the topic and also suitable for the audience you are addressing – clearly, it would be foolish to write about laser printers, and then include a picture of a dot matrix printer. In this book the audience is you, the students, and many of the images used here would be too complex if the book was aimed to introduce computers to 6–7-year-olds – but why do we use images?

Activity

Why do we use images? Look back through the book and choose two different types of image, which you feel were particularly helpful to your understanding and enjoyment of the topic. Don't rush, choosing the first image you notice, but think carefully and identify why you felt these particular images were effective. Compare your views with the rest of the group. Did many people choose the same images, or was there a variety of choice?

Important!

The assignments for the mandatory units provide plenty of opportunities to use images, but do remember that unless you actually **use images**, you cannot be credited with this core skill element.

Element 2.4 Read and respond to written materials

For this element you are expected to:

1 select and read *materials* for a *purpose*
2 extract the necessary *information* for a *purpose*
3 use appropriate *sources of reference* to clarify understanding of the *subject*

4 *summarise* the *information* extracted.

We read for all kinds of reasons:

- entertainment
- to gain information
- to check information
- to follow instructions
- receiving messages.

We read all kinds of documents:

- bills
- letters
- magazines
- newspapers
- books
- advertisements
- instructions.

We read in different ways:

- scanning the text looking for key words or pieces of information
- skimming all the text quickly to decide whether it's worth reading it in detail
- reading every word carefully, if necessary rereading to ensure we fully understand the text.

In the context of this core skill element, you will mainly be concerned with obtaining or checking information, to help you with your assignments and also to prepare for the unit tests. Apart from this textbook, you will need to refer to other books, newspaper/magazine articles, and frequently much of the information will not be relevant.

For example, the evidence assignment for Element 4.3 (page 157) includes a task relating to pornography and the Internet. When researching this information, having found an article about the Internet, you could first scan the text for the word 'pornography'. If you found the word, you would then read the section carefully. If it proved interesting and useful, you might scan the rest of the article to check whether it was worth reading it all in detail. Having found suitable references, a good technique to follow is to highlight the significant section. It is amazing how difficult it can be to find a particular sentence again, even when you know you read it previously.

Once you have extracted enough information to provide a basis for the assignment, the next stage is to summarise the key points in your own words. It is perfectly acceptable to quote some phrases or sentences, perhaps where a particularly interesting example has been used, but you will no doubt find the same points made in a slightly different way in each of the extracts. It would be boring and repetitive if you kept saying the same thing over and over.

Next, check the summary to ensure that:

- it is expressed clearly
- all the important facts have been included
- the facts are presented in a logical order.

 ### Evidence assignment

You have been asked to write a short article as follows:

1 The heading – 'Playing games on computer'.

2 Opening paragraph – a short introduction stating that there have been a number of recent innovations/improvements for playing computer games.
3 Make a list of recent innovations/improvements.
4 A concluding paragraph – state briefly which of the innovations/improvements you felt was most important and why.

Read the following extracts (reproduced with permission from the *Daily Telegraph*) for information to prepare the above article. When you have completed it, check with your tutor whether you have included all the relevant points.

PCs join in the party fun

WITH faster and funkier machines knocking at the door, the games console makers are looking forward to a renewal of the party atmosphere. However, a familiar gatecrasher is gearing up to spoil the fun: the humble personal computer.

PCs used to be the plain child of the games world. But the combination of Windows 95 and add-on hardware, such as Creative Labs' forthcoming 3D Blaster video card, has, in the eyes of the games software manufacturers, made the PC into the belle of the ball.

Games software manufacturers have preferred to develop their best games for consoles, because the PC was geared so strongly towards office use that they could not cope with the specialised demands of all but a few genres of computer games.

But there are estimated to be 30 million PCs in homes worldwide, sales which no single games console comes close to. Microsoft saw an opportunity and, with its soon-to-be-released Games Software Develop-ment Unit for Windows 95, has given the games manufacturers the tools with which to develop popular games for the PC.

Using the Windows 95 Games SDK, manufacturers will be able to bypass layers of software and give games the ability to make full use of the PC's powerful hardware. In addition, Windows 95's Plug and Play capabilities make it easy to add hardware, and games CD-ROMs can be instantly loaded.

But games consoles are cheaper than PCs, and most PC games need at least a Pentium to run smoothly. Creative Labs is preparing a 3D graphics accelerator card called the 3D Blaster which, it claims, will give 486-based PCs Pentium-like performance. Available for Christmas, this will run only rewritten DOS and Windows-based games although, using the Windows 95 Games SDK, games manufacturers will be able to create games which support it automatically. It will cost around £250.

STEVE BOXER

Now arcade high-tech is all yours in the sitting room

ONE OF the main aims of Windows 95 is to attract games players, who regard previous personal computer systems as slow and unattractive compared with specialised consoles such as the Nintendo and Sega.

The speed of Windows 95 will allow games previously limited to arcades to be loaded on to personal computers, according to David Hirst, development director of Europress Software in Macclesfield – a leading British games supplier for the educational market.

'Games will be much faster under Windows 95. It is much more user-friendly, and much more robust,' he said. 'From now on, all our new products will be for Windows 95.'

Initially, most offerings will be upgraded versions of Windows games, rewritten to exploit the speed of Windows 95. 'Our first Windows 95 product will be a CD-ROM version of *Treasure Island*, which will be out when Windows 95 is launched later this month,' Mr Hirst said.

'The first product developed especially for Windows 95 will be *Klik and Create*, which will be available in September, at around £60.'

Klik and Create, a program for making your own multi-media presentations easily and quickly, is a development of Europress's popular *Klik and Play for Windows*. It is based on 'objects' – things on screen which mimic their prototypes.

'You can choose a ball and it acts like a real ball,' Mr Hirst explained. 'It will roll around and if it hits something it will bounce. Get another ball and they will inter-act in exactly the same way that real ones would.'

The size, weight and bounciness can be controlled by simple mouse commands, and the range of objects is virtually boundless – from an earwig to an elephant.

Klik and Create will allow users to develop their own games, and will also come in a professional version. As Windows 95 reaches a wider market, personal computer versions of arcade and console games are expected to proliferate.

That does not mean, though, that Windows 95 is going to kill off the console market. 'It will make the personal computer a proper family machine, but the new generation of consoles, such as the Sony Play Station, will continue to take most of the games market,' said Mr Hirst.

CHRIS PARTRIDGE

It's good to talk chess moves

COMPUTER games players will soon be able to compete against each other over the telephone if a system demonstrated by BT for the first time today is adopted by the software industry.

Many game publishers include remote-play options which allow two or more people to play games head-to-head, either over a network or via a modem across the Internet, but these systems can be difficult to set up and expensive to use.

BT's Wireplay hopes to change all that. The system, to be introduced next summer, promises to make on-line gaming an affordable reality for anyone with a PC and modem.

Games will have a Wireplay option that will set the modem to dial automatically into a local Wireplay exchange to discover opponents waiting to play. Or a player may instruct the system to call up a friend to issue a challenge.

Once two computers have linked through the Wireplay network, the game begins. Messages can also be sent so that they pop up automatically on the opponent's screen.

Wireplay will run national games leagues and knock-out tournaments. An e-mail system will allow competition games to be arranged.

BT will introduce a tariff for Wireplay to make long calls affordable. This is likely to be a modest increase on the local call rate (BT recently introduced a '1p per minute off-peak local calls' charge). No subscription fee is planned.

Ultimately, Wireplay's success will depend on cost, convenience and the willingness of games publishers to support it: BT's plans provide no royalties to publishers; Wireplay compatibility is simply offered as an extra feature.

Will Wireplay be a viable answer to the problems of current Internet-based linking systems? John Kavanagh, vice-president of Domark, was impressed: 'It certainly has possibilities. This would suit Championship Manager [a popular football management game] ideally. We're definitely interested in hearing more.'

STEVE JACKSON

Important!

Evidence for this element must be presented as both written and oral summaries. It is important to include with the assignment your source material or to quote the source for verification that your summary is correct.

Information technology Level 2 and Level 3

Information technology has had an enormous impact on life in the twentieth century. No matter what kind of employment you have, you will almost certainly find part of your work is related to using a computer. There seems little connection between computers and a company which repairs or replaces tyres and car exhaust pipes, but almost certainly it will use a computerised till to record the sale, provide a guarantee for the work and print the bill.

Because every aspect of business is so dependent on computers, information technology has been made a requirement of every GNVQ programme of study. As you are studying an information technology course, you are clearly at an advantage, as the related core skill should be relatively easy for you to achieve. Indeed, you may well find it possible to achieve this core skill at Level 3.

At the end of this section you will find two tracking sheets – one for IT Core Level 2 and one for Level 3 – to help you identify which evidence assignments provide evidence towards particular performance criteria for the IT core skills at both levels. It is worth repeating that although one assignment may enable you to *tick all the performance criteria* of an element, you will still need the other pieces of evidence to cover *all the range*.

Element 2.1 Prepare information

For this element you are required to prepare information to enter into the computer, by selecting appropriate information from existing sources or developing information during input.

An existing source might be:

- price lists or catalogues from which information is obtained
- a scanned image
- hand-written notes – perhaps the minutes of a meeting
- the results of a survey.

Information developed during input would be any work you have created/written yourself, which did not previously exist in hard copy, such as:

- a drawing you created yourself
- ideas to be drafted in a letter or report
- formulae created in a spreadsheet
- a graph produced from data in a spreadsheet.

As always **accuracy** is very important and any errors you notice should be corrected immediately. You must also use the spelling and grammar checking facilities and proof-read your work.

You should be able to correct **simple equipment faults** such as loose cables, equipment switched off or wrongly set up. It is not uncommon on a network for a printer problem to occur, and often the easiest way to resolve it is by switching off the printer, pausing for a few seconds and switching on again. **Keep a log or diary** of any occasions when you deal with such simple faults and the action you took to correct them. If possible ask your lecturer to sign to indicate that the log entry is true.

Learn to use the online help facilities, only asking for help when it is really necessary. The help files in modern software are very good; you can print the instructions if necessary, and if you are fortunate to have the very latest software, a practical demonstration, which guides you step by step through a process, is often available.

Examples of creating work on the computer in ways which are easy to edit include:

- allowing text to word-wrap at the end of a line
- using the tab key rather than the space bar to reach a specific point
- creating formulae in a spreadsheet
- using appropriate types of fields in a database rather than creating only text fields.

Storing input **systematically** is the area where most students fall down – even many people who are at work are not systematic. So what do we mean by being systematic?

Naming files sensibly – this does *not* mean using your name or your boy or girlfriend's name, e.g. Sarah1, Sarah2, Jim1, Jim2, Jim3, etc. Doc1, doc2, doc3 is not sensible either. This topic has been mentioned earlier in the book, but it is worth repeating, as you cannot provide evidence for this core skill element unless you use sensible names. A sensible name is one which helps you identify the content of the file so that, if you want to access it again, you can find it easily. By the time you have reached Sarah25.doc/Jim25.doc and you need to open up your work for a particular evidence assignment, you will have absolutely no idea which is the correct file. It is not always appropriate to use a footer with the file name, but sometimes this can be a very useful way of identifying the file for future use. In a business context it is also important that if someone is away from the office, another person can easily find the file if necessary.

Activity

What might be a suitable name to use when this particular section of the book was written?

Check your own files and if the file names are not suitable, then rename them. If you are using Windows this is easy to do through the file manager. If you do not know how, then find out from the online help facilities.

Creating and using directories. It is no coincidence that the icon for the file manager in Windows is a filing cabinet, but a filing cabinet is useless if all the papers are simply thrown into the drawers. Certainly, given long enough, you could find the piece of paper you want, but if they are filed in order – alphabetical, numerical, geographical – it is so much easier and quicker.

By the end of this course, you will have saved many, many files on to disk and it will be much simpler to find a particular one if you have created directories and subdirectories. We looked at this extensively for Element 4.4 and, if you have not already reached that part of the book, it would be a good idea to turn to page 159. If you do follow what are known as good housekeeping practices, you will automatically provide evidence for the range **locating files conveniently for subsequent use**.

Saving work regularly is essential and we have previously discussed this in Element 3.4 on page 118.

Important!

To be sure you have all the evidence you need for this element, it is essential to:

1 include with your assignments any notes you may have taken in class, or any other source of information to cover the range 'information taken from existing sources' and 'keep source information required for the task'

2 name files sensibly
3 store files in suitable directories
4 back-up files
5 annotate some of your printouts to explain why the work is easy to edit. Another way of proving the work is easy to edit is to print a spreadsheet report showing the formulae, or to make a screen dump of work on a word processor, showing the formatting commands – that is, showing the symbols which indicate the space bar, return key and tab key have been pressed. See Figure IT.1 for an example.

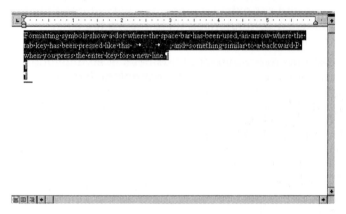

Figure IT.1 A screen dump showing formatting commands

Element 2.2 Process information

This element is concerned with what happens to the information *after* it has been entered into the computer. You need to demonstrate that you:

- can *find specific information*
  e.g. searching in the right directory, looking for files with a given name, searching a database for specific records
- are able to *edit* text, graphics and numbers
  e.g. this may be as simple as underlining or emboldening a single word, changing a number format to currency/two decimal places, or altering paragraph styles, shading a diagram, altering column widths in a table or spreadsheet
- know how to use *software* to make calculations
  e.g. create formulae in a spreadsheet or a database
- are able to *reorganise information*
  e.g. sort into alphabetical or numerical order, move paragraphs around or reorganise into headings and subheadings, change the order of rows or columns in a spreadsheet

- are aware of the importance of *saving regularly* and you should have printouts before and after processing. Again the printouts need to be annotated to explain the effects of the changes you have made
- are able to resolve differences of *format* and *style* when *combining information* from different sources

e.g. *If I imported text from another document created in a different font style, it would improve the format and style if I change the font to match the main text.*

Importing information from another source might include pictures from clip-art, a scanned image, a graph from a spreadsheet, text extracted from another document, downloading information from a CD-ROM or electronic mail. The imported material should match the style of the original document, which may require altering the font style or size, paragraph layouts, margins, tabs, format of numbers. Printouts **before and after** resolving differences would provide the necessary evidence for Performance Criterion 6.

Element 2.3 Present information

This element is concerned with the way information is presented.

For example, you might include data from a spreadsheet into a report, as in Figure IT.2.

La Baguette Cake Sales for 4 Weeks ending 12/10/9?				
	Price per unit	Price per dozen	Total no. sold (dozens)	Total sales
Carrot Cake	1.00	12.00	10	£120.00
Luxury Cakes	0.75	9.00	18	£162.00
Luxury Cookies	0.30	3.60	104	£374.40
Muffins	0.75	9.00	47	£423.00
			Grand Total:-	£1,079.40

Figure IT.2 A table reporting cake sales

Or alternatively you could present the information as a chart or graph, as in Figure IT.3.

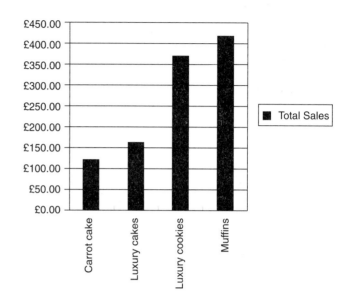

La Baguette Cake Sales for 4 weeks ending 12/10/9?

Figure IT.3 A bar chart reporting cake sales

Look at the section above for Element 2.2, Process information. You will notice that the points have been highlighted with bullets. This technique of numbering or bulleting points has been used frequently in this book. It would have been just as possible to make all the same points as one continuous paragraph, like this:

You need to demonstrate that you can find specific information, e.g. searching in the right directory, looking for files with a given name, searching a database for specific records. You must be able to edit text, graphics and numbers, e.g. this may be as simple as underlining or emboldening a single word, changing a number format to currency/two decimal places, or altering paragraph styles, shading a diagram, altering column widths in a table or spreadsheet. You should also know how to use software to make calculations, e.g. create formulae in a spreadsheet or a database, and be able to reorganise information, e.g. sort into alphabetical or numerical order, move paragraphs around or reorganise into headings and subheadings, change the order of rows or columns in a spreadsheet.

Activity

1 Study the different ways of presenting information shown above and discuss which you prefer and why. Which method is clearer/best suited to the purpose? Is either method more accurate? Which method is best matched to the audience? Would the method you consider best on this occasion always be the best method of presenting similar information?

2 Look also at any of the chapters in the book. Why do you think pictures and diagrams are often included? Do you find them helpful or do you think it would be just as easy to understand the topics without them?

As students on an IT course, you will automatically be using appropriate software and producing hard copy of information you create. As has already been mentioned for Element 2.2, when combining information from different sources, be sure to check the presentation to ensure that:

■ font styles and size are consistent
■ information is clear and presented in manageable portions – in other words, you do not want paragraphs that continue for pages
■ page breaks occur at suitable points and adjust if necessary
■ headings and subheadings use the same style throughout.

The information should be saved and back-up copies made. If you are saving work on a hard disk, then a back-up can be made on a floppy disk. If you do not have access to a hard disk, then a back-up should be made on a second floppy disk.

To demonstrate your competence for this element, you must be able to present information in different ways, and select which method is best in different circumstances. Refer to the evidence assignment for Element 4.1 on page 138. If you follow the guidelines given, you will have evidence for Performance Criteria 1 and 6.

Element 2.4 Evaluate the use of information technology

This element is concerned with understanding why we use information technology, *comparing* the different *methods* used to present and process information technology and which software facilities are appropriate for particular tasks. In addition you must demonstrate an understanding of the *problems* which occur when using information technology and also the importance of *working safely* and maintaining good practice in an information technology environment.

Although there may be some evidence towards this element from the assignments completed for the mandatory units, in the main, evidence for these performance criteria will not automatically occur. Therefore an evidence assignment has been written specifically for this element.

Perhaps before you begin, consideration should be given to what is meant by the word *evaluate*. An evaluation is more than just a description. The thesaurus compares the word 'evaluate' to words such as judge, review, assess, consider. So let's consider some examples:

1 You have been given £60 for your birthday and want to buy a new jacket. You see three jackets of quite different styles and colours – two of them cost about £30 each, and the other one costs £60. You have to decide what to do – i.e. *evaluate* whether it is better to buy two for £30 each or spend £60 on one. When making your decision you might consider the following points:

■ You like having a choice of what to wear.
■ You don't really need two jackets.
■ You could buy one of the cheaper ones and spend the rest of the money on something else.
■ The more expensive item is much better quality, has a better cut and looks really good when you try it on.
■ The more expensive item will last longer, but it may go out of fashion before it is worn out.

Having *evaluated* the options, you would then be able to *judge* whether it is better to buy one expensive garment or two cheaper ones. You might decide to go for quality, but your friend might prefer quantity. Either way, you have considered the options and made a decision.

2 Look back to pages 169–170 and the two versions of the same CV. Evaluate the merits of both and then make a judgement on which you think is most likely to catch the attention of a prospective employer, and gain that absolutely essential interview.

3 In terms of documents prepared using IT, when evaluating whether to present information in a spreadsheet or in a graph, you might consider the following points:

■ Do I need to show exact numbers? Then the spreadsheet is probably the better choice.
■ Do I only need to give a general visual picture? Then the graph is quite suitable.

Word processor	Spreadsheet	Graphics	Database
Hand-written ↓ Manual typewriter – hard to correct mistakes ↓ Electric typewriter with error correcting ribbon, as long as error noticed fairly quickly ↓ Electronic typewriter with error correcting ribbon and limited memory capacity ↓ With all typewriters, if major changes were made to a document, the whole thing would need to be retyped ↓ Original word processors with comparatively basic functions, but work saved and easy to edit. No need to retype the whole document if changes are made ↓ Latest word processors with very sophisticated functions, e.g. ability to include graphics, create drawings and newspaper-style layouts	Hand-written ledgers ↓ Manual adding machines – numbers keyed in and the column of figures could be totalled – any errors would necessitate starting again ↓ Calculators which add, subtract, multiply, divide, work out percentages – but no long-term memory facility ↓ Spreadsheets/accounting software – work can be saved and is easy to edit. Can create formulae so that when rates such as VAT are altered, the new one can be entered in one cell and the spreadsheet will automatically alter appropriate totals. Can create graphs from the spreadsheet to present data visually	Drawings such as technical plans for new buildings, design in manufacturing, layout of fitted kitchens/bathrooms – all had to be done by hand ↓ CAD – computer-aided design – software assists a designer to create fast, accurate drawings ↓ CAM – computer-aided manufacture – software assists in the manufacture of products, and enables modifications to the products to be made quickly and inexpensively	Records were hand-written on cards or in a book, such as an address book ↓ For Unit 3 we looked in detail at computerised databases which store the same kind of information ↓ Searching for information is much more flexible and quicker than in a manual system

Figure IT.4 The progression to modern software facilities

Evidence assignment

Before you prepare your evidence for this core skill element, examine the chart in Figure IT.4. It shows the impact IT has had on the methods used for preparing, processing and presenting information, by charting the developments culminating in modern computer programs.

Figure IT.5 Modern offices have progressed a long way from traditional handwritten records and correspondence

1 Keeping in mind the changes resulting in the use of IT mentioned in Figure IT.4 and also thinking about your own knowledge and experience, refer back to the assignments you have done and produce a report describing the following points. It is not necessary to describe every single assignment, but select at least three to demonstrate your understanding across a range of software. The evidence assignments for Elements 1.3 (see page 33) and 3.2 (see page 101) would be particularly relevant for this discussion.

a Which software facilities were used to meet the requirements of the task – refer back to mandatory Unit 2, Elements 2.1, 2.2 and 2.3, where you learned about the benefits such as templates.

b Your reasons for using the particular software program, such as:

■ more effective
■ easier when processing large volumes of information
■ quicker when undertaking activities which will take a long time manually
■ quicker when searching large volumes of stored information.

c The advantages of using IT compared to manual methods for the assignments, taking particular note of benefits in respect of:

■ speed
■ ease of use
■ effort and accuracy.

d (This section relates to Level 3 – Performance Criterion 3.4.3 – and is therefore required only if you are aiming to achieve IT Core at this level.)

In addition to explaining the reasons for using IT, you should also *evaluate* manual systems compared to computer systems, in respect of:

■ effectiveness
■ cost
■ effects on employment (have jobs been lost as a result of IT, have other jobs been created?)
■ benefits to individuals and organisations
■ disadvantages to individuals and organisations.

When considering the benefits and disadvantages, think about the personal angle. For example, bank clerks today are no doubt very glad that many boring, repetitive tasks are dealt with by computer. On the other hand, customers often find that errors made in the computer system are not noticed, whereas they would have been by a *person*. Also it can be surprisingly difficult to resolve any problem even when it has been spotted – refer back to the *Did You Know* on page 125, describing the problems one man in America endured, because the computer systems said he had died!

2 Computers are amazing in respect of their ability to handle data, especially large volumes of data, quickly, accurately, efficiently, **but**, like all machines, they are not without problems and can

be temperamental. A few years ago a colleague of mine had prepared a practical word processing exam for students, but on the day of the test the weather was very humid and in the middle of the test, the computers *crashed*. You can imagine the frustration and annoyance.

Loss of work owing to a power failure, poorly connected cables, an overload of the system producing error messages such as 'General protection fault' and forcing you to close the application, printers producing either nothing or pages of total rubbish – these are all problems which can make you wonder whether IT really is easier or quicker! Sometimes the problems are caused by mistakes made when data is entered, or when unsuitable processing *requests* are made.

Use a log sheet like the one on the next page to record any problems you encounter during the course of this GNVQ programme. If you are well into the year by the time you reach this point in the book, think back and make a list of any difficulties you have encountered. I am sure there will have been some! Indicate on your log or list how the problem was overcome and whether:

- the problem was outside your control, or

- was caused by you in some way, e.g. you were unable to make the searches required for the database for Element 3.3, because the design of the field type was unsuitable; or the results in a spreadsheet were incorrect because of the wrong formulae.

3 There are very specific laws relating to the use of computers, and if you are employed with VDUs (visual display units) your employer must ensure that you are aware of these laws. However, you must also use your common sense and be responsible for working safely in respect of the user, the equipment and the data.

The evidence assignment for Element 3.4 (in the mandatory units) will also provide the evidence for Performance Criteria 2.4.5 and 3.4.6 in IT core skills, because both relate to the importance of working safely and in line with good working practice.

LOG SHEET FOR IT CORE SKILLS 2.4.4 or 3.4.5		
Problem	**Cause**	**How I overcame the difficulty**

Application of number

Numbers get a bad press. In school they're usually associated with calculations you are never going to make, and maths words like trigonometry or algebraic equations. But that's only half the picture. In fact for most people working in IT, it's probably only 25%. The other 75% of the picture – the application of number – is a highly valued professional and personal skill.

Most aspects of computing are either founded on numbers or understood through numbers. This is because computers are basically calculating machines with programs and memory attached to them. Another word for 'calculate' is 'compute', and it is from this word that the name 'computers' comes. When you talk about a type of computer, you usually talk in numbers (speed – 486 Mhz, size of memories – 4 Mb RAM, 560 Mb hard disk, and so on).

Since you are interested in IT, the chances are that you already have a basic natural ability with numbers. This unit will develop your skills:

- **by revising some basic ideas such as fractions and percentages**
- **by introducing some new ones such as tolerances, means and modes**
- **by showing you how their application makes your working and personal life richer and easier.**

Element 2.1 Collect and record data

This element will show you basic techniques for choosing and handling data, describing situations with numbers, and making estimates. It will also explain how to measure shapes and spaces, and to work at the best level of accuracy.

After studying this element you should be able to:

1 make decisions about what data should be collected
2 choose and use **techniques** which suit the task
3 perform the **techniques** in a correct order
4 choose and work to an appropriate **level of accuracy**

5 record data in appropriate **units** and in an appropriate format
6 make sure that records are accurate and complete.

Handling data

Data means facts that are used to draw a conclusion or make a decision. For example, if you wanted to buy a new printer, the way to make a wise buying decision is to compare facts, such as quality of print and price, between different models. You then use these facts or data to choose the best model for the money. Before you are in a position to make that choice, the first step is to collect the data.

Data collection

Data is collected (and recorded) in surveys. Surveys that lead to wise decisions are carefully designed to collect the right type of data and from the right sources. This requires an effective data collection sheet.

When you buy new hardware or software for yourself or your company, you want to make sure you obtain the best possible deal. You do this by conducting a survey of prices and then comparing them. There are so many different dealers, in different shops and different magazines, offering different prices, that you can't possibly remember them all (especially as some include VAT and/or delivery while others do not). This means you need to design a data collection sheet that will contain all the information you need.

Activity

Your starting point in data collection is to decide exactly what data it is that you need. This strictly depends on your objective. For example, if your objective is to find the dealer with the best price on a particular model of laser printer, then you should only collect dealer names and contact numbers, prices and any additional costs. Do not include any data that is not strictly relevant to your objective – such as data on other printers – no matter how interesting you think it might be. The following are the headings you might need on a data collection sheet for the purchase of a laser printer:

Dealer	Phone no.	Price	Delivery	VAT	Total

An advertising company with over 50 employees has gradually become computerised and, over the past few years, it has built up a collection of different machines. Some employees use Macs and others use PCs. In order to get a discounted price, the management has decided to buy all new machines of one type or the other. Working in the computer services department, you have been asked to find out which type most employees would prefer. Design your data collection sheet.

Samples

If you had to survey a company with thousands of employees, it would take weeks to collect all the data by asking each person individually. So instead of boring yourself to death and wasting your employer's

time, you can take a shortcut called a 'sample'. A sample is a small part that represents a whole. For instance, if you sample someone's chips, you eat one or two and from those you know what the rest of them probably taste like.

Did you know?

The same idea is used in computer quality control: when you buy a new PC it usually has an operating system and other software already loaded. Large PC distributors preload these programs on to tens or hundreds of machines at a time. They then choose, say, five machines in a batch of 100 as a sample. If this 5% sample works properly, then there is a very high probability that the other 95% work properly as well.

Data sources

There are two basic sources from which you can obtain your data: written and people. Written sources include magazines, information stored on CD-ROM in the library, books, newspapers and so on – for example, a chart from a database showing software sales over a year, or figures from a spreadsheet on a telecom company's annual profit.

Collecting data from written sources is called desk research and is often much easier than field research. Field research means going out and asking people questions such as which computer programs they use most often and for how many hours per week. Sometimes they are helpful and polite; at other times they are just too busy to answer questions that don't directly concern them.

As a general rule, get all the information you can through desk research first – especially as someone else may have already done fieldwork you can use. Then, time your fieldwork for a nice sunny day!

Data types

There are also two basic types of data. The first is discrete and the second is grouped. Discrete data means data that is separate and distinct – not part of a group – for example, number of computers per household in your town. Grouped data is, as its name suggests, part of a group – for example, the number of computers per household in your town, at two-year intervals over the past 10 years, drawn up into a chart showing how fast computer use is growing.

Techniques with numbers

The results of most surveys are expressed in numbers – for example, 'Half (fraction), 50% (percentage), 0.5 (decimal fraction), 2 out of 4 (ratio), or even –0.5 (negative number) of the people surveyed can't tell the difference between margarine and butter'.

Fractions

Fractions are numbers that represent parts of a whole. Simple fractions are a convenient and easy way to think about, communicate and understand quantities. For example, many programs need at least 4 Mb of RAM to run, so if your machine has 16 Mb available, they will use $\frac{1}{4}$ of your computer's RAM capacity.

Simple fractions are most frequently used to give estimates. For example, if you're wondering how long it will take to get through this book, your tutor might say you'll study $\frac{1}{4}$ of this term and $\frac{1}{2}$ the next term, at which point you'll have studied $\frac{3}{4}$ of the book and know you have $\frac{1}{4}$ left for the final term. There is no advantage in specifying the exact number of pages.

Decimal fractions

Rather than writing $\frac{3}{4}$ or three-quarters, you can use a decimal fraction, 0.75. Like ordinary fractions, decimal fractions are a useful way to talk about size and quantity. The main practical difference is that you can input decimal fractions to spreadsheets and calculators. You can also be more accurate while still being clear. For example, a standard floppy disk has a capacity of 1.44 Mb. This is much easier to understand than $1\frac{11}{25}$ Mb.

Did you know?

When writing out decimal fractions, places to the left of the decimal represent whole numbers (e.g. 1.00, 3.00), tens (e.g. 10.00, 30.00), hundreds (e.g. 100.00, 300.00) and so on. Places to the right of the decimal represent places for tenths (e.g. 0.10, 0.30) hundredths (0.01, 0.03), thousandths (0.001, 0.003) and so on.

When converting ordinary fractions to decimal fractions, simply divide the denominator (the number at the bottom) by the numerator (the number at the top). For example, to turn 4/7ths into a decimal, divide the 7 by the 4, and you get 0.57.

The decimal fraction 0.57 is 57/100ths. In other words, to convert a decimal fraction into an ordinary fraction, put the decimal over 100. For example, 0.25 is the same as 25/100ths. Because 25 goes into 100 four times, the ordinary fraction reduces to $\frac{1}{4}$.

Did you know?

Estimating numbers is also a very useful skill to develop. It acts as a quick check or prediction to test whether your calculation is on the right track or is completely wrong. For example, you can see that the fraction 4/7ths is just over half. So you can estimate that the answer must be something just over 0.5. If you got an answer of 3.6 or even 0.7 your estimate would tell you there was something wrong.

Percentages

Per cent means out of each hundred, or per hundred. So if you have £100 and you spend £15 on a music CD and £30 on a CD-ROM you have spent (15 + 30 = 45) 45% of your money. At work and in your private life you often need to find the percentage of a number. For example, how much will 17.5% VAT add to your bill?

Did you know?

To calculate a percentage, multiply the number by the percentage and divide by

100. For example, if your bill is £16 + VAT at 17.5%, your calculation for the VAT is:

$$17.5/100 \times 16 = 2.80$$

Your total is the £16 + £2.80 = £18.80.

If you have a calculator handy, just enter the number (16) and press $\times$ 17.5%.

A useful technique when you just need to know the total is to enter the number (16) and press $\times$ 117.5%. The 100% represents the original number and the 17.5% is the percentage increase. This way saves you the trouble of adding the number found from the percentage (the £2.80) to the original number (£16).

Percentages are also useful for giving estimates – for example, 'under 5%' to describe the amount of time a computer network is failing to work, or 'over 80%' to describe how much time a graphic designer uses computer-aided design (CAD) packages.

Ratios

A ratio is a proportion of one quantity in relation to another. Ratios are a good way of making comparisons. For example, if you survey 100 computer users and find that 30 use Macs and 70 use PCs, the ratio of Mac to PC users is 30:70 or 3:7.

Negative numbers

Numbers describe situations: how many people are in your class, the score in a football match, the speed a car can travel at. Some numbers can represent negative situations such as winter temperature, for example, –7°C. One of the commonest negative

situations involves money. If you have £10 in the bank and you take £20 out, you are in a negative situation: you owe £10 or have –£10.

A business manager in, for example, a company selling IT services, needs to know the financial situation. If he adds up all the money that comes in from sales then takes away all the money that the company spends on buying equipment, paying wages and so on, he can describe the financial situation. If business is good, it will be positive. If business is bad, it will be a negative situation such as –£20,000.

Activity

Difficult maths test

1 A friend asks you if there's enough room on her hard disk to load a new games program. When you check, you find she has a 156 megabyte hard disk that is already $\frac{1}{3}$ full and the new games program takes up 49 megabytes. Approximately what fraction of her hard disk is still free?

2 Write the following hard disk sizes in decimal fractions:

$\frac{1}{2}$ GB $\frac{3}{4}$ GB $\frac{1}{5}$ GB $1\frac{1}{5}$ GB $2\frac{2}{3}$ GB

3 Express the following as percentages. First, however, predict the answer by estimation, then make the calculation (write out your estimate and your calculation):

14% of 150   12% of 200   27% of 154

4 A computer services department has an annual budget of £10,000. If they spend £7,299.45 on hardware and £1,701.89 on software, roughly what percentage of their budget is left?

5 Your tutor is trying to persuade your school or college to buy more computers. At the moment there are 30 computers and 240 students. What is the computer to student ratio? If the school or college bought another 30 computers, what would the new ratio be?

6 The good thing about portable computers is that you can use them wherever you are. Well, not quite. There are some places where temperatures are so cold that the machine would not work. Manufacturers supply this information with the computer. Look in a magazine or a shop to find an example, and write down the minimum operating temperature.

Levels of accuracy

Information technology generally requires a very high level of accuracy. If you type a line of code into a computer and you make one little mistake such as forgetting a space or dot, it won't work. Most microprocessor chips are engineered to a thickness of 0.05 cm (0.02 in) – look at a ruler to see just how thick (or thin) this is.

Rounding

Working in IT, you will have to select a suitable level of accuracy for data collection and for measuring tasks. For example, you might need to measure the amount of space available in a computer to see whether there is enough room for a sound card or fax modem. As numbers are commonly given to two decimal places (3.27 cm, £17.56), if you work to three places then round down to two, you can be sure that your figures will be accurate. Here's how:

- If a number is 0.4 or less, round down. For example, round 3.274 down to 3.27.
- If a number is 0.5 or more, round up. For example, round 3.275 up to 3.28.

Large numbers

IT also requires you to work with large numbers. For example, a standard high-density (HD) floppy disk can hold 1.44 Mb of information. As 1 Mb is roughly one million bytes (actually, it's 1,048,576 bytes), so 1.44 Mb is roughly 1,440,000 bytes. If you have two files on your hard disk and your file management system tells you that each of them takes up 800,000 bytes, you know that you won't be able to back them both up on to the same disk.

Activity

One kilobyte (abbreviated to 1 K or 1 Kb or 1 Kbyte) is 1,024 bytes. If your file management system tells you that you have 10 files of 40 Kb each, could you back them up on to a 1.44 Mb floppy disk?

To answer this question you don't need to find your calculator to work out exactly how many bytes there are in ten 40 Kb files. You don't need to know exactly, so you can just make a quick calculation in your head: 1 Kb = just over 1,000 bytes so 40 Kb is something over 40,000 bytes. Ten files this size = something over

400,000 bytes, so there's plenty of space on a 1.44 Mb (1,440,000 byte) disk.

Tolerance

When, for example, you calculate in kilobytes, you don't usually need to be absolutely accurate – you don't need to bother with the extra 24 bytes over a thousand. You just need an answer that is correct, give or take a few bytes. The limits of this 'give or take a few . . .' are called tolerance.

It is the same for many other calculations: if your boss asks you how long it will take you to install a CD-ROM drive, you wouldn't say 'between 1 hour, 35 minutes and 2 hours, 13 minutes', you'd just say '2 hours give or take half an hour'. Being able to say how long something will take is an important work skill: it allows you to manage your time and so to give yourself realistic work targets.

If you were measuring pieces of equipment in millimetres, you might decide that 5 mm was a reasonable tolerance. You could express this by writing '± 5 mm'.

Shape, space and measures

When you take the lid off a computer and check, add or adjust components, you are dealing with shape, space and measures. This requires a proper set of tools that are, in the main, screwdrivers. A useful tip is to keep a ruler in your kit so that you can measure component shapes and the spaces between them.

Units of measurement

There are two different systems of measurement – imperial and metric. Because the metric system is easier to understand and to work with, it is the standard in EU countries and is slowly becoming the world standard.

Metric units are related to each other by powers of 10. This simply means that when you divide or multiply from one unit to another you just shift the decimal point. For example, 1 centimetre is 0.1 of a metre, 1 metre is 0.001 kilometre, 1 Kb is 0.001 Mb. This is much easier than working with 12 inches in a foot, 36 inches in a yard, 16 ounces in a pound, 14 pounds in a stone and so on.

However, as many countries such as Britain and America still use both systems, you need to understand each system and how to convert between them. The most important units you will have to measure and convert between are money, physical dimensions and weight.

Money

Computer components and other personal electronics are much cheaper in the USA than in Britain. Many items are pound for dollar equivalents. For example, a sound card that cost £100 in Britain costs $100 in the USA. So what's the difference?

Well, the exchange rate is usually somewhere around $1.53 to the pound. To make the calculation, divide the number of dollars by the rate. In the example, 100 divided by 1.53 = 65.359, which rounds to 65.36. In other words you pay nearly $\frac{1}{3}$ more (to the tax authorities) for exactly the same card in Britain.

In this example, you use division to calculate from dollars to pounds. Most of the time you will probably start with pounds and want to know how many dollars you'll receive. Find out by using multiplication: £100 × 1.53 = (shift the decimal) $153. So you would get $153 dollars for your £100.

Physical dimensions

Do you know how tall you are in the metric system? The metric system of measurement expresses length, breadth, height and distance in parts of a metre. The imperial system expresses them in inches, feet, yards and miles. Here are the conversion factors, to three decimal places:

Multiply the number of	by	to obtain the equivalent number in
centimetres (cm)	0.393	inches
metres (m)	1.093	yards
kilometres (km)	0.621	miles
inches (in)	2.54	centimetres
yards (yd)	0.914	metres
miles	1.609	kilometres

Weight

When manufacturers advertise portable computers, they usually begin by saying how light they are: 'Only 3.3 pounds/kilograms and it'll fit in your briefcase.' So how heavy is 3.3 pounds or kilograms? You can get an idea of how much things weigh by comparing them with your own weight. But first you need to know what you weigh in each system (remember there are 16 oz in 1 lb and 14 lb in 1 st). Here are the conversion factors, rounded to three decimal places:

Multiply the number of	by	to obtain the equivalent number in
ounces (oz)	28.349	grams
pounds (lb)	0.453	kilograms
grams (g)	0.032	ounces
kilograms (k)	2.204	pounds

Figure N.1 You can get an idea of how much things weigh by comparing them with your own weight

Activity

Difficult maths test

1 For £100, what would you receive in the following currencies?

French francs at FF8.14 to the pound
Italian lire at L2,401 to the pound
German marks at DM2.34 to the pound
Spanish pesetas at pta188 to the pound.

2 What is:

a 3.5-inch floppy disk in centimetres?
a 0.93-metre monitor packing case in feet?
a 44-mile drive to another town in kilometres?

3 How much do you weigh in pounds and ounces and in kilograms and grams? Here are three portable computer makes and their weights in pounds. How heavy are they in kilograms and grams?

IBM ThinkPad	5.8
Gateway Liberty	4.2
Hewlitt Packard Omnibook	3.8

Evidence assignment

Information Technology has given us access to a vast amount of data on almost any subject. Individuals and organisations can select and use this information to help them to make better decisions. As a rule, quality information leads to better decision making.

For example, if you were looking for a cellphone, you wouldn't just buy the first one you found. You would look around, talk to different people, compare features and prices, then use your information to make the best choice. The same is true in organisations, except that they are often dealing in large amounts of money – not buying just a cellphone, but whole communi-cations systems, sych as phones, faxes and other communicating devices, all on a Local Area Network. When an organisation makes this sort of buying decision, they too want to be sure they have the best information to help them to make the best decision.

How do organisations access quality information? There are three phases, each covered by the elements in this Application of Number unit: research, analysis and presentation. Start by collecting the data, next make the calculations, and then present the information in an easily understood format.

As you work through this unit you are going to prepare and carry out two quality information projects, and write them up into reports. Here are your project briefings:

Project 1   Pentium prices

Scenario

The computer industry is always talking about how quickly prices are falling and how this is making powerful technology available to everyone. However, they rarely give us any factual information such as price comparisons, so we need to know how much of this is marketing talk and how much is hard fact. How fast are prices falling, and when would be a good time to buy a better machine?

Your task in Project 1 is to find out how fast the general public think computer prices are falling, to research actual price decreases over the past two years, and then to compare your findings.

Project 2   Cellphones

Scenario

The IT industry has been so successful in developing cellphones that the market is almost flooded. The first cellphones were big and ugly, very heavy, and cost a fortune to buy and to use. Nowadays conveniently sized, light-weight phones are often given away free. This means that manufacturers need new cellphone ideas that will help them sell their products.

Your task in Project 2 is to design an 'adventure cellphone' for use in extreme conditions (mountain cold and desert heat), based on an ideal size and a maximum acceptable weight. To complete this task you will need to research existing models, survey potential cellphone buyers, then use this information to present your ideas.

Each project is divided into three phases. You can complete both reports at the same time, phase by phase as the unit progresses. Alternatively, you can study all three elements then complete each report individually. Discuss this with your tutor.

Project 1 – Phase 1

Phase 1 is the data collection phase. Carefully review the Project 1 briefing above, then design one data collection sheet to use for surveying people and another for your desk-work.

People   Question 15 people about computer prices in general. You will need to know first if people think prices are getting cheaper, and then by how much expressed as a percentage (it is up to you to decide on an appropriate level of accuracy).

Desk-work Research your data from a minimum of two different sources. Find 12 advertisements in magazines or other sources, which appeared at approximately two-month intervals over the past two years. Focus only on prices for Pentium 120Mhz processors, or this project will take up the rest of your life! Pentiums are a reasonably accurate measure of price changes.

When you are happy with the design of your data collection sheets, carry out the research and keep your data safe. Then write the first part of your report. You should write up the project briefing in your own words, explaining your reasons for:

■ collecting the data
■ choosing the methods for collecting the data
■ choosing means of recording the data.

Project 2 – Phase 1

Carefully review the Project 2 briefing above, then design one data collection sheet to use for surveying the general public and another for your desk-work.

People Question 15 people about the dimensions they would prefer and the maximum acceptable weight for a cellphone. Take a ruler or other measuring device to help them be specific with the dimensions. At this point it doesn't matter whether they use inches or centimetres. You might also take with you something that weighs around one pound or 0.5 kilo, to give people an idea of an acceptable weight.

Desk-work Your desk-work should cover the dimensions, weight, and minimum and maximum operating temperatures for twelve different phones currently on the market.

When you are happy with the design of your data collection sheets, carry out the research and keep your data safe. Then write the first part of your report. You should write up the project briefing in your own words, explaining your reasons for:

■ collecting the data
■ choosing the methods for collecting the data
■ choosing means of recording the data.

Element 2.2   Tackle problems

In Element 2.1 you learnt how to collect and record the correct types of data and to apply basic calculations. The next step is to use the number-crunching techniques of formulae, conversions and averages. These techniques are shortcuts that let you tackle problems with two- and three-dimensional shapes and whole sets of numbers at one time.

After studying this element you should be able to:

1 choose and use *techniques* which suit the problem
2 perform the *techniques* in a correct order
3 choose and use appropriate units
4 choose and use an appropriate *level of accuracy*
5 use mathematical terms correctly
6 carry out calculations correctly
7 use *checking procedures* to confirm the results of calculations
8 check that the results make sense in respect of the problem being tackled.

Formulae

Formulae are another area where your choice of IT puts you ahead in the application of number. In Unit 2, you used formulae to make calculations in spreadsheets. For example, instead of adding up a list of numbers to find the total, you just enter a formula that tells the spreadsheet to do it for you. In this case the formula would look something like =sum(A1:A7).

You already know what 'equals' means. You also know that 'sum' is another way of saying 'add up'. In this formula 'A1' is the reference for the first number on your list and 'A7' is the reference for the last number on your list. So the formula simply means add up all the numbers from A1 to A7.

Formulae express a logical relationship. They say that one value (such as a total) is the same as another value (such as a list of numbers). You can easily see this from the formulae you have already been using in Element 2.1, when you made conversions. For example:

■ subtotal + VAT = total
■ kilobyte times one thousand equals megabyte
■ US$ $\times$ 1.53 = UK£.

One of the best things about formulae is that you can make them up to suit your own data. For example, if you are often asked to obtain software or hardware for other people, you might decide to add 10% to the total price to cover your time and efforts. Then you would quote a price using the following formula:

$$C +10\% = P$$

C is the cost in the shop or magazine and *P* is the total price including your fee.

Formulae in words and symbols

As you will have noticed, most formulae can be expressed in words and in symbols. When you use a formula everyday and know it by heart, it is quicker to express it in symbols than in words. Therefore, you are much more likely to say or write 'Kb × 1,000 = Mb' than 'kilobyte times one thousand equals megabyte'. Symbols take up a lot less room as well as a lot less breath!

Activity

The following are some formulae written in words. Write them out in symbols:

- speed equals distance over time
- Fahrenheit equals nine divided by five degrees Celsius plus thirty-two
- total cost equals cost of production plus distribution plus profit.

Shapes and sizes

IT hardware comes in all different shapes and sizes, and you will be expected to explain what different components are and to fit them together. For example, you may be asked the difference between a desk-top and a tower system. Your answer would probably begin with hand movements to give the general idea.

You might then mention that most tower systems can hold more internal components. To know whether a particular box (desk top or tower) could take an additional drive, you would need to measure the drive size and the available space. In all your measurements you will be dealing with two basic categories of shape: two dimensional and three dimensional.

Two dimensions (2D)

All 2D shapes are flat. Most 2D shapes in IT are rectangles, squares (squares are special rectangles where all the sides are the same length) and circles.

Squares and rectangles

The top of your desk is a 2D shape and so is your mouse-mat. Both of them are probably rectangular, so if you need to make a calculation that involves

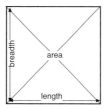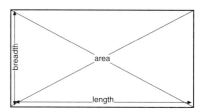

Figure N.2 The area of a square or rectangle equals length multiplied by breadth

them you would need to know their area, length and width.

For example, you might have to install a number of workstations in a crowded office. To save space in this situation, monitors are often placed on a central table with people working around it. Your instructions are to install four monitors on the table with a minimum space around each for air-flow, wires, keyboards and so on. Before transporting the equipment, taking it out of the boxes and setting it up, you want to be sure it will all fit.

If you find out the area each monitor will take up and the total area of the table, you can answer your question. The formula for finding the area of a square or a rectangle is $a = l \times w$ or, in words, area equals length multiplied by width (or breadth, which is the same thing).

Activity

In the above example, the monitors are 30 cm × 30 cm (30 cm square) and the minimum space between them is 20 cm. This means that each monitor needs a space of 40 cm × 40 cm. The table is 1 m × 1.2 m. Without using a calculator, what do you think? Will they fit? Draw a rough sketch, write on the measurements and make an estimate. Remember that 1 m is 100 cm.

Now calculate the area needed for each monitor, and the total area needed for all four monitors. Next calculate the area of the table. Will they fit?

Circles

If you look at the bottom of your mouse and the gate that holds the tracking ball in place, you'll see that it's circular. So are CD-ROMs and other computer disks. If you need to make a calculation that involves these or any other circles, you need to understand area, radius and circumference.

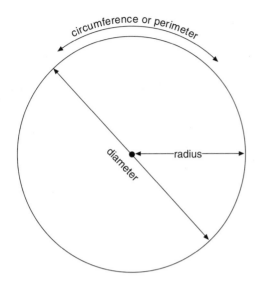

Figure N.3 Measuring a circle

For example, you may be working for a multimedia company that decides a circular casing for their CDs would be more practical and attractive, and cheaper as it would use less material. They design the cover picture and information then ask you to find out how much paper they need to produce 1,000 inserts. Where do you begin?

To make calculations with circles you need to know what circumference, radius and diameter are, and then the formulas for working with them. The circumference or perimeter is the distance around a circle. The radius is the distance from the centre to the outside of a circle. Diameter is the distance straight across a circle at its widest point (this is the same as the radius × 2).

The formula for finding the circumference of a circle is $C = 2\pi r$ or πd. The symbol π is 3.1416 (an unchanging number pronounced *pi*). What do the C, r and d stand for? The formula for finding the area of a circle is $A = \pi r^2$.

Activity

Find out the circumference, radius and diameter of a CD-ROM, then work out its area. Multiply by 1,000 and you'll know how much paper is required for inserts in the multimedia company's new casing.

Three dimensions (3D)

CDs, mouse-mats and pieces of paper are actually 3D not 2D. They all have height or thickness as well as length and breadth. We sometimes work with 2D and ignore height or thickness, just because it is convenient – as in the CD inserts example. So, 3D shapes have length, breadth and height. In IT, the main 3D shapes you will work with are cubes, cuboids and cylinders.

Cubes and cuboids

A cube is a 3D shape that has six square faces. Think of dice – they have six square faces, each distinguished by one to six dots. A cuboid is the same thing as a cube except that all its faces are rectangles. Cubes and cuboids are everywhere in IT – every box for every piece of equipment is a cube or cuboid. Understanding how to calculate the volume of cubes and cuboids makes it easier to work with them.

For example, you often need to move fragile equipment. If you are moving it further than around a workspace, and particularly if you have to transport it by car or van, you must package it. If you were asked the approximate volume of polystyrene chips needed to pack around a sound card in its delivery box, you would need to know the volume of the

Figure N.4 Cubes and cuboids in everyday life

box. The formula for calculating the volume of cubes and cuboids is simply $l \times b \times h$ (length times breadth times height).

Activity

The cooling fan in your computer doesn't work anymore – something to do with the bearing. A friend offers you one she has salvaged from an old machine. It is the right electrical specification so the only question is, will it fit? The maximum fan space in your machine is 20 cm × 7.5 cm × 6 cm. What is the volume?

Cylinders

A cylinder is a tube shape with circles at either end. For example, Pepsi and Coke and other drinks are often sold in aluminium cylinders (cans). Some of the commonest cylinders in IT (apart from electronic components such as transistors and diodes) are toner cartridges and the rollers that help paper through printers, photocopiers and other devices.

Companies that make printers need to know how much toner a cartridge will hold. The formula for this calculation is $V = \pi r^2 \times$ length.

Activity

What are the volumes of these cartridges?
- $r = 2$ cm, length = 15 cm
- $r = 1$ cm, length = 15 cm
- $r = 1$ cm, length = 7.5 cm

Conversions

In Element 2.1 above, you studied and applied conversion formulae between weights and measures, and between currencies. At work you usually have to make conversions many times. For example, if your company deals with equipment from the USA, you may constantly have to convert between pounds and dollars and back again. As Americans still use imperial measurements you would also have to convert these to metric. Instead of making a new conversion each time, you can construct a graph or scale that shows the differences, and then just read them off.

Activity

Construct a **conversion graph** between pounds and kilograms:

1 If possible, get a piece of graph paper.
2 Draw a right angle (an L shape). The line going down, the vertical line, is your Y axis. The line going across, the horizontal line, is your X axis.
3 Mark and number intervals of equal distance on each axis. (If you are using graph paper, mark every fifth line. If you're not using graph paper, measure and mark every centimetre.)
4 Label the Y axis 'kilograms' and the X axis 'pounds'.
5 Check how many pounds in a kilogram.
6 Draw a line from the 1 k mark on the Y axis across to meet another line coming up from the 2.2 lb mark on the X axis. Mark the meeting point with an asterisk.
7 Draw another line from the 5 k mark on the Y axis across to meet another line coming up from the 10.10 lb mark on the X axis. Mark the meeting point with an asterisk.
8 Draw a diagonal line between the two asterisks.

You have now constructed your graph. To use it, read any weight on the kilograms or pounds line, move up or across to the diagonal line, then read down or across to the equivalent weight. Try it out. Check your own weight first, then check three other people's weight.

Activity

Construct a **conversion scale** between pounds and dollars:

1 Use graph paper if possible.
2 Draw a vertical line 10 cm long.
3 Label one side £ and the other side $.

4 Mark and number £ every 1 cm.

5 Check the exchange rate.

6 At the £1 mark write 1.53 (the rate) on the $ side.

7 At the £2 mark write 3.06 on the $ side.

8 At the £3 mark write 4.59 on the $ side and so on up to the £10 mark.

You have now constructed your scale. To read off £20, check £2 then move the decimal point on the $ side, one place to the left. This should be $30.60.

- How many dollars would you get for £50, and for £100?
- How many would you get for £500, and for £1,000?
- If you were a millionaire in pounds, how many dollars would you have?

Check your answers with your tutor.

Averages

The commonest type of number-crunching is working with averages. The attraction of averages is that, although they are just one number, they can represent tens, hundreds, thousands or even millions of other numbers. Any market report on IT will include averages to describe all sorts of situations – for example, the number of families with PCs in 1996, the number of telephones per British home, the number of factories using robots in the production process and so on. There are three sorts of averages: mean, median and mode.

Mean

Mean is the everyday use of the word 'average'. It is found by adding up all the numbers in a set, then dividing by however many numbers there are. The formula for finding the mean uses the word values instead of numbers but it means the same thing:

$$X = s/n$$

or, in words, mean = sum of values/number of values in the set.

For example, in your printer survey you find three different prices for the same device. The first is £400, the second is £420 and the third is £450. The sum of these values is, £1,270 and there are three values so divide by 3. The answer: £423.34 – the mean price.

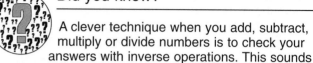

Did you know?

A clever technique when you add, subtract, multiply or divide numbers is to check your answers with inverse operations. This sounds complicated, but it's actually very simple. For example, you can check:

- addition by subtraction
- subtraction by addition
- multiplication by division
- division by multiplication.

Does 20 + 33 + 14 = 67? Check by starting with 67 and subtracting 14 and then 33. If you arrive back at 20, then you know you are right.

Does 14 − 5 − 3 = 6? Check by starting with 6, adding 3 then adding 5. If you arrive at 15 you're wrong. If you arrive back at 14, you're right.

Does 20 × 17 = 340? You can check by dividing 340 by 17. If the answer is 20 then you are correct. Alternatively you can divide 340 by 20 and your answer should be 17.

Does 48 ÷ 11 = 4.364? Check by multiplying 4.364 by 11. If your answer is 72.14 you're way out. If your answer rounds to 48, you're right.

Median

You now know how to calculate (and check) the mean. Another type of average is the median. The median is the middle number in any range. For example, if the results from one of your surveys, in the order you receive them, are 44, 52, 54, 54, **57**, 61, 62, 63, 79 the number in the middle of the string of answers, 57, is the median.

Mode

If you survey 10 offices to find out how many telephone handsets each has, the mean will not be a very useful average, especially as it will probably have a decimal place (what is 0.4 of a telephone?). In this case the most common number of handsets is the most useful average. The 'most common number' average is called the mode. For example, of 2, 3, 4, 4, 4, 6, 6, 7, the mode for office telephones is **4**.

Evidence assignment

Project 1 – Phase 2

In Phase 2 of your project work, you are going to collate your data into more easily understood forms. First, review your work on Project 1 to date.

People Find the number of respondents who thought computer prices are getting cheaper and the number who did not. Next, calculate the mean, median and mode for the percentages. Once you have the average percentages, first estimate them (remembering to record your workings) then calculate them as fractions and decimal fractions. Check your results carefully, using appropriate procedures.

Desk-work Calculate the mean, median and mode price of Pentiums over the two-year period, then identify the highest and lowest prices you found and specify their dates.

Important: Keep all your notes and workings in preparation for Phase 3, and to attach as appendices to your report.

Project 2 – Phase 2

Review your work on Project 2 to date.

People Find the mean, median and mode for the dimensions and the weights that respondents gave. Express them in both imperial and metric measurements to an appropriate level of accuracy. Check your results carefully, using appropriate procedures.

Desk-work Find the mean, median and mode for the dimensions, weights and operating temperatures of the cellphones. Express the dimensions and weights in both imperial and metric measurements. Express the minimum and maximum operating temperatures in terms of both Celsius and Fahrenheit. Check your results carefully, using appropriate procedures.

Important: Keep your notes and workings in preparation for Phase 3, and to attach as appendices to your report.

Element 2.3 Interpret and present data

Having learnt how to design surveys, collect data and perform various number-crunching routines on it, you now have results that represent your data. So what do they all mean and what is the best way to explain them to your manager? This element will show you how to identify the main features of your results, then interpret them in relation to the problem being tackled.

After studying this element you should be able to:

1 identify and *explain the main* features of the data
2 choose and use *techniques* which will present the data effectively
3 follow *conventions* for presenting the data
4 present the results with an appropriate *level of accuracy*
5 explain how the results make sense in respect of the problem being tackled.

Presentation

When you've collected all your data, even in a relatively small survey, you will have amassed a great deal of information. This needs to be organised into a presentable form. The most important objective of your explanation and presentation is to answer the question you set out to solve.

Like any answer, the clearer and more concise the explanation the better. With numbers, the clearest, most concise explanations allow the reader or listener to understand the main points within the whole picture. The most effective techniques use probabilities, diagrams of 2D and 3D objects, and statistical diagrams.

Probabilities

Whenever you toss a coin the probability or chance of it being heads or tails is expressed in the ratio 50:50. The outcome is a simple either/or result. Probabilities are numerical descriptions of the chances of something happening.

Most of the time when we deal with probability our assessments are based on facts and experience. For example, if the computer services department have resolved all software problems in seven out of the past ten months, then the probability of their solving all problems in the next month is 0:7. Or, in other words, they have a 70% chance.

Activity

Express the probability of the following as ratios and as percentages. Look back at Element 2.1 if you need to check on how to make the calculations:

- The sun will shine tomorrow because it has done so for three out of six days already this week.
- The next modem off the production line will be faulty because four in the last batch of 100 were faulty.
- The next time the phone rings it will be a wrong number because seven out of the last 28 calls have been a wrong number.

Diagrams of 2D and 3D objects

In Element 2.2 you discovered whether the monitors would all fit on a table by drawing a sketch. Computer-aided design (CAD) packages or features enable you to construct highly accurate diagrams on the screen or printed out on to paper.

Did you know?

While the objects that these diagrams represent can be 2D or 3D, the diagrams themselves are always in 2D. This is because they are on the screen or a piece of paper – screens and pieces of paper have length and breadth, 2D. For example, a plan or drawing showing how to connect up a computer is in 2D. The computer illustrated in the plan is, of course, 3D.

Activity

Because of its position on a desk or table, the back of a computer is often difficult to see or to get at. If you need to plug or unplug different devices or to change switches over, and you have memorised the layout, it's much easier. The best way to memorise a layout is to make a drawing in 2D that shows the position of the switches and plugs, and label it. Try it and keep the drawing for later.

Figure N.5 below shows the top of your desk or table – at home, school, college or work – from a bird's-eye view. In the actual positions, or the positions you would like them, draw the computer, keyboard, mouse and any other equipment.

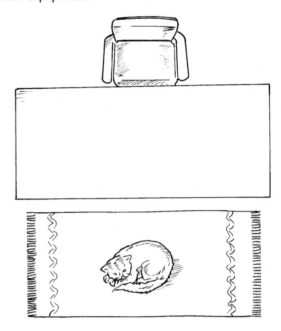

Figure N.5 A bird's-eye view of your desk

2D is particularly useful for explaining layout, as you can see from these two activities and from any IT manual. When you are trying to explain objects rather than layout, it is often clearer with 3D. For example, the size of equipment is often an important factor when selecting the best for the workplace or home.

Figure N.6 is an outline diagram of a typical IT cuboid – a printer.

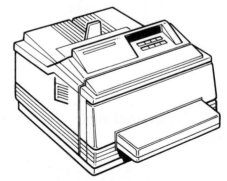

Figure N.6 A diagram of a printer

This drawing of a printer gives you some idea of its size, but not a very accurate idea. This is because it is not to scale. To scale means that the length of the lines in the drawing are in direct proportion to the length of the actual lines. This principle is used in a map that gives a scale of 1 inch to 1 mile: you know that if the distance between two towns is 4 inches, then it is actually 4 miles.

When you produce drawings to scale remember that the best technique is to choose a simple scale, for example, 1 cm = 1 m. If you choose 1 cm = 0.56 cm or even worse, 1 cm = 4 in, you'll get a bad headache when you do the calculations.

Activity

Try this for yourself. Find a printer that is more or less cuboid and measure up its main dimensions – length, breadth and height. Then, forgetting any details, draw it to scale.

Statistical diagrams

Statistical diagrams are charts and graphs. Just as 2D diagrams can often represent objects more clearly than words, statistical diagrams can represent numbers more clearly. For example, Figure N.7 shows a list of computer system sales over the past 12 months, and a chart that gives the same information.

Month	Sales
Jan	23
Feb	25
Mar	23
Apr	17
May	15
Jun	13
Jul	13
Aug	12
Sep	26
Oct	33
Nov	30
Dec	34

Computer sales

Figure N.7 A bar chart is a clear way to present numerical information

It is easier to see the picture that this bar chart presents than it is to try to form a picture in your mind from the list. It is also easier to interpret what the numbers are saying: you can see that fewer computers are sold in the summer months than in the winter. Why do you think this is? Perhaps the cold winter weather keeps people indoors and in the summer people prefer to spend their money on holidays rather than computers. Why do you think most computers are sold in October, November, December and then sales drop in January?

Activity

Do you remember the X and Y axes from your graph in Element 2.2? In this chart, which is which?

- Which axis represents frequency (number of computers sold)?
- Which axis represents intervals (months)?

Charts

Another advantage of IT is that you learn how to prepare charts like the one above, using software charting tools. Two of the most common types of chart are the bar chart and the pie chart.

Bar charts show individual figures at a specific time or illustrate comparisons among items. The chart in Figure N.7, showing computer sales by month, is a typical bar chart: it compares sales over different months.

Activity

The following data comes from a survey on the number of people planning to take courses in different software over the next 12 months. Present it in a bar chart using the computer sales chart as your model:

Software	Applicants
Word	77
PowerPoint	23
WordPerfect	60
Visual C++	11
PageMaker	53
CorelDRAW	44

Pie charts show the relationship of one part to the whole. For example, Figure N.8 is a pie chart showing the distribution of mobile telephones in eastern Europe.

Graphs

Graphs are the second type of statistical diagram. In Element 2.2 you constructed a line graph to show

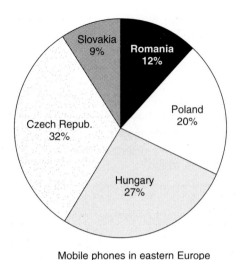

Mobile phones in eastern Europe

Figure N.8 A pie chart

the pound/dollar conversion rate. Line graphs are a straightforward way to make comparisons between different categories on the same graph. For example, Figure N.9 is a graph that shows the rates of use of photocopiers in different departments (marketing and production) over a six-week period.

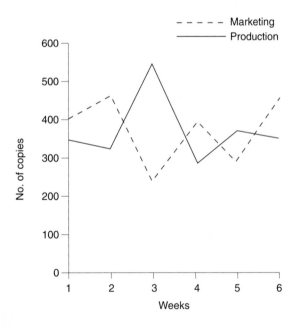

Figure N.9 A line chart

Activity

The following data comes from a survey into people connected to the Internet. The numbers are in millions, and 1996–9 are estimates. Present this information in a graph:

Year	No. of people (millions)
1990	7
1991	8
1992	10
1993	12
1994	15
1995	19
1996	28
1997	37
1998	52
1999	74

Pictograms

Information can also be displayed in a picture diagram called a pictogram. This is usually used to show general information in a visually striking way (see Figure N.10) – for example, in a sales presentation. A pictogram may show growing numbers by enlarging each illustration or increasing the number of illustrations, and will usually need a key to show what each picture represents.

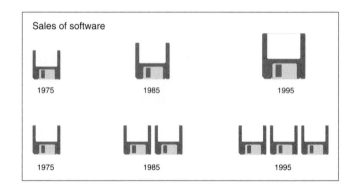

Figure N.10 Two ways of showing increasing sales by pictogram

That is the end of this unit in the application of number. You have covered all the basic number skills that you will need for IT. As you work through the chapters in this book, you will develop and practise these skills further.

Evidence assignment

Project 1 – Phase 3

In Phase 3 of your project work, you are going to present and explain the results of your findings, and complete your report. Review your work on Project 1 to date.

Select and prepare an appropriate statistical diagram to represent your results. You should show your findings on what people think has happened to prices and what your desk-work shows has actually happened, on the same diagram.

When your diagram is clear and complete, use the calculations you made at Phase 2 to help you write a report interpreting it. In the first paragraph, explain how your diagram works – what the different axes and the lines or bars (or whatever you have chosen) represent. In the next paragraph, state the averages. In the following paragraph(s), compare and explain any differences in the averages and suggest reasons why they differ.

Add your diagram to the report, and attach your workings from Phase 2 as appendices.

Project 2 – Phase 3

Review your work on Project 2 to date.

Select and prepare two statistical diagrams. The first should represent existing cellphone weights and the maximum weights that people think are acceptable. The second should show the minimum and maximum operating temperatures of the existing cellphones you researched.

When your diagrams are clear and complete, use the calculations you made at Phase 2 to help you write separate interpretations for each. In the first paragraph, explain how the diagram works. In the next paragraph, state the averages you found. In the following paragraph(s) compare and explain any differences in the averages and suggest reasons why they differ.

Using the mean of the dimensions which people said they would prefer, draw an outline 3D diagram of the ideal adventure cellphone, to scale. Explain the diagram, especially its dimensions and scale.

Add your diagrams to the report, and attach your workings from Phase 2 as appendices.

Answers

Element 1.1 Revision test

1 Booking, electronic funds transfer, electronic point of sale systems, stock control, order processing, payroll processing.
2 Design, process production control, robotics.
4 Spot-welding in a car factory, photographing speeding motorists, connecting telephone calls, automatic pilot systems.
5 Perform set routines faster, more cheaply and more accurately than humans.
6 Electronic funds transfer.
7 Point of sale.
8 Accuracy, cost, speed, efficiency, environment.
9 Costs, security, health, safety, environment.
10 Data, hardware, software, processing, effectiveness, purpose.
11 Computer-aided design, computer-aided manufacture.

Element 1.2 Revision test

1 Qwerty.
2 Visual display unit, cathode ray tube, dots per inch, digital audio tape, graphical user interface, enhanced graphics adaptor, multimedia personal computer, read only memory, random access memory, dynamic random access memory, central processing unit, super video graphics adaptor.
3 Mouse, keyboard, joystick, light pen, sensor, scanner.
4 a Keyboard; b Mouse; c Dot-matrix printer; d Ink-jet printer; e Laser-jet printer; f 3.5-inch floppy disk; g 5.25-inch floppy disk; h hard disk i CD-ROM disk.
10 File management, graphic user interface, system control.
11 Screen windows, drop-down menus, user-friendly.

Element 1.3 Revision test

1 Purpose, type of processing activity, method of processing.
2 Input device, main processor unit, output devices, cables and connectors.

4 Mouse, keyboard, printer, monitor, speakers.
10 Power, applications, enter, save, retrieve, print.

Element 1.4 Revision test

1 Reduce input error, speed up processing, standardise procedures.
2 Repetitive key stroke sequences, templates, set defaults.
3 Spell-check function, document default, template.
4 Template, sum.
5 Applications software to be used, purpose of using macro, uses of macro, method of executing macro, data to be embedded in macro, layout styles, tests to be applied.
6 Commands, activated.
7 Recorder, sequence, menu, toolbar, shortcut, save.
8 Implemented, procedures.

Element 2.1 Revision test

1 Letter, legal, A4, B4.
2 Newspaper columns, positioned columns, columns in tables.
3 First-line indent, negative indent, hanging indent.
4 Anti-theft procedures, regular saving and backing up, non-disclosure of confidential information, adhering to data and software copyright.
5 Orientation, size, portrait, landscape.
6 Format, appearance.
7 Distance, margin.
8 Vertical, line, single, double.
9 Saving, letters, numbers, symbols.

Element 2.2 Revision test

1 Line, shape, text, brush, colour palette.
2 Fills, styles, line thicknesses, colours and shades, height and width.
3 Rectangle, circle, polygon.
4 Solid, shaded, patterns, textures.
5 Type, format.
6 Arrow, dotted, dashed, shade.

Element 2.3   Revision test

1 Calculating break-even points, budgeting, conversion tables.
2 Developing military strategy, understanding political and economic situations.
3 Data, calculations, layout.
4 Characters, numbers, dates, formulae.
5 Rows, columns, cells.
6 Numerical, forecast, demonstrate, changes.
7 Set, rules, difficult.
8 Numbers, cell references, operators, equals sign.
9 Rows, columns, cells.

Element 2.4   Revision test

1 Heating and cooling systems, smoke alarms, intruder alarms, traffic lights, street lights, washing machines, cooking timers.
2 Environmental control, process production control, quality control, security.
3 a They can be programmed to handle many information processing tasks.
   b They can be connected to external memories and other systems.
4 Timer systems to switch lights on and off; video cameras programmed to switch on when movement or body heat is detected; shoplifting detection systems.
5 Purpose, process control limits, response time, sensors, type of feedback.
6 Feedback loop, sense, compare, pre-set limits, adjust output.
7 Sensors, processors, control, output, interconnecting.

Element 3.1   Revision test

1 False.
2 True.
3 True.
4 False.
5 Commercial.
6 Thrill, service, holiday.
7 Purchase order.
8 Delivery note.
9 The VAT reg. no. and the order no.
10 The order no.
11 Because the two organisations have different VAT reference numbers.

12 So that when the invoice is received, it can be checked against what has been delivered to ensure that only goods received are paid for.

Element 3.2   Revision test

1 False.
2 True.
3 True.
4 Payroll.
5 Personal.
6 Bar-code.
7 Questionnaire.
8 Because you do not want to run out of popular lines and have to turn customers away, or reorder lines which are not selling well because this is not profitable.
9 Because people sometimes have the same name and it is important to be sure that the correct person is identified. Products often have similar descriptions, and again a unique reference number will ensure that the correct item is identified.
10 Sensors can be contact, heat, light, proximity or sound. Information received by the sensor controls a reaction, e.g. when a thermostat registers that the temperature has dropped below a certain level, a heater is switched on.
11 a transaction – because it needs to be up to date.
   b batch – because it is done at a set time – usually monthly – and the whole batch can be processed together.
   c transaction – because it needs to be up to date.

Element 3.3   Revision test

1 False.
2 True.
3 True.
4 False.
5 True.
6 Amend.
7 Append.
8 Delete.
9 Amend – when someone has married and changed her name, or moved to a new address; append – when a new employee has joined a company, or a new product has been introduced to a shop; delete – when a student leaves a school/college, or a product is discontinued.
10 Greater than, less than, equal to. Refer to text for examples, and think up some of your own.
11 And, or, not.

Element 3.4 Activity, page 117

Order no. can be limited to an integer with a maximum of 6 digits, or even a fixed length of 6 digits, so that the computer will indicate if only 5 or fewer are entered.

Goods reference number – if all the company's product reference numbers are similar, the field could be designed to require 2 characters, followed by 1 digit, followed by 2 characters, e.g. VM2SP.

Unit price – the field could be designed with a suitable range check, and also 3 digits to the left of the decimal and 2 to the right.

Customer order number – it is impossible to know what variety of customer order numbers might be received, and therefore it would have to be a character field.

Element 3.4 Revision test

1 True.
2 True – if the format for the month is given as 1 for January, etc.
3 False.
4 False – it is not personal data.
5 False – employees are also responsible.
6 Verification, correctness.
7 Radiation.
8 Back-up.
9 Yes – selling copies of software packages does break the copyright law.
10 Yes – even giving away copies of software packages breaks the copyright law. In both 9 and 10, the action deprives the rightful author of his or her payment.
11 No – because it is permitted to keep a back-up copy of software disks you have purchased, in case the originals are lost or damaged.
12 No – because the data listed is all relevant to the needs of a college.
13 Yes – because the college is not giving you a loan, and therefore your credit rating is not relevant.
14 No – because the tutor would be considered an authorised person and is entitled to contact a student.
15 Yes – because another student is not an authorised user, and however harmless the request may seem, the member of staff should not give out these details.

Element 4.1 Revision test

1 False.
2 True.
3 False.
4 True.
5 True.
6 Network.
7 Fax.
8 Bit, bits, byte.
9 Parity.
10 Emulation.
11 See page 129.
12 It informs the receiver that a character or byte of data is completed.
13 See page 136.
14 See page 137.

Element 4.2 Revision test

1 True.
2 False.
3 True.
4 True.
5 False.
6 Communication software.
7 Protocols.
8 Passwords.
9 Echo.
10 If the various protocols do not agree, either the data will not transmit at all, or it will be corrupted during transmission.
11 The process of transposing data into a code as a security check.

Element 4.3 Revision test

1 False.
2 True.
3 True.
4 False.
5 True.
6 Local area network, wide area network.
7 Cable.
8 Telephone lines, satellite, microwave.
9 Bus, ring, star and mesh.
10 Star.
11 See pages 147–8.
12 Users with a high security will have access to all or most of the data, whereas those with low security will have limited access to data.

13 If the file has been write-protected, you may read the file but you cannot write to the file, i.e. add or modify the data, unless you have the password.

Element 4.4   Revision test

1 False – you can create access privileges on a network.
2 True – one copy as a back-up.
3 False – you can read the file, but if you make any changes, you have to save under another name, so preserving the original.
4 False.
5 True.
6 Back up.
7 Write protect.
8 Logon.
9 Data Protection Act.

Core Skills Communication – Apostrophes exercise, page 174

The cat's milk is hot, so he shouldn't drink it until it cools down.

Anytown High School's players were delighted because the grammar school's team hadn't beaten them for the first time.

The cars' engines had overheated in the traffic jam, because the drivers hadn't switched off the engines.

EVIDENCE ASSIGNMENT TRACKING SHEET FOR COMMUNICATION LEVEL 2

Evidence assignment for element:	Unit 1				Unit 2				Unit 3				Unit 4				Communication 2.4	Appl. of Number	
	1.1	1.2	1.3	1.4	2.1	2.2	2.3	2.4	3.1	3.2	3.3	3.4	4.1	4.2	4.3	4.4	2.4	2.1	2.3
Communication Element 2.1 — 1	✓	✓										✓			✓			✓	
2	✓	✓										✓			✓			✓	
3	✓	✓										✓			✓			✓	
4	✓	✓										✓			✓			✓	
Communication Element 2.2 — 1	✓	✓	✓	✓		✓		✓	✓	✓	✓		✓		✓				✓
2	✓	✓	✓	✓		✓		✓	✓	✓	✓		✓		✓				✓
3	✓	✓	✓	✓		✓		✓	✓	✓	✓		✓		✓				✓
4	✓	✓	✓	✓		✓		✓	✓	✓	✓		✓		✓				✓
5	✓	✓	✓	✓		✓		✓	✓	✓	✓		✓		✓				✓
Communication Element 2.3 — 1	✓	✓	✓	✓		✓				✓			✓		✓				✓
2	✓	✓	✓	✓		✓				✓			✓		✓				✓
3	✓	✓	✓	✓		✓				✓			✓		✓				✓
Communication Element 2.4 — 1	✓	✓	✓			✓		✓	✓	✓			✓		✓		✓	✓	
2	✓	✓	✓			✓		✓	✓	✓			✓		✓		✓	✓	
3	✓	✓	✓			✓		✓	✓	✓			✓		✓		✓	✓	
4	✓	✓	✓			✓		✓	✓	✓			✓		✓		✓	✓	

EVIDENCE ASSIGNMENT TRACKING SHEET FOR IT LEVEL 2

Evidence assignment for element:	Unit 1				Unit 2				Unit 3				Unit 4				IT
	1.1	1.2	1.3	1.4	2.1	2.2	2.3	2.4	3.1	3.2	3.3	3.4	4.1	4.2	4.3	4.4	2.4
IT Element 2.1 1	✓	✓	✓	✓	✓	✓	✓		✓	✓	✓		✓	✓	✓		
2	✓	✓	✓	✓	✓	✓	✓		✓	✓	✓		✓	✓	✓		
3	✓	✓		✓		✓				✓			✓	✓	✓		
4	✓	✓		✓	✓	✓	✓		✓	✓	✓		✓	✓	✓	✓	
IT Element 2.2 1				✓		✓	✓				✓		✓				
2		✓		✓	✓	✓	✓		✓	✓	✓		✓	✓	✓		
3				✓		✓	✓							✓			
4				✓	✓	✓	✓		✓	✓	✓		✓		✓		
5				✓	✓	✓	✓		✓						✓		
6						✓											
IT Element 2.3 1	✓	✓		✓	✓	✓	✓		✓	✓	✓		✓		✓		
2	✓	✓		✓	✓	✓	✓		✓	✓	✓		✓		✓		
3	✓	✓		✓			✓		✓				✓		✓		
4	✓	✓															
5	✓			✓							✓		✓		✓		
IT Element 2.4 1			✓							✓							✓
2			✓							✓							✓
3			✓							✓							✓
4			✓							✓							✓
5												✓					

EVIDENCE ASSIGNMENT TRACKING SHEET FOR IT LEVEL 3

Evidence assignment for element:	1.1	1.2	1.3	1.4	2.1	2.2	2.3	2.4	3.1	3.2	3.3	3.4	4.1	4.2	4.3	4.4	IT 3.4
IT Element 2.1 — 1	✓	✓		✓	✓	✓	✓		✓	✓	✓		✓	✓	✓		
2	✓	✓	✓	✓	✓	✓	✓		✓	✓	✓		✓	✓	✓		
3	✓	✓	✓	✓		✓				✓			✓	✓	✓		
4	✓	✓		✓	✓	✓	✓		✓	✓	✓		✓	✓	✓	✓	
5				✓	✓		✓*				✓						
IT Element 2.2 — 1				✓							✓						
2				✓	✓		✓		✓	✓	✓		✓		✓		
3		✓		✓	✓	✓	✓							✓			
4				✓		✓	✓				✓		✓		✓		
5				✓	✓	✓	✓		✓	✓	✓			✓			
6						✓	✓										
7				✓		✓											
IT Element 2.3 — 1	✓	✓			✓	✓	✓		✓				✓		✓		
2	✓	✓		✓	✓	✓	✓		✓		✓		✓		✓		
3	✓	✓		✓			✓		✓		✓		✓		✓		
4	✓	✓		✓			✓						✓		✓		
5	✓	✓							✓		✓		✓		✓		
6	✓												✓		✓		
IT Element 2.4 — 1	✓		✓							✓							✓
2			✓							✓							✓
3																	✓
4			✓							✓							✓
5			✓							✓							✓
6												✓					

*needs a spreadsheet template

EVIDENCE ASSIGNMENT TRACKING SHEET FOR APPLICATION OF NUMBER LEVEL 2

Evidence assignment for element:	Unit 1				Unit 2				Unit 3				Unit 4				Appl. of Number		
	1.1	1.2	1.3	1.4	2.1	2.2	2.3	2.4	3.1	3.2	3.3	3.4	4.1	4.2	4.3	4.4	2.1	2.2	2.3
Number Element 2.1 — 1	✓	✓					✓		✓								✓		
2	✓	✓					✓		✓								✓		
3	✓	✓					✓		✓								✓		
4							✓		✓								✓		
5							✓		✓								✓		
6							✓		✓								✓		
Number Element 2.2 — 1				✓			✓		✓									✓	
2				✓			✓		✓									✓	
3				✓			✓		✓									✓	
4							✓		✓									✓	
5							✓		✓									✓	
6				✓			✓		✓									✓	
7				✓			✓		✓									✓	
8				✓			✓		✓									✓	
Number Element 2.3 — 1		✓					✓												✓
2		✓					✓												✓
3		✓					✓		✓										✓
4		✓					✓		✓										✓
5		✓					✓												✓

COMPUTER CONSULTANTS LTD
108 King Street
Anytown
AT2 3RJ

Tel: 0132 549 261
Fax: 0132 319 734

PURCHASE ORDER

VAT Reg. No.: 482/83742/95

To:

Date:

Order No.:

Please supply

QUANTITY	DESCRIPTION	REF. NO.	UNIT PRICE

Blue copy: File

PC Manufacturing Co. plc

Unit 24
The Industrial Estate
Anytown
AN1 6HS

TEL: 0132 283 535

VAT Reg No: 632/84173/41

INVOICE

To:

Deliver to:

Date:

Your order no.	Invoice date/tax point	Invoice no.	Despatch date

Quantity	Description	Cat. no.	Unit price	Total price	VAT rate	VAT amount
		Delivery charges				
		Sub-total				
		VAT				
		Total amount due				

Terms:
E & OE

213

COMPUTER CONSULTANTS LTD

108 King Street
Anytown
AT2 3RJ

TEL: 0132 549 261

VAT Reg. No.: 482/83742/95

INVOICE

To:

Deliver to:

Date:

Invoice no.	Invoice date/tax point	Your order no.	Despatch date

Quantity	Description	Cat. no.	Unit price	Total price	VAT rate	VAT amount
			Delivery charges			
			Sub-total			
			VAT		Terms: E & OE	
			Total amount due			

214

Index

V

Validation 115
VDUs – visual display units 16, 20, 21, 121–122
  CRT – cathode-ray tube 17
Vector graphics 57, 58
Verification 90, 116, 117

VGA – video graphics adapter 16
Viewdata 129
Viruses 54, 124, 156
Visual display units – VDUs 16, 20, 21, 121–122
  CRT – cathode-ray tube 17

W

WANs – wide area networks 7, 131, 148–149
What if queries 69
Wide area networks – WANs 7, 131, 148–149
Windows 31, 52, 159
Word processing 22, 28, 29, 51
Workstations 154